KITE CRAFT

OTHER BOOKS BY THE AUTHORS

PLASTICS FOR THE CRAFTSMAN

with Thelma R. Newman
PAPER AS ART AND CRAFT
THE FRAME BOOK

KITE CRAFT

The History and Processes of Kitemaking Throughout the World

Lee Scott Newman

Jay Hartley Newman

Crown Publishers, Inc., New York

For Brandt Aymar, and his special brandt of humor

Inquiries should be addressed to Crown Publishers, Inc., One Park Avenue, New York, N.Y. 10016

Library of Congress Catalog Card Number: 73–91154
ISBN: 0–517–514702
ISBN: 0–517–514710 pbk

Printed in the United States of America. Published simultaneously in Canada by General Publishing Company Limited
Design by Nedda Balter

Sixth Printing, July, 1977

ACKNOWLEDGMENTS

A book such as this owes its existence to countless people who have contributed to kite legend and design. Many individuals, institutions, and companies helped us, and the information and work gathered here could never have been compiled without their generous cooperation.

William Bigge, Frank Rodriguez, and Keith Shields, three master kite craftsmen, contributed their time, energies, and experience. Our special thanks go as well to Robert Ingraham, President of the American Kitefliers Association, whose advice and suggestions we fully appreciate.

Andrea Bahadur, whose Go Fly a Kite Shop in New York City is well known, was extremely helpful. Our appreciation goes to Sally Fontana of The Kite Shop, New Orleans, as well.

We owe a great deal to the generosity of Ichiro Hike and Shingo Modegi, leaders of the Japan Kite Association, who took time from busy schedules to help us in Japan.

To Norm Smith our very great thanks for his excellent photoprocessing even in the clinch.

The individuals, companies, and institutions listed below were all helpful and encouraging. Our debt to them is great.

Bermuda News Bureau
Benn Blinn
British Museum
Du Pont
Paul Garber
A. D. Goddard
Charles Henry
Tsutomu Hiroi
Ray Holland, Jr., of the Airplane Kite Company
Howe & Bainbridge, Inc., makers of Zephyrlite and Stabilkote
Domina Jalbert
Huot Kimleang
E. Ted Maciag
Jackie Monnier
The National Geographic Society
Ted Norton
Harry Sauls
Science Museum, London
Frank Scott
Mendel Silbert
Smithsonian Institution
Tal Streeter
Hod Taylor
Paul Thomas
Vincent Tuzo
Fumio Yoshimura

Nothing would have been accomplished without the support of our encouraging parents, Thelma and Jack Newman. Their suggestions, criticisms, and assistance helped to make the entire project worthwhile.

L.S.N.
J.H.N.

All photographs by the authors unless otherwise noted.

PREFACE

Kites straddle a curious position. Although best known as children's toys, the most exciting and innovative designs have been developed by artists, scientists, and engineers pursuing solutions to problems of design and aerodynamics.

At this point in history, too, kites occupy a rather special position. In the Far East, where kites were born and where the craft became a fine art, the kite has become an object of the past—less a current art form than a piece of folklore. The few kitemakers who remain often cannot find apprentices. Those who want to learn are often foreign artists and students. In western countries—especially the United States—a resurgence of interest in all craft forms has buoyed the ranks of kite enthusiasts.

There is no mystery to the kite's appeal. Kites are simultaneously a means of defining space, utilizing the wind, and overcoming gravity. They challenge our creativity to devise structures that will respond to natural phenomena and design criteria as well. At a time when work takes most people indoors, kite flying brings us outside and heightens our appreciation of the elements, seasonal changes, and beauties. Kites entail special interest in both craft and sport, and as a sport compare with fishing and sailing.

Working with kites is a discovery process. The technical and design concepts presented in KITE CRAFT are transferrable; they can be no more than a beginning. The value of traditional and modern materials and techniques lies in their application. The alteration of old forms and the discovery of new materials and solutions are central to the full enjoyment of kites.

We hope that this compilation of techniques and design suggestions will result in a greater curiosity about the form and its potential. The parameter of the kite's potential is your own creative thought—it can explode a new realm of possibility.

L.S.N.
J.H.N.

CONTENTS

KITE CRAFT

A Maori bird kite with a fiber frame and feathered tail. Courtesy: The British Museum.

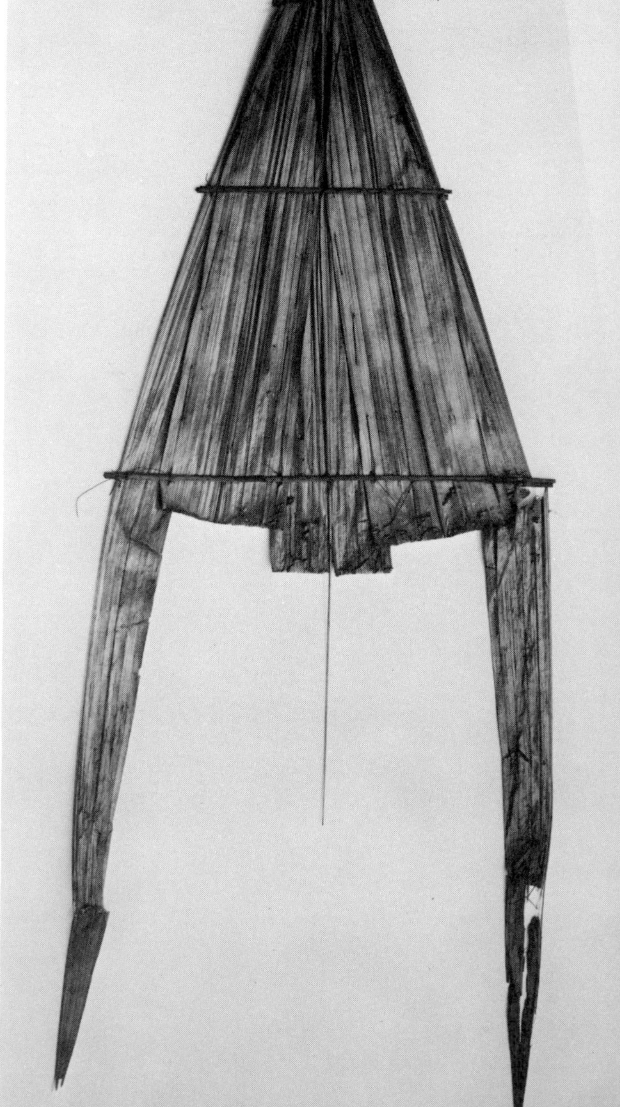

This Solomon Islands fishing kite is constructed of twigs and plaited leaves. Courtesy: The British Museum.

A HISTORY OF KITES

Chapter 1

How the kite was discovered is a matter for conjecture. Perhaps a farmer lost his hat on a windy day, or a mariner's sail escaped in the breeze. Or, as Clive Hart suggests, the kite may have been the logical extension of banners and pennants which, when stiffened with crosspieces, became kites. In any case, we sense that the kite resulted from the random observation of objects acted upon by a natural phenomenon, and because the phenomenon is the wind—uncontrollable, perhaps unfathomable—early observers and kitemakers felt a very special, spiritual relationship with this toy or tool which allowed them to become a part of such a distant and powerful force.

Within this context, it is easy to see how the kite achieved and maintained a mythical and religious significance in many cultures, mainly in the Orient. From records of its earliest uses we find the kite used continually as a vane of the fates, as a tool for prophesying, and as an object for celebration of birth, happiness, fertility, and victory. The kite began, not as the reasoned invention of a scientific mind, but as a wondrous and even magical link with the heavens.

Almost certainly the kite originated in

China over 2000 years ago. No matter what we choose to accept as its inspiration, the materials for kitemaking surely existed there: bamboo for frame, and silk for material and line. From China, the kite spread rapidly throughout Asia.

Japan, which absorbed so much of Chinese culture, was the first to embrace the kite, and it was also adopted in Korea, Burma, Malaysia, Indonesia, and India where substantially different designs developed. Kites were also know early in Polynesia, and forms existed on Easter Island as well. In Europe there is a record of a kite being flown by the Greek scholar Archytas who lived in the fifth century B.C., but evidence suggests that this could have been an import from the east. The American continent knew no indigenous kites in ancient times.

ORIENTAL KITE LORE

Chinese folklore is rich in tales of kites flown for purpose and pleasure. Most interesting are the military uses which the Chinese found for kite forms. In fact, the most widespread account of the kite's origin describes the use of a kite by General Han Hsin. While laying siege to a palace, the general is said to have flown a kite over the walls in order to gauge the distance between his forces and the fortress. Using the length of line as a guide, he tunneled under the walls to surprise the defenders.

Around the beginning of the Christian era, during the Han Dynasty, kites, according to legend, caused troops to flee in terror. They had been flown over the camp of the invading army one night with bamboo hummers attached. As the legend goes, spies within the camp spread rumors that the horrible moans and screeches were the voices of the gods declaring defeat for the invaders. The enemy was thus routed.

Chinese skill in creating kites both fine and huge appears to have reached high levels. Man-lifting kites were employed as observation posts—and the danger involved in such flights was capitalized upon as a grave punishment as well.

Though China was the birthplace of the kite, other eastern cultures developed distinctive kite designs and traditions, too. Japan, in contrast to Chinese exploitation of the kite as a technological and functional object, welcomed the kite for its ceremonial and religious value. Kites figure in religious episodes and are present in many paintings relating to religious subjects. And, of course, Japanese history is rich in the lore of kite shenanigans.

The famed and daring thief Kakinkoki Kinsuke is said to have built a man-sized kite which carried him to the roof of the Nagoya Castle dungeon, allowing him to steal the solid gold fins of the dolphins perched there. A practical application was devised by the architect Kawamura Zuiken who lifted materials to his workmen with the help of kites.

Indeed, not only did the Japanese show great ingenuity in their use of kites, but they proved to be incredibly talented at designing improvements for high fliers. There are hundreds of kite designs, many with symbolic importance.

Japanese folk hero Kintoki (said to have been raised by bears in the mountains, and to have become the strongest man in Japan and an aide to the emperor) has been forever immortalized through the kite. His face is painted on Sagara kites which are given by friends and family to children as congratulatory gifts.

Kites decorated with a crane or turtle symbolize long life; the famed dragon kite denotes prosperity because of the dragon's ability to rise to the heavens. Other kites are said to bring luck, frighten evil spirits, give hope for knowledge and learning, abet fertility, provide good fishing, and so on.

From the basic rectangular form that originated in China, each culture began its own design exploration. In Japan, figurative designs were especially important. Human, animal, and object forms were all inspirations for the Japanese kitemakers, as they were for the Chinese. Even forms as modern as the airplane are represented in current designs.

An exceptionally versatile and innovative invention by the Japanese was the Nagasaki fighting kite. This kite is one of the most

3

Another fishing kite, from Banks Island, provides an interesting lesson in kite construction. Tiny bamboo tacks are used to hold the covering in place. Courtesy: The British Museum.

finely tuned fighters ever designed. Usually no more than a yard long, it will fly in any direction at great speed with or without a tail. It is constructed with a carefully formed horizontal spar of bamboo, a single vertical spine, and paper reinforced with string. Balance and symmetry are essential, but the responsiveness makes those efforts worthwhile. (The construction of this kite is described in Chapter 3.)

In Nagasaki, these kites were used, along with others of Korean design, for kite fights. In order to provide kites with weapons with which to sever an opponent's string, the line was often doctored ("glazed") with powdered glass or porcelain bonded with egg white or another natural adhesive. Special knives were also developed, and the goal was always to set the other kite free of its owner. The loss of a kite meant a blow to the ego of the flier, to be sure, but it was expensive as well. The defeated might lose substantial amounts of silk line as well as the kite. Skillful fliers could (and still do) encircle and ensnare the defeated opponent's severed kite, bring it back to earth, and claim it as spoils.

Control, of course, is an admirable goal, but the Japanese sought to build very large kites as well. The nineteenth century charted a path of increased development of kites—culminating in the construction of the *wan-wan.* The *wan-wan,* 20 yards in diameter, with a tail 480 feet long, a weight of nearly a ton and a 35-leg bridle was the result of intense community planning, launching, and flying. The tradition, though devoid of some of the frenzy that marked the originals, persists today. A notable festival occurs yearly at Hamamatsu, where hundreds participate in the construction and flying of the largest of kites.

Malaysia also has long had a kite culture. Leaf-shaped fishing kites from which line was strung provided native fishermen with a means of lightly suspending their baited hooks without frightening the prey. Often these kites were made of leaves reinforced with sticks or bamboo. A variety of kite shapes evolved there as well. Of special interest is the moon kite or *wau bulan,* the bottom half of which is shaped like a new moon. Variations of this kite are constructed: some as large as a man, some 10 feet high. The construction makes them particularly maneuverable and popular for kite fighting, although for many years kite fighting in Malaysia has been forbidden because of the large number of disputes that have arisen from them.

In Polynesia, kites have long been important as a means of making contact with the heavens. Folklore records many incidents where kites have symbolized gods or have been the toys of the gods. In many cases, Polynesian kites were associated with birds and constructed in that configuration. But again, turtles, human figures, and abstract shapes were known even in early times. Most often, a native bark cloth (*tapa*) was used there in combination with wood, rushes, feathers, and shells, which produced a rattle in flight.

KITES IN THE WEST

In comparison to these cultures, kites came rather late to the West. There is some suggestion that a Greek mathematician, Archytas, flew what might have been a kite as early as 400 B.C. It could, conceivably, have been an import of a Chinese invention, but little evidence supports either a claim for invention or importation. There is speculation that the Cretan legend of Icarus (who flew too close to the sun on wax wings and perished) might have been inspired by stories of men flying aboard kites. And, although other references to kites are present in both Greek and Egyptian cultures, it is still assumed that the role of kites fell far short of their role in the Orient. Hart traces a chain of discovery through the Dacian wind-

From its birthplace in China, the kite spread to the rest of the world.

A wood block print records an early English kite. Notice the two-leg bridle. Courtesy: The Science Museum, London.

An Indian miniature shows two women playing with Tukkal kites. Courtesy: Andrea Bahadur, Go Fly a Kite Store.

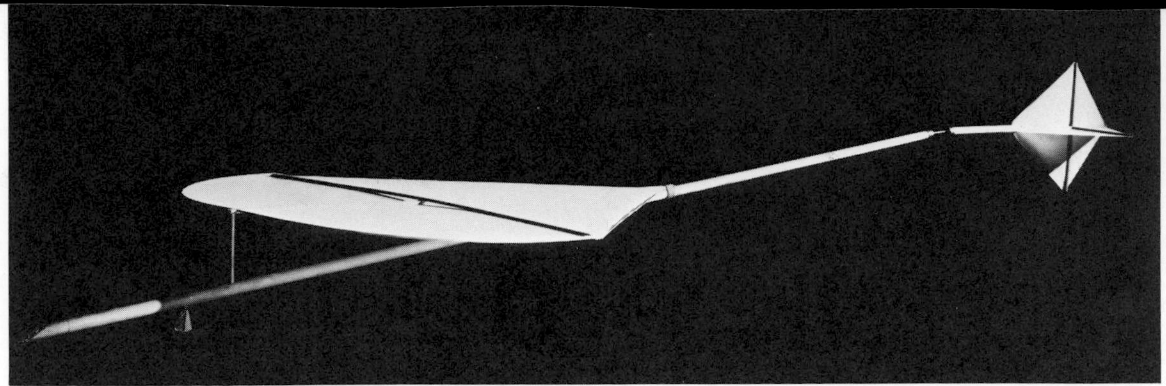

The sophisticated design of Sir George Cayley's glider, executed in 1803, suggests that, had an adequate power source been available, the airplane might have been invented much sooner. Courtesy: Science Museum, London.

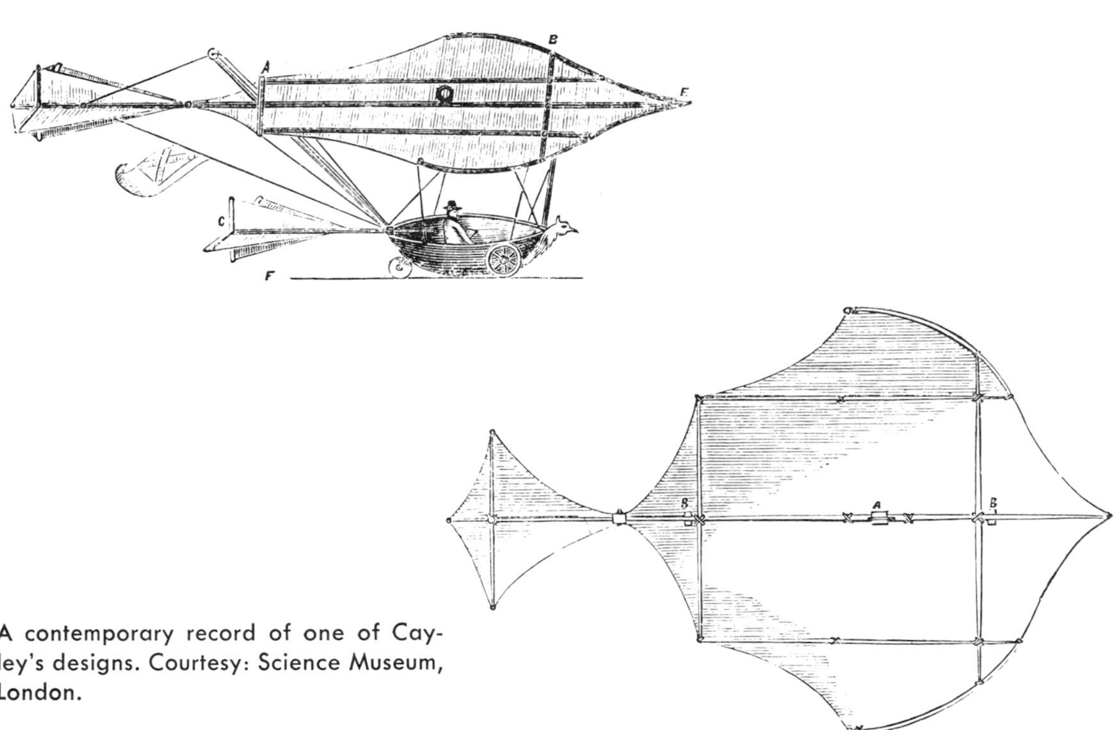

A contemporary record of one of Cayley's designs. Courtesy: Science Museum, London.

sock standard, *draco*. This device was often used by the legions. Faced like otherworldly dragons, these pennons gave inspiration to the fighters and, hopefully, frightened their enemies. Later innovations apparently involved the use of fire—perhaps as an added dragonlike illusion—but, as is its wont, hot air forced through the wind sock caused it to rise, suggesting the kitelike potential.

Diamond-, lozenge-, and pear-shaped kites were designed in Europe in the fifteenth, sixteenth, and seventeenth centuries. But the eighteenth century ushered in a new era in the use of kites in the West. The development of kites as flying machines and as tools of scientific inquiry became the passion of many men.

The first record of a scientific experiment using kites describes the work of Alexander Wilson in 1749, using a series of kites flown in train with thermometers attached. The objective was to determine the variation in temperatures at different altitudes. This preceded the most famous of all kite experiments by just a few years.

In the famous experiment of raising a kite during a thunderstorm during June 1752, Benjamin Franklin provided one of

Although Pocock's Charvolant did travel briskly when the wind was blowing, it never became quite as popular as this rendering suggests. Courtesy: Science Museum, London.

the very first evidences of the existence and effect of electric current. He later gave very detailed instructions as to how the experiment might be repeated, and he cautioned that the end of the string should be kept quite dry, lest the experimenter receive the full shock of the current.

Other experimenters, of course, followed Franklin's lead. They used different wires and different subjects (like animals) to judge the effects of electricity. Of special note is the fact that most kites built to be raised during storms were protected in some measure against the elements. Some varnished their papers, and others, like Franklin, used silk handkerchiefs which would not absorb much water and would also maintain high tear resistance.

Though there was a great deal of interest in applications of kites, no substantial design changes were made during the eighteenth century. During the next century, however, kites aroused the curiosity and stirred the creativity of many people.

Meteorologists are among the most avid kitefliers because of the observations that can be made by attaching cameras and other instruments to kites. Another group working with kites sought to make kiteflying unnecessary for observation of the clouds; they wanted to fly.

Some of these precursors of flying machines had other objectives. Experimenters would often want to see how high they could fly kites. Others wanted to see how much weight kites could lift. A Frenchman, Maillot, designed a man-lifter in 1885. Nine years later B. F. S. Baden-Powell developed the tandem system in which several smaller kites (each 110 square feet in area) were attached and flown in train for great lifting power. His original goal was to provide the army with a readily available observation post. At nearly the same time, but independently of Baden-Powell, Lawrence Hargrave built a successful man-lifting kite with a train of four cellular kites. Hargrave's cellular forms were later capitalized on by Jimmy Wise, who claimed several successful ascents over New York in 1932.

Of some contemporary interest to those interested in pollution-free vehicles is the Charvolant designed by one George Pocock in the 1820s. His special lightweight carriage was drawn not by horses but by two kites arranged in tandem so that the smaller of the two acted as the pilot or leader kite. Pocock thought that the principle could be successfully applied to other modes of transport as well, and, in fact, boats have been successfully powered with kites alone.

The most significant applications of kite experiments must, however, be recognized as the tests and design experiments which led directly to the development of the airplane.

The first form in airplane configuration employed the basic arch kite. It had a rear rudder and elevator as well and was designed by Sir George Cayley in 1804. The Cayley glider also employed a dihedral angle, which anticipated the Eddy kite and others of modern design. It seems reasonable to sug-

A Chinese bat kite built in the late 19th century shows the use of a three-dimensional head. The use of three-dimensional bodies in kites persists in China today. Courtesy: Smithsonian Institution.

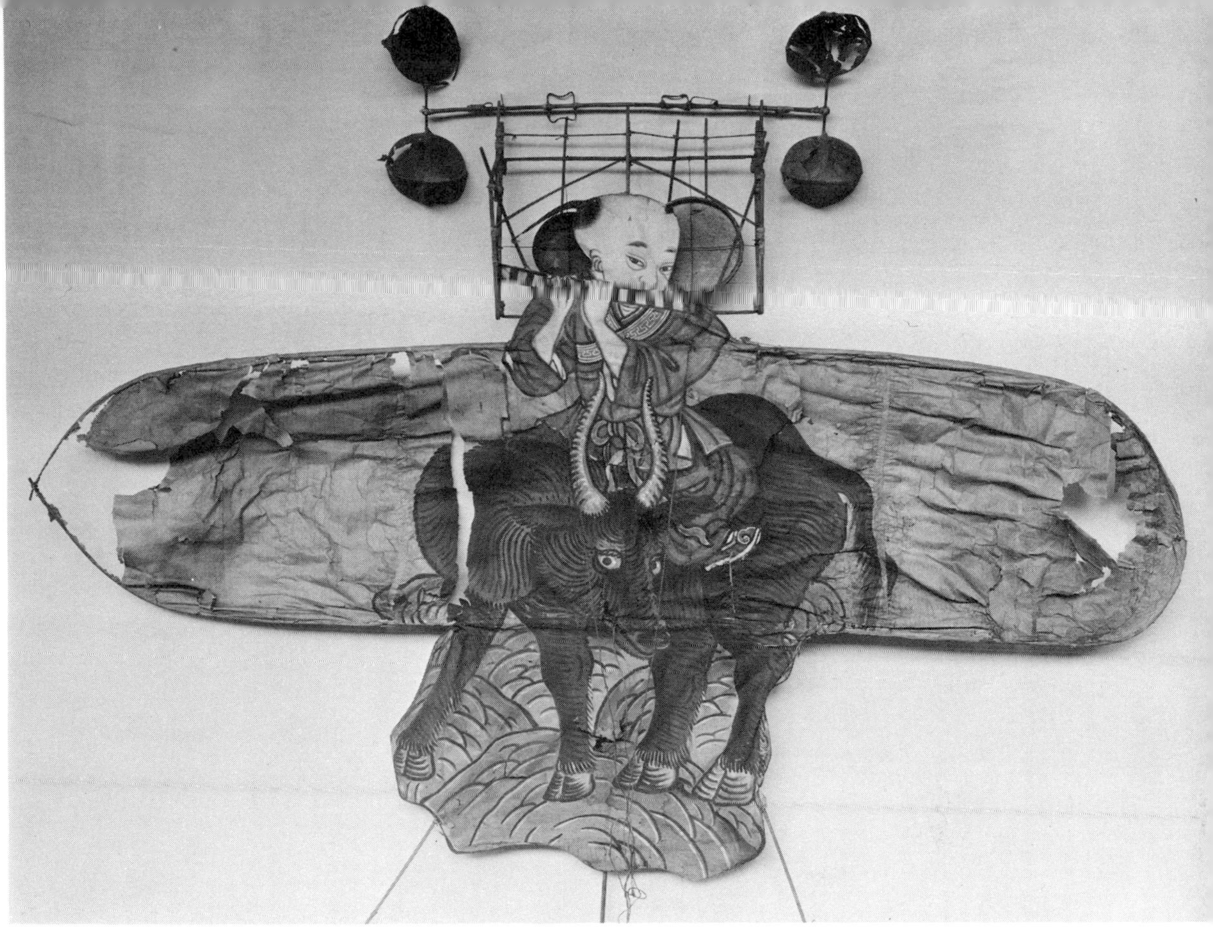

This Chinese kite, of the same period played a song as it flew. The disks, when rotated by the wind, triggered sticks which struck the small drums visible on the back. Courtesy: Smithsonian Institution.

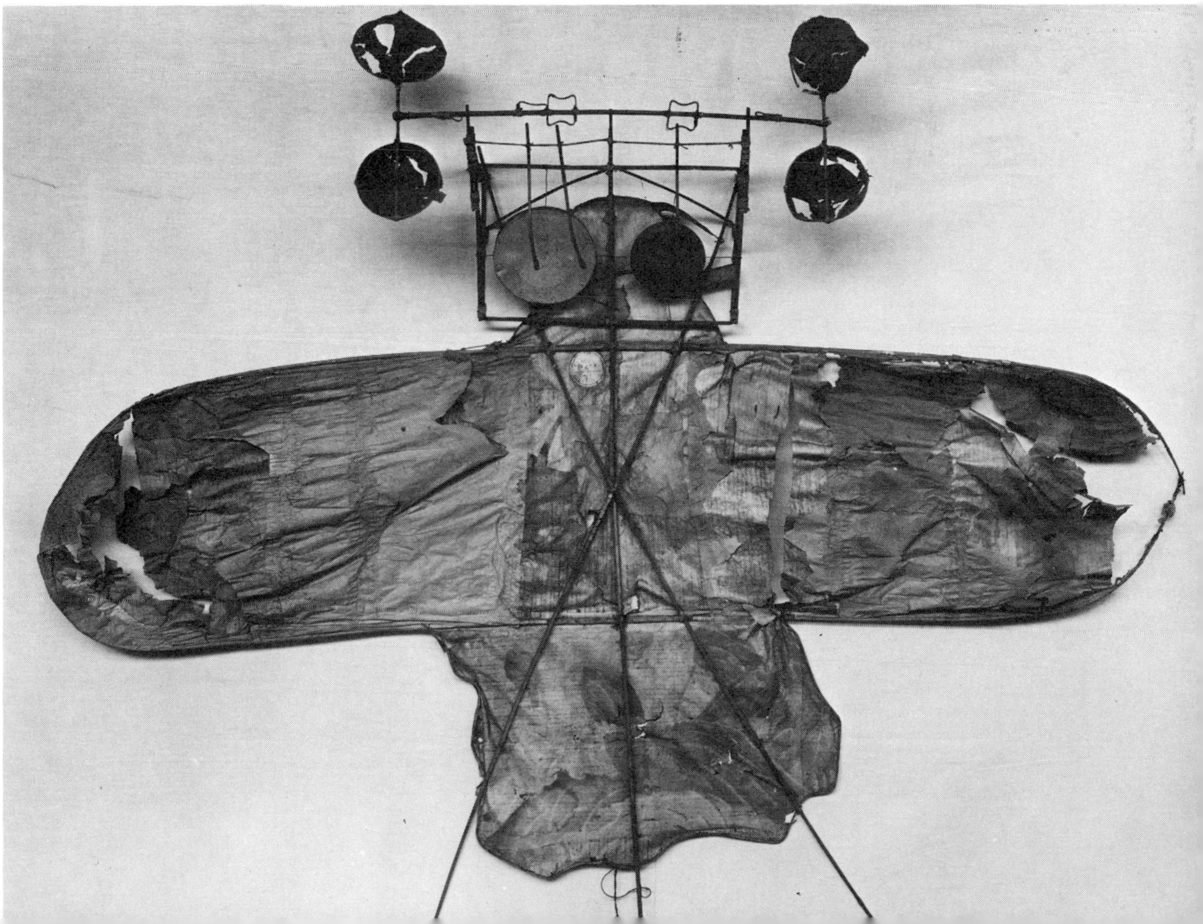

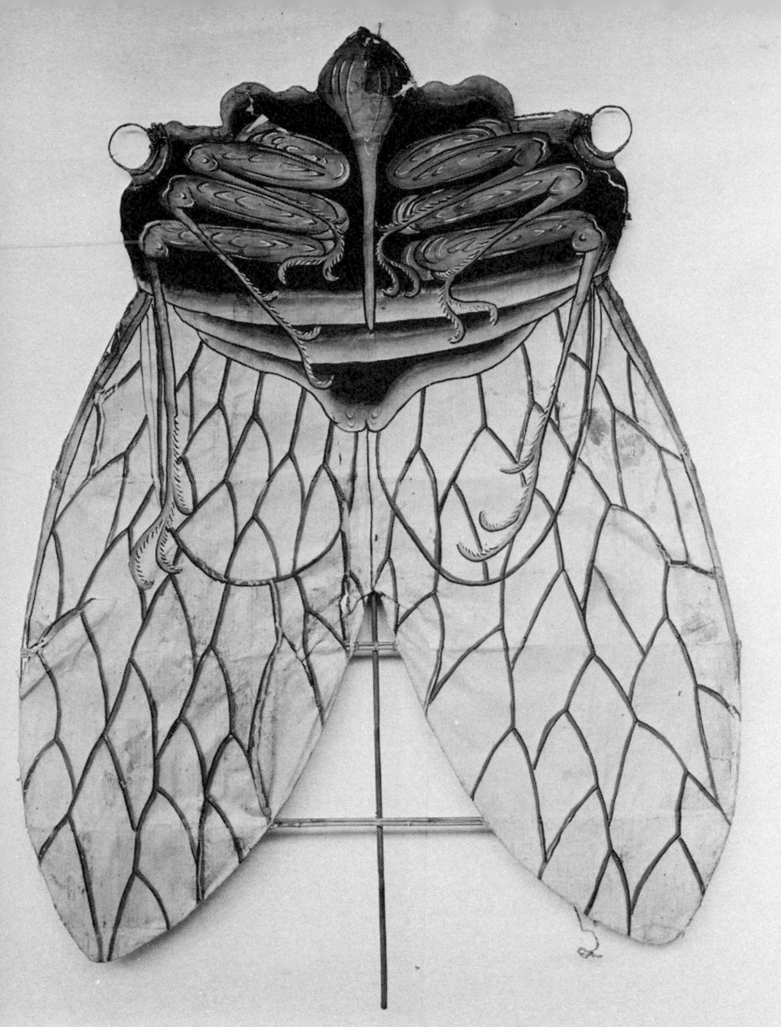

The cicada design has long been popular in both Chinese and Japanese kites. Courtesy: Smithsonian Institution.

gest that if a suitable power source had been available to Cayley, the airplane might have been invented one hundred years earlier than it was.

To be sure, the Wright brothers pursued the most systematic search for a means of allowing men to fly, and kites played an important part in their initial researches. They experimented with changes in the positioning of lifting surfaces—toward which end they developed and flew a special warping kite, the planes of which could be controlled and changed to determine the effect of different configurations upon flight.

Two other individuals became intensely involved in the design of kites as well: Lawrence Hargrave and Alexander Graham Bell. The Hargrave box kite provided the basis for many subsequent designs, and his work suggested plane designs for powered flight to many others involved in this research.

By far the most fantastic kite designs are those by Bell. He began with the Hargrave box kite which he referred to as "the highwater mark of progress [in kite design] in the nineteenth century." One of Bell's intense concerns was stability, and within the constraints of maximum rigidity, lifting power, and minimal weight, his results are striking.

The advance in kite design for which Bell is most famous, though, is the introduction of the regular tetrahedron as an element of kite construction. Not only is this structure a very rigid one which does not require any external bracings, but any number of cells can be connected without changing the surface-to-weight ratio—meaning that the kites could be made very, very large indeed. Some of his designs had as many as four thousand cells.

That the popularity of kiteflying and kite designing decreased noticeably with the advent of the airplane is not surprising. The kite flourished in quite a different era from that of its flying relatives which now move faster than sound. Recently, however, the sport of kiteflying has enjoyed a noticeable renaissance in the West. Part of this undoubtedly stems from a resurgence in interest in the out-of-doors and in craftsmanship,

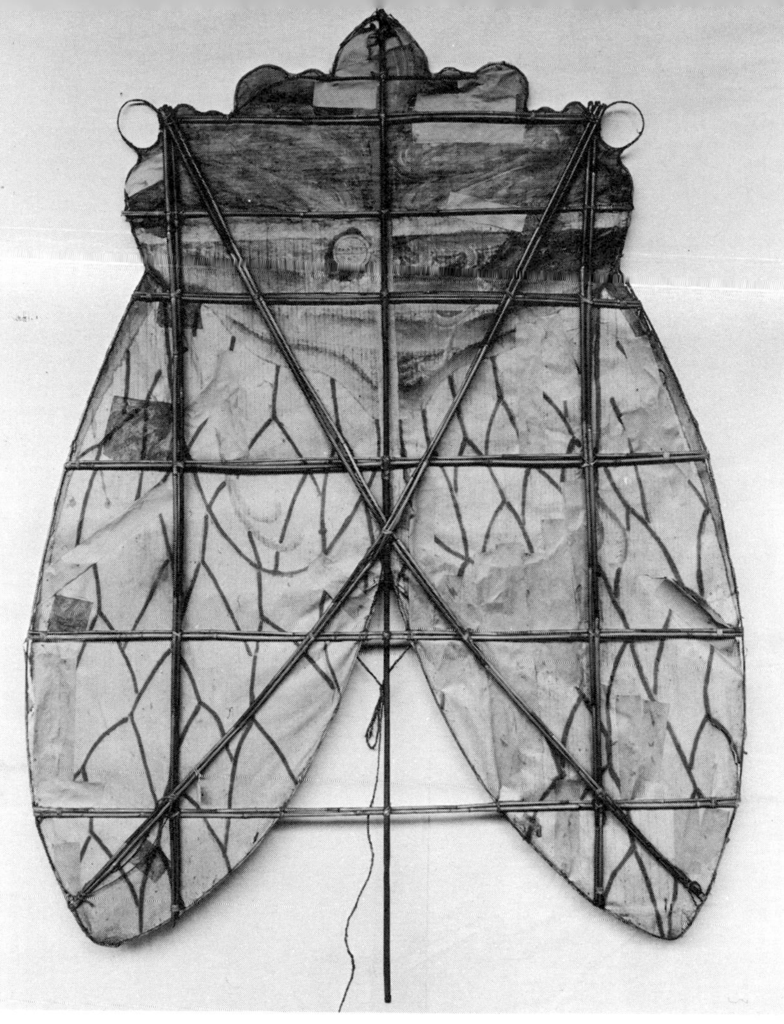

but some modern kite designers have been flying and building kites for many years.

Of the more recent innovations in kite design is the Flexi-kite® or parawing designed by Dr. Francis Rogallo. This cloth kite is entirely flexible and is given form by a multileg bridle system. Rogallo originally designed this wing to act as a glider/parachute. It is, in fact, used for both purposes today—most popularly in the sport of hang gliding. With the addition of rigid members, this kite has been adapted to water skiing where the skier, with the kite strapped to his back, is lifted into the air from the water as he is pulled along by a boat.

Another invention is the Scott Sled kite. Supported only by two vertical reinforcements, the sled flies very well in most winds. It is constructed in vented and unvented formations.

One of the most interesting new inventions with practical uses is the Jalbert parafoil. Designed by Domina Jalbert to provide great lift and to stand up to very strong winds, this entirely flexible kite is something of a revolution in kite design. Discussed later in this book, the parafoil was the result of necessity. A western university, in need of a kite which would lift instruments in 100 mph winds, made their problem known, and Jalbert responded with a magnificent solution. The last chapter describes these and other modern kite designs in detail.

Quite apart from the technical aspects of kite flight, artists have found the kite an exciting sculptural form. Fumio Yoshimura designs fanciful kites in bamboo—as sculptures rather than as flying objects. Charles Henry works with fiber glass rod and synthetic fabrics. Jackie Monnier paints fantastically long kite tails. Tal Streeter finds inspiration in traditional Japanese kitemaking materials. Their work also extends the range and standards of kite design by creating aesthetically appealing forms. The kite is more than a simple machine, and kitemaking can be more than craft: it can be an art.

This Hargrave box kite shows the heavy, solid structure. Visible here is the single point bridle which Hargrave favored. Lent to the Science Museum, London, by Sir Richard Threlfell.

An American kite designer poses with two box kites. The kite on the left makes use of a dihedral angle for stability; the one on the right has both the dihedral of the cell walls and a rudder. Courtesy: Smithsonian Institution.

Hargrave with one of his three-celled box kites. Once again the bridling is to a single point determined by balancing the kite carefully. The strong, braided flying line attests to the wind power harnessed as lift by Hargrave's kites. Courtesy: Science Museum, London.

A train of Saconney military kites, developed and flown by the French in the early 1900s, were popular as man-lifters. Courtesy: Smithsonian Institution.

One of Alexander Graham Bell's giant multicellular kites rises into the air. Bell constructed many kites using tetrahedrons; one had nearly four thousand cells. © Bell Family, Courtesy: *National Geographic Society*.

Man-carrying kites were the craze in the early part of this century. In these photos, Conyne kites in train were used. Conyne kites, because of the dihedral angle of their wings, are stable and develop a great deal of lift. Courtesy: Smithsonian Institution.

ST. LOUIS POST-DISPATCH

DEMONSTRATIONS OF MAN-CARRYING KITES MADE BY THE POST-DISPATCH IN FOREST PARK, ST. LOUIS.

SUNDAY PICTURE SUPPLEMENT

ST. LOUIS, MO., DEC. 4, 1910.

First photograph made in the United States from man-carrying kites.

Sending up the first pair in the train of kites.

Post-Dispatch photographer making pictures from a height of 200 feet.

Samuel F. Perkins, the kite man, 350 feet in the air.

The swing seat used by Perkins.

S. Louis Von Phul Saluting Friends 100 Feet Below.

The parawing, a totally flexible kite, has a sophisticated bridling system which maintains the kite at the proper angle to the wind. Courtesy: Kite Tales.

The Rogallo parawing has also been adapted for use as a parachute. The design is now "jumped" regularly by the U.S. Army parachute team. Courtesy: Kite Tales.

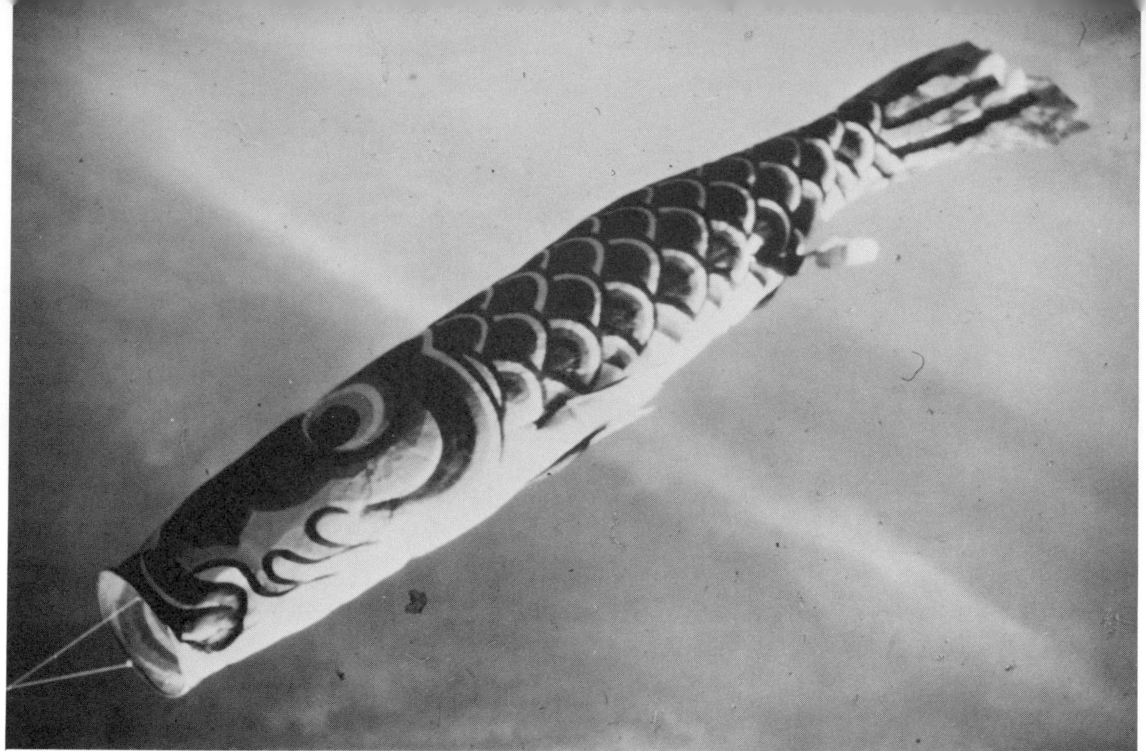

Although not a kite in the normal sense of lift and flying, this Japanese fish acts as a wind sock and flies in the wind. It has a hole in the front through which wind enters, bloating the tubular form. Wind rushes out the open-ended tail. It is strung on a pole in front of Japanese homes to celebrate a male child on Boys' Day. One carp is hung out for each male child.

A modern kite manufactured in Taiwan.

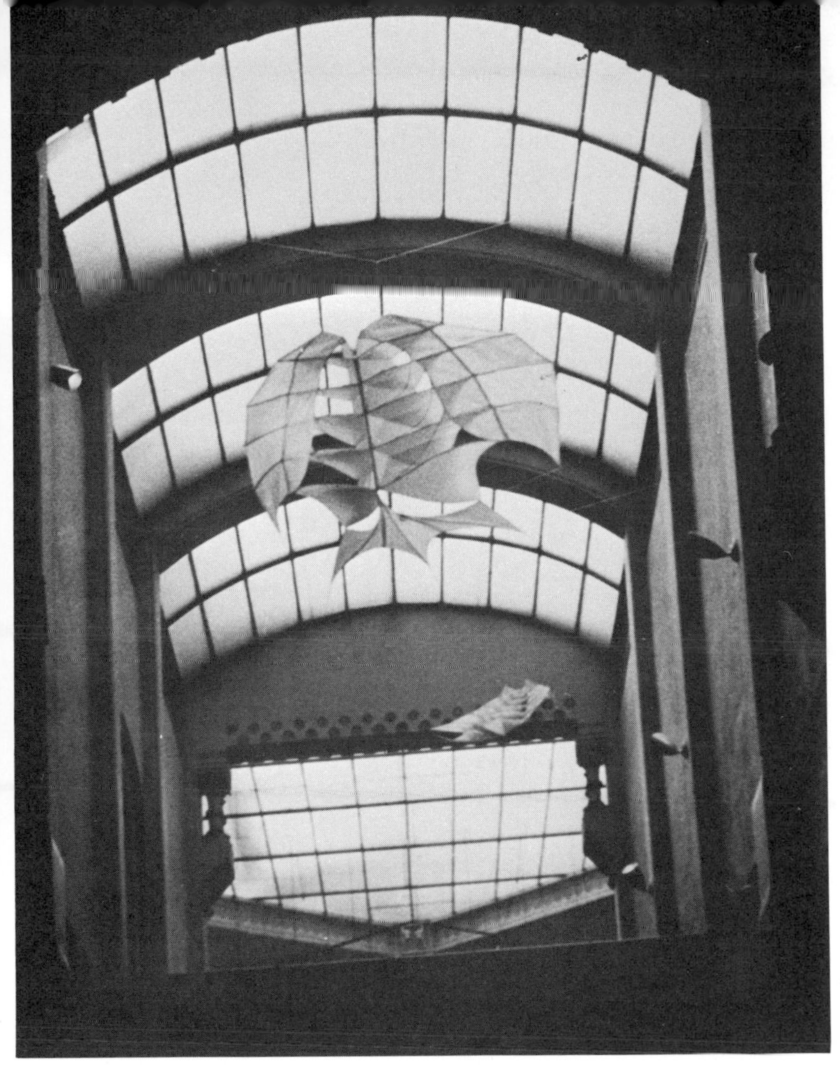

Fumio Yoshimura, inspired by the beauty of kite form and the simplicity of materials, builds fanciful kite sculptures with bamboo and Japanese papers. Courtesy: Fumio Yoshimura.

This classic Japanese centipede kite is made up of eleven circular, paper-covered bamboo frames. Each is 10″ in diameter, and the full kite extends to 6′. Because of its length and the need for extremely precise balancing, this is one of the most difficult kites to fly.

Although Yoshimura's sculptures are not built to fly, their beauty as "kites" and as works of art is undiminished. Courtesy: Fumio Yoshimura.

Jackie Monnier, one of several modern artists who have found kites an appealing form to experiment with, decorates the long long tails for which her kites are known.

The Glite®, one of the simplest and very best commercial kites, is shown in flight. The secret to its successful and easy flying lies in a molded plastic nose cone which holds the keel and spars at the proper angle.

A bug kite sculpture, made in 1965 by Fumio Yoshimura of *seki-shu* paper on a bamboo frame, stands 39½″ x 32″ x 13½″. Courtesy: Container Corporation of America and the Museum of Contemporary Crafts.

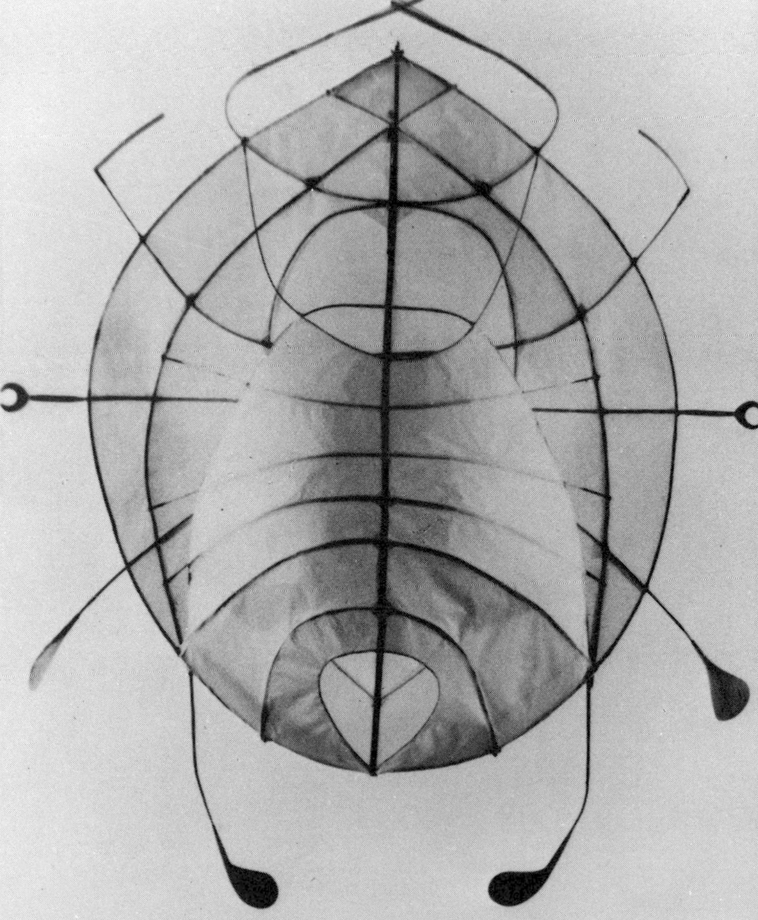

Charles Henry came to kites through his work as a sculptor. This elegant form was constructed of fiber glass rod and nylon cloth. The photo illustrates how the flexible rod reacts to a sudden gust of wind.

The Puffer® kite suggests the relationship between kite and balloon. It is an inflated plastic sheet which has been heat sealed to retain the air. Extremely light, the Puffer will fly in almost any breeze.

The sport of sky-surfing, using an adaptation of the Rogallo parawing, is gaining increasing popularity. Necessarily, the rule to follow is not to fly farther than you would like to fall. Courtesy: Canadian Club.

Flying Lips, by an unknown maker, was flown at a kite festival in Charlotte, N.C. Courtesy: Tal Streeter.

The first gyro-kites were designed in Germany during WW II. They are meant to be towed behind a moving vehicle; when released the gyro-kite slowly settles to the ground. Courtesy: Smithsonian Institution.

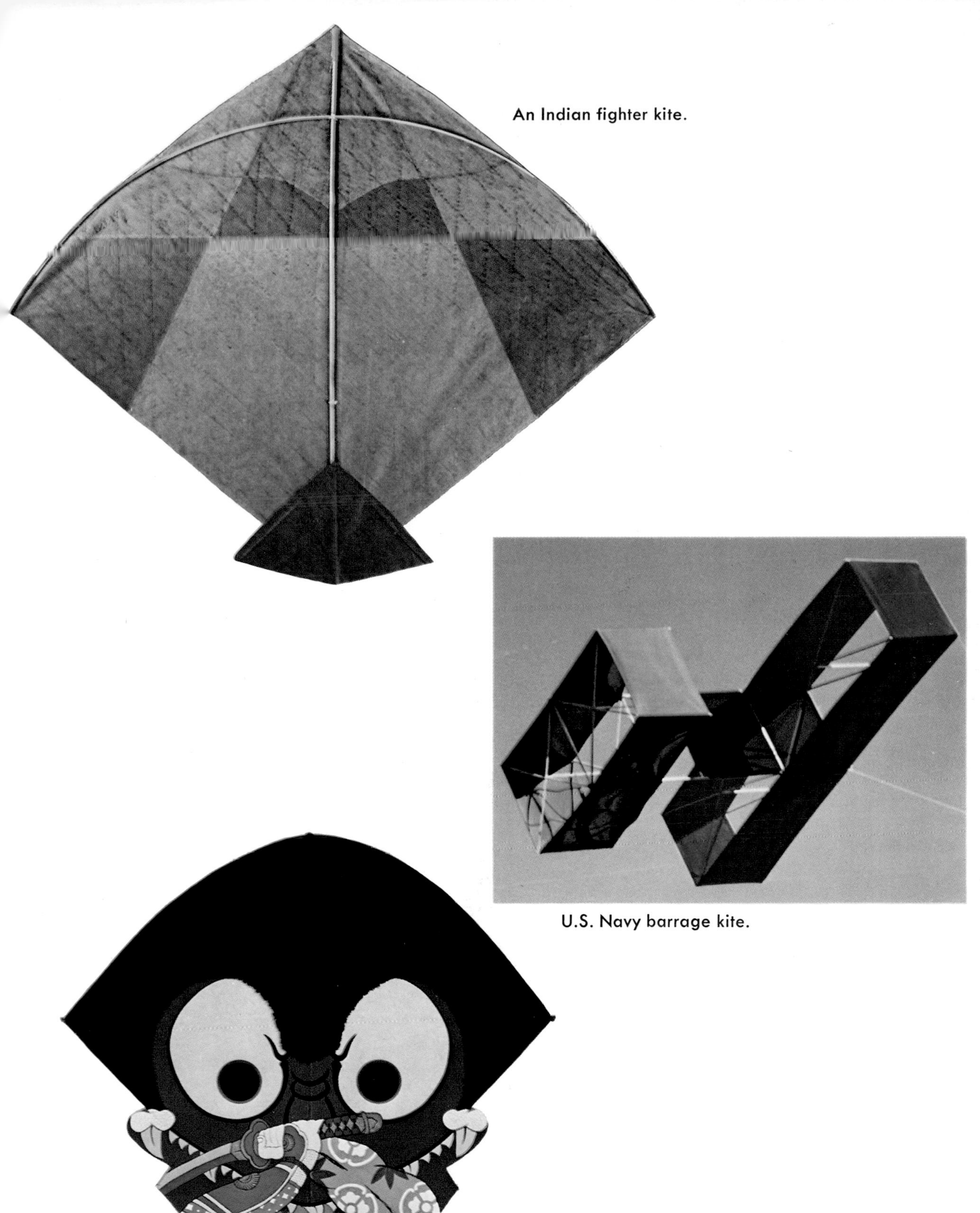

An Indian fighter kite.

U.S. Navy barrage kite.

Japanese warrior kite.

A Jalbert parafoil. Courtesy: Go Fly a Kite Store.

A towering delta wing. Courtesy: Frank Rodriguez.

Sleeve kite: a samurai's servant.

Bermudian head-stick kites. Courtesy: Bermuda News Bureau.

Bird kites by Bevan Brown.

Ted Norton's colorful centipede kite. Courtesy: Ted Norton.

Cicada kite from Japan. Courtesy: Tal Streeter from "The Art of the Japanese Kite."

A butterfly kite.

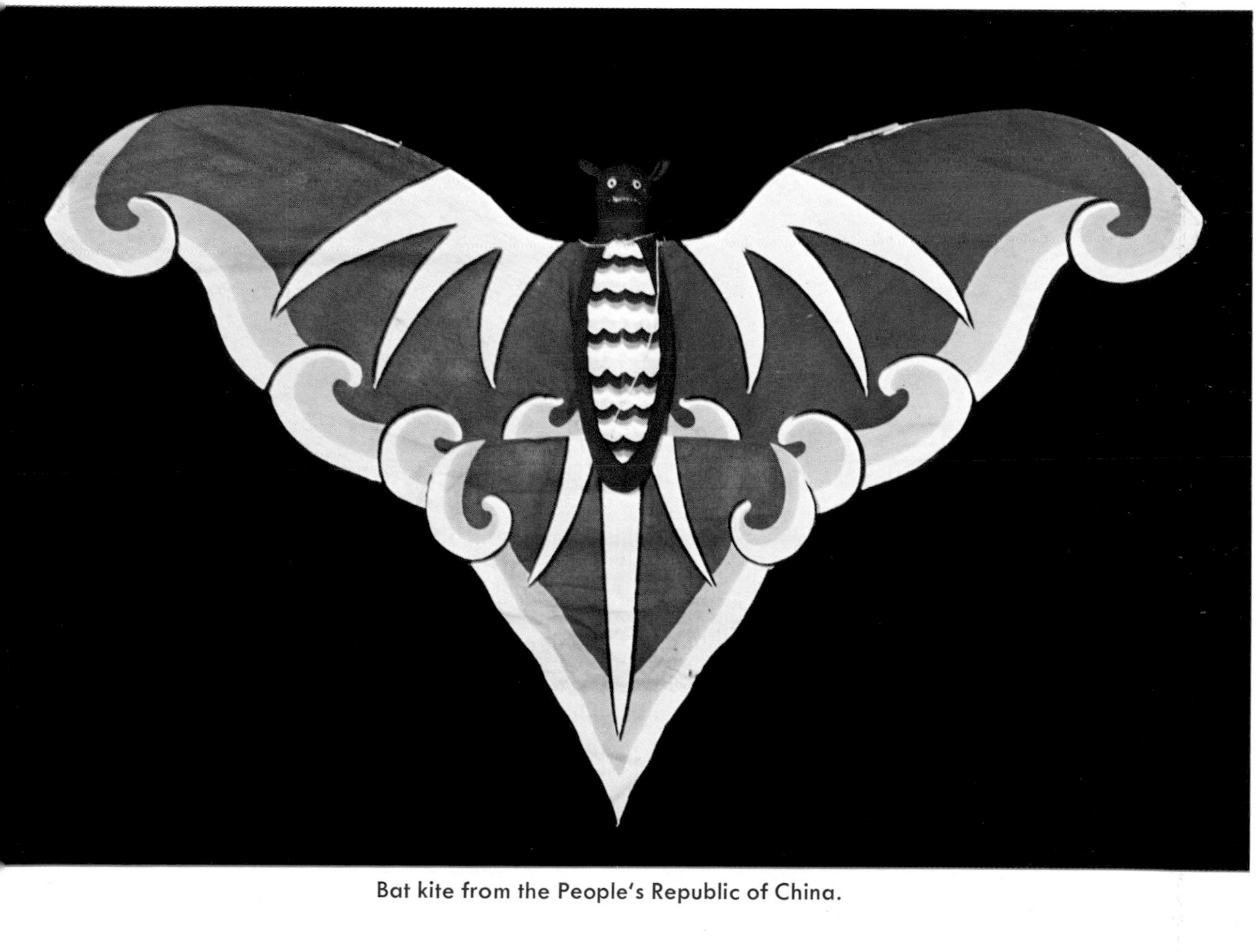

Bat kite from the People's Republic of China.

Nagasaki-hata, archetypal Japanese fighter.

Thai man kite with keel.

Classic confrontations of priest and general.

A realistic eagle by Zeke Contreras. Courtesy: Kite Tales.

Japanese wind-sock carp for Boys' Day Festival. Courtesy: Go Fly a Kite Store.

Chinese bug kite.

One of the giant kites of Japan flown at an annual festival in Shirone, Japan. Eight to twelve men fly the 22′ x 16½′ kite. More than 300 such kites may be flown in combat, one against the other, over the three-day festival period. Courtesy: Tal Streeter, *The Art of the Japanese Kite*.

Tal Streeter, an American sculptor who studied the art of kitemaking in Japan, built this *Flying Red Line*. The kite is pictured in the artist's studio. Courtesy: Tal Streeter.

The Flying Man kite designed by Jean-Michel Folon is built on the principle of the Conyne kite. Courtesy: Entec.

THE AERODYNAMICS OF KITES

Chapter 2

At the heart of every creative and successful kite design is some command of the scientific principles of how a kite flies. Without first mastering a few of the essential concepts of kite aerodynamics, your kite will never perform as well as you would like, and the most fantastic flights of design imagination will never get off the ground. Good design is aesthetically appealing, but it must be functional as well.

By definition, *a kite is a tethered aircraft.* As with all aircraft, from Lawrence Hargrave's first box kite to the SST, certain conditions of air affect flight. Some kites are better fliers than others, and some will fly better on certain days—all because of small differences in a few variables of air, kite construction, and tethering. Weight of kite, balance, size, bridling, speed and steadiness of wind, wind pressure, altitude, terrain, tension of line, permeability of paper or cloth, size of tail or depth of bow, rigidity of form: all affect flight and should be considered in design.

Of course, "good flight" is a relative consideration whose definition depends solely on the kitemaker/flier. Some kitemakers seek products with the greatest lift-to-drag ratios, creating kites which can fly extremely high. At the turn of the century the United States Weather Bureau pursued this objective, raising instruments on a train of ten kites to an altitude of 24,000 feet (over 4½ miles).

But at about the same time, telephone inventor Alexander Graham Bell was experimenting with the application of kites to possible powered flight. He dedicated his research on kite structure not to "ascertain how high a kite may be flown or to make one fly at any very great altitude.

"I have had especially in mind this," he wrote in 1903, "that the equilibrium of the structure in the air should be perfect: that the kite should fly steadily and not move about from side to side or dive suddenly when struck by a squall and that when released should drop slowly and gently to the ground without material oscillation." In this pursuit, Bell also noted the need for a framework possessing "great strength with little weight." This has always been a requisite for efficient tethered flight.

In these two examples, one aimed for *height* and the other for *stability*. But other flight motivations exist in the kiting world, particularly outside the Western countries where we often rely on measures of size or strength as sole expressions of success. Kites were introduced to the West late in comparison to their use in the East. Their history here has been marked by many more scientific than romantic applications. Quite aside from mere height or stability (both admirable traits, by the way), the Orientals have long used kites for sport and recreation. People seeking entertainment build kites for decorations or to do acrobatic feats. In India and Far Eastern countries, kite fights have been the order of the winds for centuries.

The kite craftsman should consider the fact that kites should be designed and constructed for different purposes. But all kites will have one thing in common: they will obey basic rules of aerodynamics, and will therefore fly (if the aerodynamic concepts are sensibly applied). This axiom underlies all kite construction. The rules of aerodynamics must be adhered to in tethered flight.

Kites, being heavier-than-air crafts (aerodynes), defy the forces of gravity which pull all objects toward the earth's center. To stay aloft the kite must apply some force to counteract gravity, and this force is derived from the wind. Air is made up of atoms —constantly moving particles—and when the wind blows, the kite must be able to redirect the force of these onrushing particles in order to rise.

Alexander Graham Bell sought strength and stability in his multicelled tetrahedral kites. His goal was to gain an understanding of kite aerodynamics and apply that knowledge to the development of manned aircraft. Courtesy: National Geographic Society.

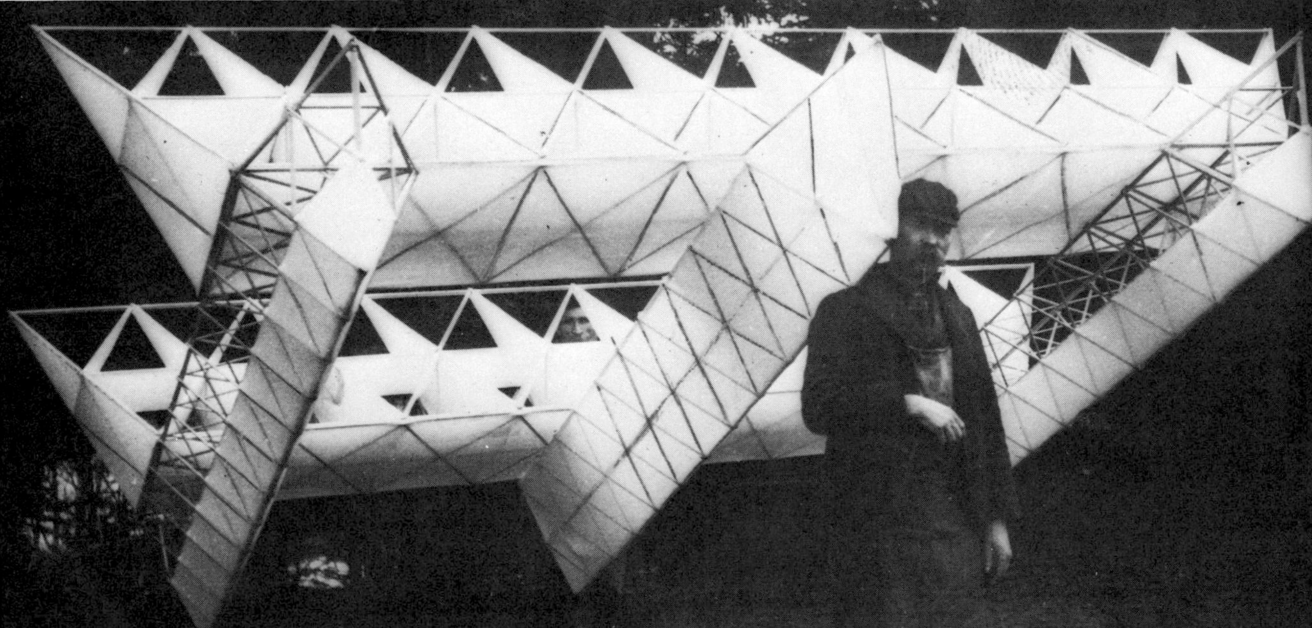

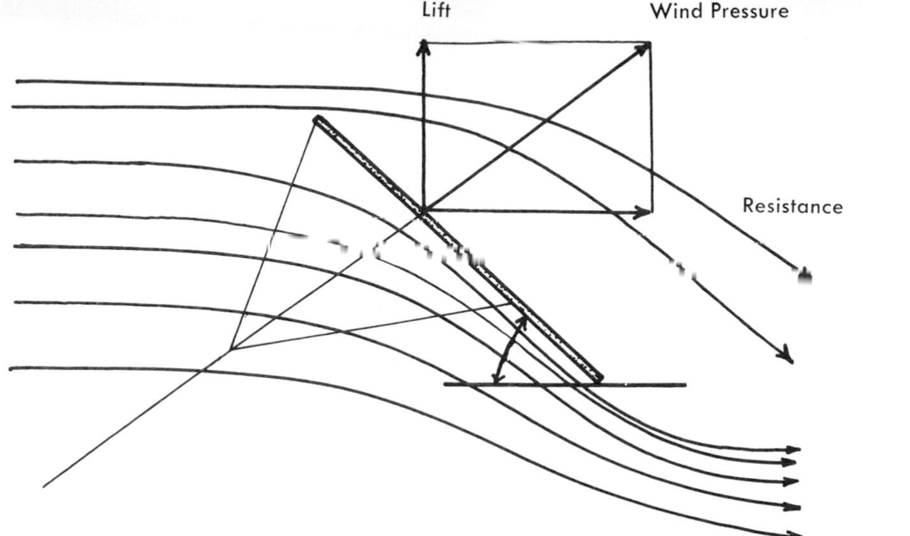

Air resists the passage of any object through it. The kite is angled so that it takes advantage of the wind's force to provide lift. When the effects of wind pressure, lift, resistance (drag) are properly judged and manipulated by construction and bridling, the kite rises most efficiently. The arrows which trace the flow of air around the kite point out that an area of lower air pressure is created on the backside of the lift surface while an area of increased air pressure results on the kite's face. Scientists reason that it is this change ,in relative pressures which actually causes lift.

This manipulation of the wind is effected by the angling of the kite. All air resists the passage of any object through it. So when a kite is sent skyward, the wind will try to force its way through that object. If the kite is angled so as to divert the wind properly, the kite will rise. This works in accordance with Bernouilli's Principle that when the wind blows on an airfoil the airflow immediately above the topside is faster and pressure (on that side) will be reduced. Similarly, the airflow diverted downward moves more slowly, causing air pressure to increase on the underside. This creates a kind of "vacuum," or reduced pressure center on the top, and this low-pressure area in relation to the increased pressure on the bottom side of the kite results in "lift." The kite rises. These changes in pressure are actually very small, but they are enough to effect the upward movement. The reasoning is that if pressure is reduced on the top side, the pressure on the underside will predominate and force the kite up.

An object which can control the flow of wind to create a change in pressure and subsequently rise on air is called an "airfoil." Airplane wings, sails, bird wings, and kites are all airfoils. An airfoil "foils" the air, redirecting it, putting it to work in the form of lift. The term "lift" is just a way of describing this manipulation of wind forces in overcoming gravity and other opposing forces.

There are other factors besides gravity that fight lift. One key opponent of lift is called "drag." Drag is the kite's or airfoil's frictional resistance to the wind—a resistance that slows skyward progress. Much of the work done in industry to "streamline" objects like jets, boats, and cars is aimed at cutting down the wind's resistance to (and drag on) the object.

All kites have lift and drag. The perfect airfoil would have only lift—no drag, but this is a theoretical ideal which can never be achieved because kites are objects with weight and dimension. The amount of lift a kite develops will always depend upon the amount of drag produced. Lift is an inverse function of drag. This relationship is called the lift-to-drag ratio. For high flight, lift should be maximized and drag should be minimized. In scientific terms, the lift-to-drag ratio should be maximized for high flight. Obviously, if drag is ever greater than lift, the kite will not fly.

It is within the framework of lift and drag that all kite designs and variations emerge. The serious kite craftsman learns quickly how best to manipulate these factors to achieve the desired characteristics. This will include reduction or introduction of protrusions which will alter resistance to the airflow; the proportion of length of a kite to span; degree of bowing (a type of streamlining), weight and length of tails, and the like.

WIND, ANGLE, BRIDLE

Setting a kite at the proper angle to the wind is one of the single most important

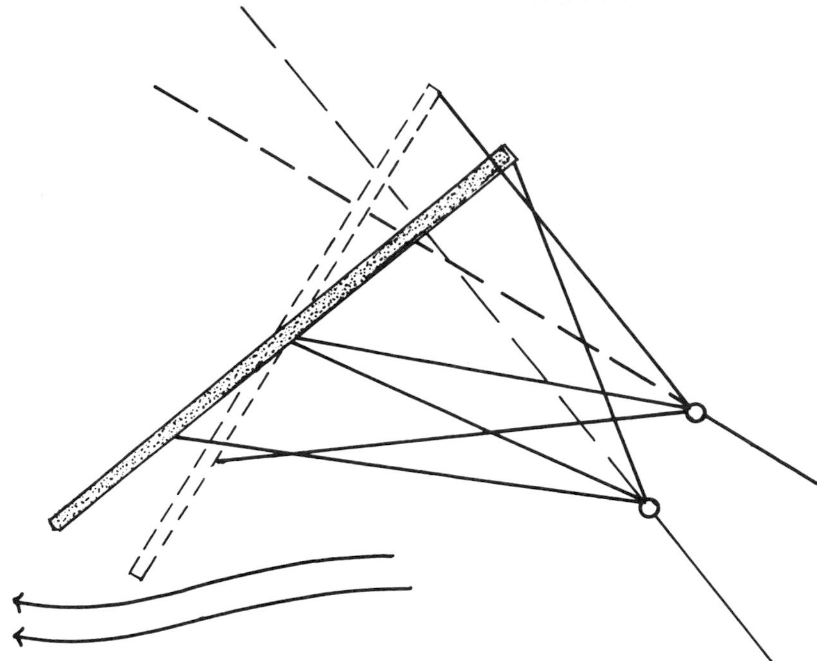

Kite angle must be adjusted for different winds. In a heavy wind most kites require a smaller flying angle than in a light breeze. This change in angle, which is accomplished by adjustments in the bridle, allows more or less air to "escape" under the trailing edge of the kite. On very windy days, if the kite faces the wind too directly, it might be destroyed by the pressure.

considerations in preparing a kite for flight. But to decide on the angle, one must know how the general and the individual airfoils react at different angles in different winds.

If the kite plane is parallel to the direction of the wind (0°–20°) it is not likely to have very great lift, even though the drag component is smallest at small angles. The angle is simply not great enough to divert enough wind to create lift and counteract the force of gravity under most conditions. At such low angles the kite is said to "stall." For most kites, an angle of flight between 20° and 35° from the horizontal will prove effective. Beyond that degree, as the kite angle approaches 45°, lift will still be great, but because of the increase in drag, the kite will not fly as well. The 45° angle of incidence to the wind is the peak of drag. Past 45°, most kites will tend to fly (if at all) like clothes on a line, flapping in unequal, inconsistent resistance to an untapped, uncontrolled wind flow. No tethered craft should be flown at such a negative angle.

Angle, then, is a singularly effective tool in achieving flight. But remember that while any particular angle might be the right one for a certain kite on a certain day, it may be the wrong one under other conditions. The Eddy bow kite, for example, is only slightly sensitive to flying angle, while some airplane kite designs cannot rise stably without just the right setting to the wind.

If an angle is wrong for the wind, the kite is likely to dive, flutter, spin about, slip, tear, do just about anything but fly right.

Finding the correct angle for flight in different wind conditions is essentially a trial-and-error matter. It requires experimentation at the launch site. Knowing the kite's stability, weight, and special idiosyncrasies helps you in determining the exact setting for the day. But you also need to know a little about the wind too.

One of the handiest ways of judging wind velocity was derived by Sir Francis Beaufort, an English rear admiral who sought to give sailors a convenient set of signs by which to estimate wind conditions. The system is called the Beaufort Scale, and it is especially useful for kitefliers in distinguishing a light breeze from a gentle or moderate breeze—a difference of up to 14 mph which may help you decide which kites can be flown.

BEAUFORT SCALE

BEAU-FORT #	*NAME*	*MPH*	*DESCRIPTION*
0	Calm	Less than 1	Calm: smoke rises vertically
1	Light air	1–3	Direction of wind shown by smoke but not by wind vanes
2	Light breeze	4–7	Wind felt on face; leaves rustle; ordinary vane moved by wind
3	Gentle breeze	8–12	Leaves and small twigs in constant motion; wind extends light flag
4	Moderate breeze	13–18	Raises dust and loose paper; small branches are moved
5	Fresh breeze	19–24	Small trees in leaf begin to sway; crested wavelets form on inland water
6	Strong breeze	25–31	Large branches in motion; telegraph wires whistle: umbrellas used with difficulty

The scale continues through moderate, fresh, strong, and whole gales, "storm" from 64–72 mph, and a variety of hurricanes (up to 136 mph) at which point the Beaufort Scale records only that "devastation occurs." Obviously, few fanatics will fly their kites much beyond a moderate or fresh breeze, the best wind velocities for kites having been generally found between 4 and 20 mph.

Wind and angle both, then, must be treated together to achieve efficient flight. But how does the kiteflier manipulate these factors? With the bridle. It is the bridle—usually a two-legged piece of cord attached to the kite at different points along the center vertical spine, which is then attached to the flying line—that fixes a kite's attitude to the wind. It is a primary tool of the kiteman working for maximum lift.

Most flat kites, for instance, fly well with a bridle spoke attached one-third of the way down from the kite top, with the second string-spoke tied to the kite bottom. Depending on the actual balance of the kite, this may vary slightly, just as this imposed angle is expected to deviate in different winds. For perfect balance, one should remember that there are three centers of force in a kite: center of pressure, center of gravity, and center of thrust (center of lift). Center of pressure is determined by kite shape and angle to wind. Center of gravity is set by the distribution of weight across the kite surface. And the center of thrust is a function of the attachment and angle of the bridle itself. The object of a good bridle attached to the face of a kite is to orient the kite at a flying position that best distributes the wind pressure to create lift. For perfect balance and stability, the bridle should be adjusted so that the kite's center of gravity coincides with the imaginary center of thrust. When these centers meet, and the lifting power proves stronger than the forces of gravity, the kite will climb smoothly skyward. If the bridle spokes do not meet at the center of lift (thrust), or, in other words, if the kite is set at the wrong angle for the wind conditions, the kite may dive, flutter, spin, wobble, slip, fly ineffectually.

One of the simple and perhaps nearly foolproof ways of finding a close to perfect bridle setting is to start by arbitrarily tying the two spokes (of a flat kite's bridle) with one at the base of the kite face, the other extending from a point one-third down from

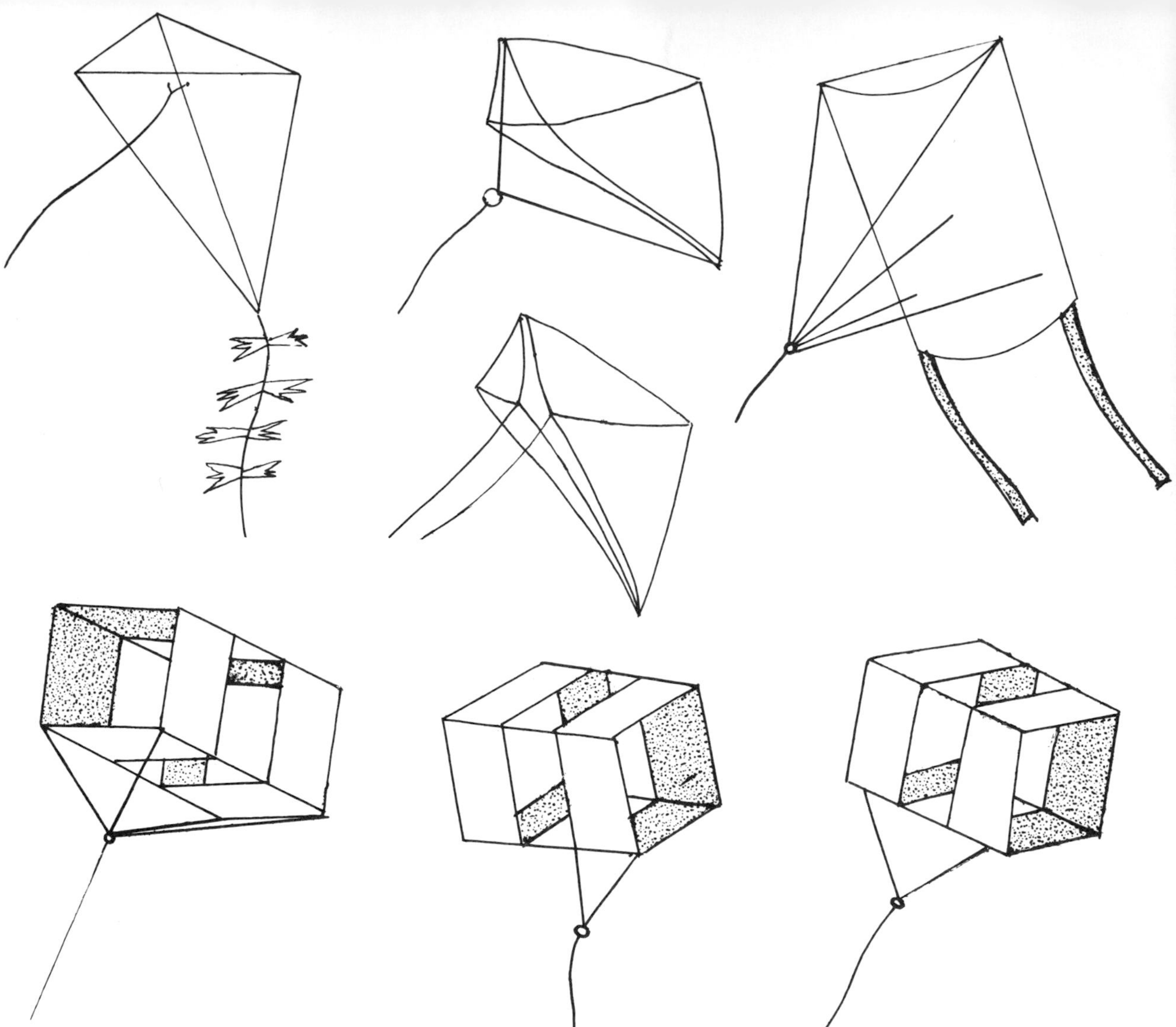

There is a wide variety of bridling methods. Any bridle which keeps the kite stable works, but some are more efficient. The use of many bridle legs, for instance, is often advisable since this helps to distribute wind pressure over the entire kite face more evenly. The diamond kites above show single-leg, double-leg, and four-leg bridles. Most Japanese kites employ bridles with numerous shroud lines, as at the upper right. There is a variety of box kite bridlings too, but the three primary techniques are shown above. Experimentation holds the key to expert bridling.

the top edge. Tie both onto the center spine of the kite. Pierce holes in the paper with an awl or knife to get the string through the paper face to the framework behind. The length of the bridle itself will vary, of course, according to the size of the kite, but as a standard, use a length of line that is approximately four times the length of the distance between the two attached points on the center spine for the entire length of bridle.

Once the holes have been made (reinforce holes with looseleaf reinforcers, tape, or use eyelets), the string looped through and tied, hold the bridle so that the top spoke is extended at a 90° angle from the kite face at a distance equal to the distance between the two spokes along the center spine. Holding at this point, correct any slack in the other spoke. Now, still grasping the kite bridle at this point, pull it and the kite into the wind and see if the kite maintains a reasonable angle (between 20° and 35°) and appears to want to rise. If this seems to be the case, tie a loop at this juncture—it will probably serve as a reasonable bridling point, approximating the center of lift.

A note on tying: It is best to use either

simple bowknots, or the clove hitch (described in Chapter 3 on techniques) to form the loop in a bridle. Both knots are easily removed and retied, and since bridling requires regular readjustment, this is quite a help. From this loop in the bridle, the flying line will be strung.

Having approximated the proper bridle, tie some flying line to the loop and send the kite aloft a few feet to check the bridling again. The winds change higher up and so the bridle may require some alterations, effected by a simple shift in the loop either closer to the top or closer to the bottom of the kite. A bridle is considered perfect when the kite rises to its maximum angle and maintains a good flight attack position throughout flight without looping, dipping, or nose-diving in gusts.

Another way of establishing the point for fixing a bridle and flying line is first to tie all the strings firmly to the kite and lay the kite on the floor, facing up. Draw the bridle strings together and lift the kite a foot off the floor. Now, choking up on a string here, or lengthening a string there, adjust bridle strings so that all are equally taut and the framework of the kite is at a 20°–35° angle to the floor with the top of the kite higher off the floor than the tail end.

Once this angle is set, and all lines are taut, tie them together in a loop, fixing the bridle for flight. Here an alternative to tying the clove hitch may be used. Tie the bridle lines onto a light brass or plastic ring at the hitching point. These loops make it extremely easy to tie on or cut off flying lines.

You may also choose to tie loops at several points about one inch apart on the bridle in the general bridling area. This way you can easily select and alter the bridle/kite angle to suit a variety of winds. Swivel fishing hooks which snap on and off the line and can rotate a full 360° may also be of some help in expediting the hook-up process.

There are a few general observations about bridling that will help in judging the best arrangement. As said earlier, the best performances usually result at an angle between 20° and 35°. An angle much lower than 25° actually has a greater tendency to throw the kite into a stall or cause numerous power dives (in which the kite rides directly overhead, begins to nose-dive, and plunges speedily downward—it can mean disaster at low altitudes, or great fun when the kite rights itself at higher levels). In any case, no two kites ever fly quite alike, but generally, in a light wind, use a bridle with a steeper angle of incidence (hitched at a lower point from the top). This increases the amount of kite surface that faces the wind, making the kite less streamlined but better able to "find" enough wind to create lift. Concomitantly, in a strong wind move the hitch to a point nearer to the kite top. The kite becomes more streamlined, permitting more air to escape around it. The kite will be less likely to be shredded by heavy gusts.

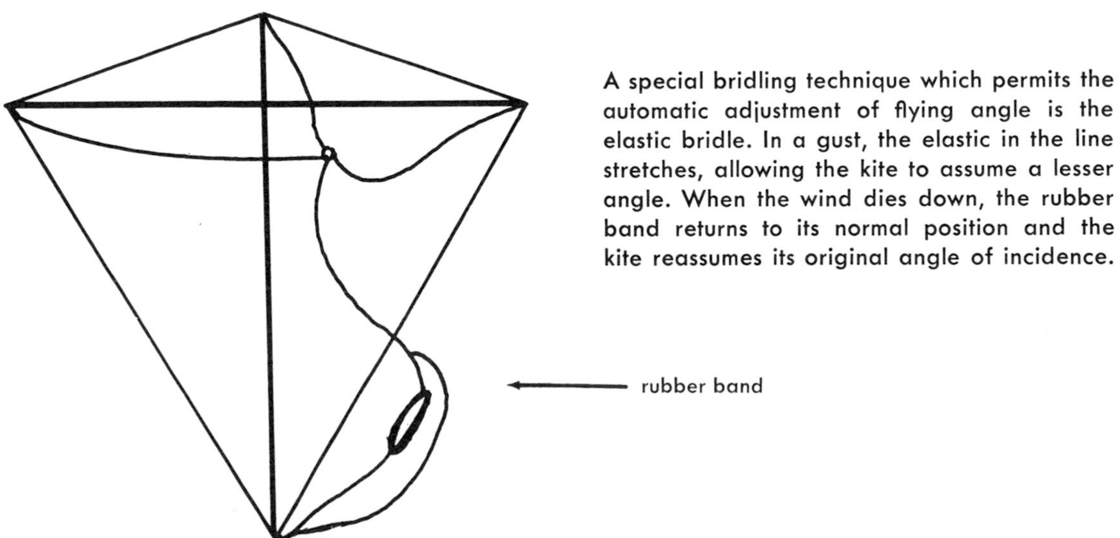

A special bridling technique which permits the automatic adjustment of flying angle is the elastic bridle. In a gust, the elastic in the line stretches, allowing the kite to assume a lesser angle. When the wind dies down, the rubber band returns to its normal position and the kite reassumes its original angle of incidence.

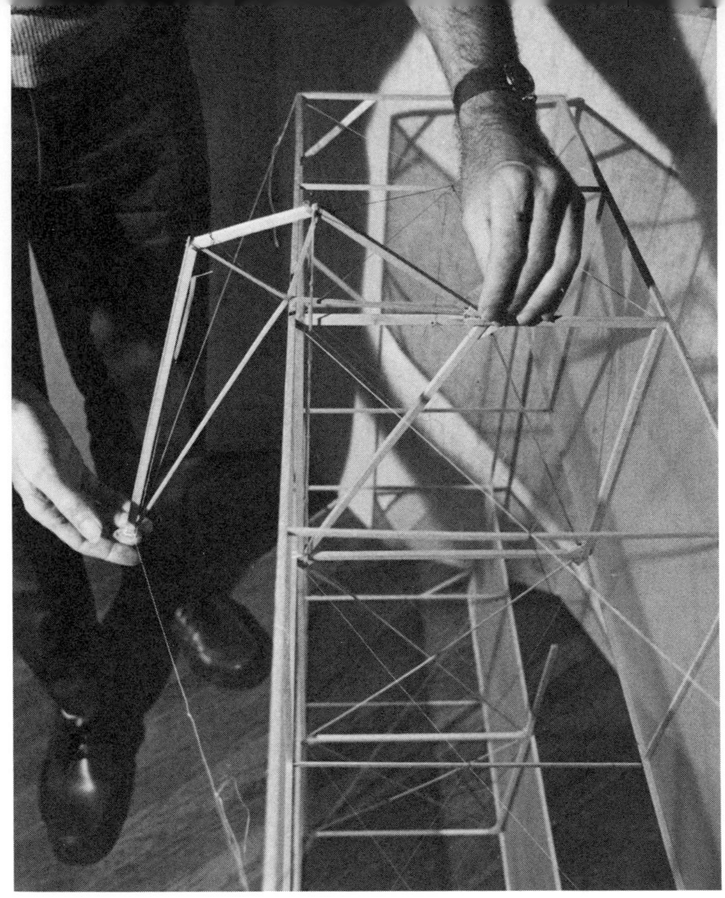

William Bigge demonstrates his own elastic bridling system for a box kite. The purpose of any elastic bridling system is to anticipate change in wind intensity and provide for the dissipation of excess wind pressure which might damage the kite.

During World War II, the Navy Target Kite, developed by Commander Paul Garber, provided gunners with a constantly moving target. The kite is flown with two lines and is manipulated with a twin-spool reel complete with a control bar, handle, and brake. Skilled fliers have proved that Garber's bridling/reel system provides the ultimate in flight control.

You will find some kites that don't even need a bridle—they achieve the proper attitude on a single line attached at the center of gravity for the kite. But it is still a good idea to bridle most kites accurately and sufficiently, since bridling can do more than just help a kite fly right. Bridles, by being attached at several effective points on the flying surface, distribute the stress placed on the kite by wind. Without proper bridles some fine kites might be damaged by wind pressure.

One notable advance in bridling was the introduction of the elastic bridle in the 1890s. Constructed exactly like the normal bridle with the exception of an intervening heavy-duty rubber band, this bridle eases excess tension on the flying caused by sudden gusts. In the strongest winds, the elastic will stretch, resulting in a change in flying angle. When normal winds again prevail, the elastic will relax and return the kite to the original flying angle.

TAILS

Tails help to stabilize kites. They are particularly effective with flat kites and extra-wide kites which require some lateral stabilization.

Part of the stabilizing force is provided by the extra drag that a tail creates. Every tail encounters the same friction and turbulent forces that the kite itself deals with, and the extra weight of the tail also helps stabilize the aircraft.

All flat kites need tails, otherwise they spin and loop uncontrollably in most instances. A good tail eliminates these tendencies while only minimally hindering lift and maneuverability.

The drag of a tail that blows out behind a kite parallel to the wind keeps the kite facing in the right direction. It maintains proper orientation, acting much as a spine does. Most tailless kites have fins of some sort which, like a tail, act as lateral stabilizers and rudders for the craft.

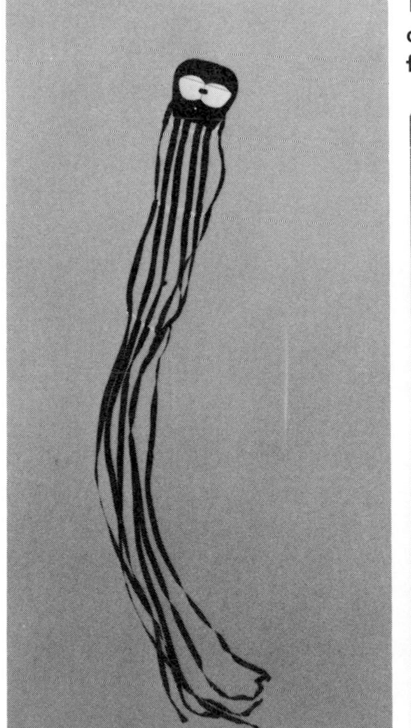

Ted Norton's streaming octopus, "Orville," shows both the decorative and practical uses of tails. The design is derived from that of the Thai snake kite. Courtesy: Ted Norton.

Artist Jackie Monnier puts great stock in the beauty and flight-worthiness of the tail. She uses a wide variety of painting and printing techniques on her airbound scrolls. The abundance of paper permits the flying of an otherwise low-wind kite on gusty days because of the increase in drag. Courtesy: Jackie Monnier.

Besides correcting the tendency to face away from the wind and to flap uncontrollably, the tail corrects the twisting and turning of a kite. In a gust, for example, the kite may suddenly twist to one side. This motion will continue down through the tail, causing it to snake from side to side. When the tail is of the correct weight and length, this swishing action counteracts the kite sway, bringing the kite back on course so it can straighten out and fly right.

A good tail should swing like a pendulum, dancing as the kite flies. But if the tail is long, too heavy, or too stiff, it will wag the kite, a reverse process that is inherently destabilizing. On the other hand, a tail that is too short will not be effective in controlling looping.

The tail need not be particularly heavy. Although in a very high wind, lighter kites may be steadied by a heavy tail, the more appropriate and common purpose of the tail is to add drag and correct instabilities resulting from variations in wind conditions.

The standard single tail is made by cutting strips of cloth approximately two inches by six inches. These strips are knotted into strong line about four to six inches apart. Knot the line around the cloth, and not the other way around, otherwise all the cloth strips will fall to the bottom of the line.

This type of tail is adjusted by lengthening and shortening, by moving the strips of cloth together or farther apart, or by adding more strips for weight, drag, and stiffness. A good procedure in adjusting the tail is to begin with a tail about four times as long as the kite's diagonal. Adjust it gradually to the wind conditions by experimentation. Do not forget, however, that as the kite goes up it will find upper winds of different velocity from the ground wind.

Typically, the stronger the wind, the longer the tail—or tails. Aesthetically, some kites look better with two or more tails. In these cases, do not use cloth tied to the string because this has a greater tendency to tangle unmanageably. Use long crepe paper strips that will flutter and wave behind a high flier actively and attractively.

DROGUE

Although a drogue is in no way closely related to the kite tail, it serves some of the same purposes. What is a drogue? Commonly called a wind cup, the drogue is a most efficient way of adding resistance and ruddering for lateral stability when stability is not guaranteed by the kite design itself.

What the drogue does is to offset, by simple leverage, the destabilizing forces of drag which affect wide kites, or kites with broad tops. So the wider the nose of the kite, or wider the wingspan, the farther back the drogue must be placed to be effective. The advantage of drogues is their simplicity, not to mention the fact that they do not adversely affect the liveliness or lift of a kite as some tails will.

First used by George Nares in the nineteenth century, the drogue or wind cup is self-regulating, hence quite efficient. As a wind picks up, the cup or cups will fly at an angle nearly horizontal to the ground, catch-

A drogue is used instead of a tail with this parasled by Domina Jalbert. The drogue is a convenient lateral stabilizer for the kite.

ing more and more air inside the cone shape, offering increased resistance and at the same time directing the kite into the wind.

A series of wind cones is often quite effective as a substitute for a tail. The force developed by air flowing through the drogues will increase the speed at which that wind travels, providing optimal stabilization in a large range of wind velocities. Kitefliers have recorded higher flights with drogue tails than with any other type. Currently, drogues have come into play as a simple stabilizing feature of the fantastically light and efficient parafoils designed by Domina Jalbert.

BOWING

In tailless kites, or in those with very little tail, the kite is kept upright by angling the surface backward along the vertical center. This is called "bowing."

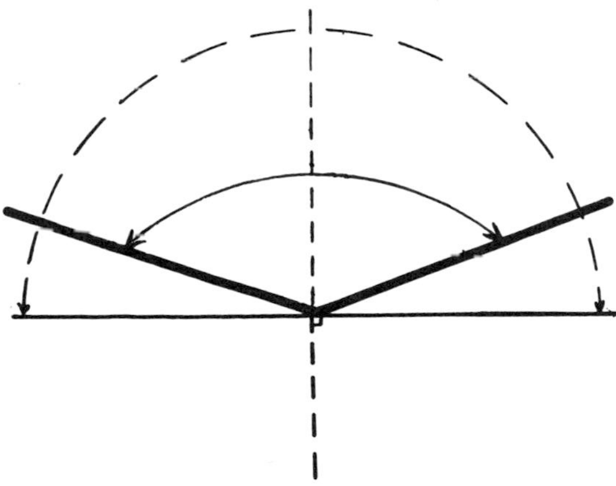

The special righting tendency of bowed kites comes from the formation of a dihedral angle surface—a surface where two butting planes intersect at an angle like the backswept wings of an airplane.

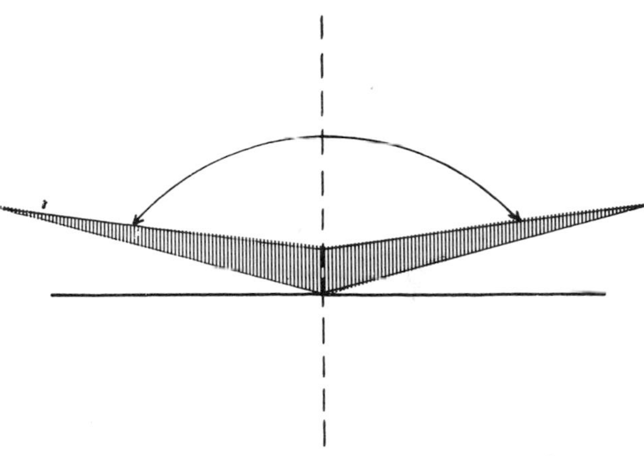

The front of a bowed kite, like the wings of a jet, form a more streamlined positive dihedral angle to the onrushing wind than a flat plane . . .

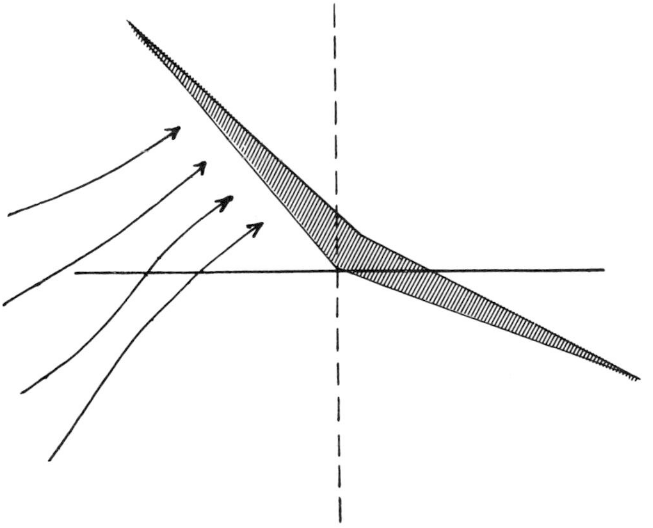

. . . if a sudden gust of wind strikes one side of the kite face more than the other, that side will tip back.

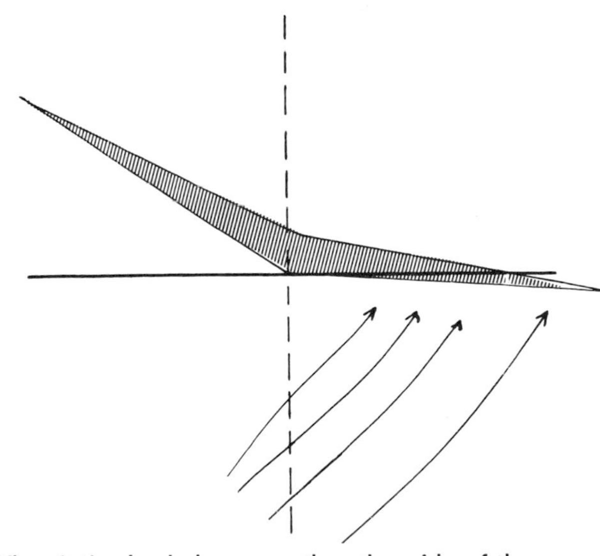

When it tips back, however, the other side of the dihedral face dips forward—increasing wind pressure on that face. This brings the pressure on both faces closer to equilibrium, thereby righting the entire kite.

Bowing effects a special righting tendency by creating a "dihedral" angle. A dihedral surface is one in which two planes (faces) butt each other at an angle, actually a bending or folding along the axis of symmetry. Dihedral angles are used in backswept wings of jets and other aircraft. In fact, the positive dihedral angle created when you bow a kite is quite like that of an airplane where the tips of the wings are higher in the wind than the center section. Bowed surfaces function much like the pointed prow of a ship, cutting the wind, reducing resistance on all sides. The bowing technique increases lateral stability and improves the tendency of a kite to return to a normal, level position in the wind after one or the other side of the kite face has been dropped suddenly by a brief gust. Bowing reduces drag by introducing a kind of streamlining, too. Continuing the ship's prow analogy, flying an unbowed kite in a heavy wind is like cruising in the ocean on a boat with a square prow.

Bows are especially important in high winds where all the faults of a kite become exaggerated. Although bowing will not necessarily remedy the instabilities of all kite designs, one of the best-balanced and stable kites known relies solely on the bowing dihedral principle for directional and lateral stability. The Eddy kite (see Chapter 3) needs no tail for stabilization and is incredibly even-tempered in flight.

Bows are formed by tying a piece of flying line at each end of the cross-spar of a kite, pulling at the string until the bamboo or wood strip begins to arc forward, making the kite face convex. At the end of each flight it is wise to undo the bow, in a sense to let the kite "relax"—this kind of tension, you will find, does quite a bit in altering the temperament of the kite. The rule of thumb in using the bow is: heavier wind, deeper bow. Of course, for some kites, bowing will not be the entire answer (this is generally the case with many flat kites). Whether the spar is bent or not, a tail or some other lower end corrective device may be advisable to provide the stability necessary for successful flight.

VENTING

Ever since Australian Lawrence Hargrave introduced cellular construction with

The dihedral principle which is applied to bowing is illustrated in this kite constructed by Lawrence Hargrave. This dihedral kite, built in 1893, is stabilized the same way bowed kites are.

This Taiwanese printed cloth kite comes with strips of cloth sewn on to act as a bowstring. It is easily adjustable.

his famed box kite, kite fanatics and experimenters have utilized open space much more in kite design. Hargrave's work became a starting point for Alexander Graham Bell's own researches toward powered flight. The Wright brothers and others employed combinations of plane surfaces separated by open space for controlling wind. As with the bow's dihedral angle, the use of attached, parallel, perpendicular, and the angled planes was discerned to be a valid, efficient means of getting a kite aloft.

While experimenting with open-sided cells, the Wrights found that the greater the space between the cells, the more stable the kite became in the fore and aft directions. Tendencies to dive or dip could be almost totally eliminated by increasing the flow of unobstructed air between the kite's faces. It was also recognized that the longer the vertical sides of the aircraft, the greater the lateral stability. Tendencies to roll, slide from side to side, or to flip over in the air were thereby reduced. Although hardly the first kites to use vents, the Hargrave box did set the pace for the use of venting in modern kites.

Vents are used not only in three-dimensional designs like the tetrahedrals, boxes, and naval barrage kites, but in two-dimensional constructions as well. The Scott Sled has been modified with vents to fly in nearly all winds; the Marconi sail kite uses the essential principles of sail formation to manipulate the wind through vents and, of course, any kite that has indentations in the flying surface just below the main lift area can be said to be "venting" air indirectly.

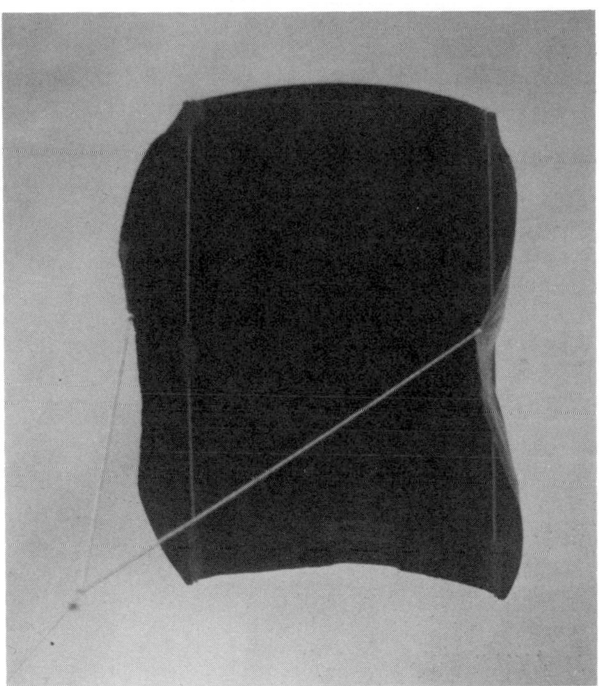

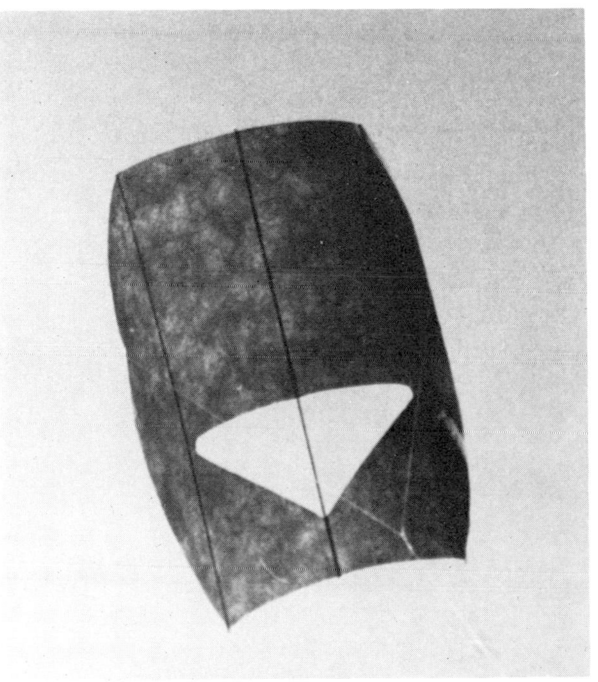

A triangular vent in the Scott Sled allows air to flow through the kite so that it sets up less resistance to the wind. Courtesy: Airplane Kite Company.

Vents can correct the destabilization that results from irregular, or too powerful, airflow by allowing air to pass through the kite. Not all air pressure need be put to work in flying a kite, some always passes above, below, and around, while some flows directly through the kite face. This flow of air through the kite helps stabilize without harming the design or interfering with lift. If the vent is on the top half of the kite, behind which the reduced pressure area is generated, lift would be destroyed, however, and the kite would not fly well at all. So proper placement of the vent is an important consideration.

Venting is an alternative to tapered kite designs which allow the air to escape in a different fashion. Malaysian moon kites, for example, although having a broad lifting surface, taper down to a much narrower surface toward the tail of the craft. This narrowing ventilates the kite, allowing air to flow as near to "through" the kite as possible, thus acting like a vent. The delta wing kite is designed in a bowed taper so that, even though it has no vent, it allows airflow to pass evenly on both sides.

The Scott Sled, although made and flown with and without vents, has been found to fly successfully in high winds only when vented. The renowned Jalbert parafoil flies quite successfully without vents, but it should be noted that ventrals provide stabilization, eliminating this need for venting. Parafoils also fly at a lower angle of attack, and are aided by drogue rudders to give proper orientation to the wind.

Vents, then, should be considered as a design tool. Many of the designs in this book illustrate how creative kite craftsmen preserve the lift surface while forming vents or use substitutes such as tapering, narrowing, bowing, and ruddering at the drag end.

The Malaysian moon kite uses another approach to venting. Its structure minimizes wind resistance while still providing an adequate lift surface.

The box kite is stabilized by the vent areas between the cells. The covered areas of a box kite must be sufficiently large to offer a lifting surface to the wind; they channel the airflow as does a set of dihedral angles. If the entire length of a box kite were covered with cloth or paper, stability would decrease. The vented open space between laterals, where the wind passes through uninterrupted, liberates the box kite from excessive wind pressure, resistance, and drag.

RUDDERS

Experiments in kite construction have shown the importance of yet another aerodynamic relationship: the aspect ratio. While the kiteman need not understand the precise calculations involved in this ratio, he should have a grasp of what it entails to be able to apply a notion of the aspect ratio to kite construction. In boats, this ratio is the relationship of the height of a rudder to its fore-aft length. For the kite it is the relationship between the width of the leading edge(s) of the kite and the distance from it that the rudder must be placed to achieve directional stability. Small kites are difficult to fly if they lack a tail or rudder. They are directionally unstable and have no fore-aft leverage on which to establish stability in the face of the wind. The pressure on a kite with a very broad lifting surface must somehow be offset by having a tail or other balancing measure at the bottom end. The general rule is: the broader the lift surface, the farther back the rudder needs to be to compensate and stabilize. Aircraft that have very wide wings with only a short distance from those wings to the rudder/tail are said to have greater aspect ratios. Skinny, long kites have a lesser aspect ratio since the wingspan is small in relation to the length.

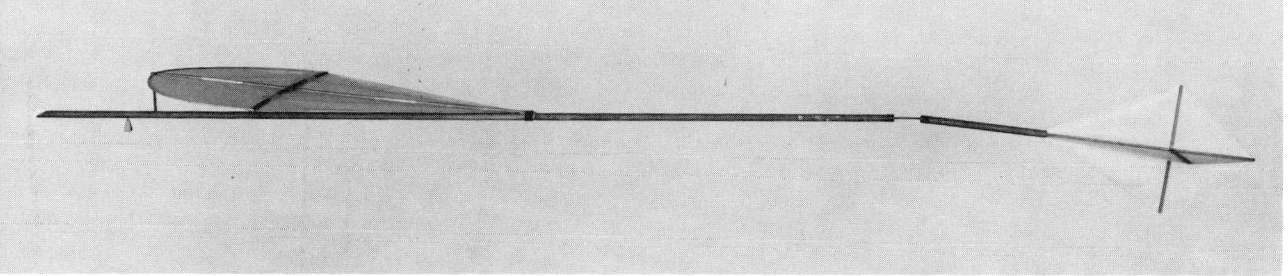

Sir George Cayley had an excellent conception of the function of the rudder in kites: the broader the lift surface, the farther back the rudder must be to provide adequate directional stability. Courtesy: The Science Museum, London.

It is a sensitive relationship, which is particularly evident in such forms as the navy barrage kite, where there is a most definite relationship between wing width and fore-aft length required for best stabilization. Venting and tapering, as well as the kite size and the proportion of wing length to distance from rudder end, alter the aspect ratio.

This aspect ratio can, of course, be described in terms of lift and drag. The larger the aspect ratio, the greater the lifting surface and the greater the lift. But there is a point of diminishing returns for those planning kites with wider and wider wings with an eye on achieving fantastic lift. Practically, a kite that has an extremely large aspect ratio can be expected to be far too unstable and structurally weak to be a reasonable design. Intelligent design implies that factors like lift and drag, span and length, venting and covering be interrelated, not in competition with no regard for *proportion*. There are reasonable limits to which any design tool may be extended; beyond these lies failure to properly analyze those elements toward the goal of efficient flight.

LAUNCHING, FLYING, LANDING

You have designed a kite with all the important considerations in mind. The kite has been bridled for the estimated wind velocity. It has the correct bow or tail, and you think it is about time to send it up. The first rule in putting the kite to flight is to stay calm and always proceed in an orderly manner.

Launching is often like a psychological battle with the winds on high. Patience is essential in this. Take the time to check and to recheck the kite's balance, wind conditions, the bridling, and knots. Attach the proper-strength flying line to to the bridling loop.

Running with a kite is an absolute no-no. Not only is it poor style, tiring, and requires two people, but it more often than not is ineffectual. Running with a kite is also a way to damage your kite, leaving you worse off than before.

In decent breezes (relative to the weight and size of the kite), a single person may launch a kite easily. With your back to the wind, cast the kite into the air, feeding out line as the wind takes hold of the kite. Let the string out gradually, sending it aloft.

Square bottom kites, box kites, and others may be stood on the ground about 50 feet downwind from where you stand and hoisted up with a quick jerk in an appropriate gust.

Yanking on a kite line increases the wind speed and turbulence on the top side of the kite. It fosters a temporary artificial lift which carries the kite to a height where the natural wind can do the lifting work without your help. Besides pumping on the kite line, you can also walk at a medium pace backward from the kite to get it to rise. Your walking speed offers a consistent extra wind velocity, giving added lift.

In a light wind, one-man hand takeoffs are sometimes impossible. Have a friend hold the kite as you walk with the attached spool of line about one hundred feet downwind. Wait for a gust to come up, and have the friend toss the kite skyward. Simultaneously, pull on the line in firm tugs. At a certain altitude the kite may catch on to a steady breeze above the ground current. In lighter winds, until the kite finds a firmer breeze, hold the line taut. Never permit slack if you can help it. Slack only limits your control. When the kite "asks" for more line by pulling at the line, feed out string gradually. Stop again, let the kite pick up slack, perhaps rising to a higher altitude and a better angle. When it asks for more line, feed it. Repeat this process until your kite reaches the desired height.

At medium heights, short tugs and pumping on the line can be particularly helpful in sending the kite higher in the air and can also bring it more squarely into the wind. If the kite tends to dart around, pumping is advised, but if it continues to dart, make quick loops, flip, or dive, do not continue to tug on the line. Feed out a little more. The kite should right itself. If not, try correcting the bridling or balance, because perhaps there is too much or too little wind.

If the kite performs some sudden sideslipping or diving from one side to the other, the release of just a few yards of line can quickly correct the dancing. But in a sharp dive, the pull only accelerates the downward progress. If the kite is slowly drifting to one side and seems to be falling, try running across the wind in the same direction as that of the falling kite, letting out extra line. The extra line often creates sufficient drag (caused by the sheer weight excess and the velocity of your run) to return the kite to the correct flight angle. It is an instance where the string works somewhat like an extended rudder.

A kite that pulls firmly while climbing steeply in the sky shows excellent aerodynamic qualities. But it is often the case with a quick-rising kite that the flier will pay out too much line too fast. The kite may pass the breeze, ride nearly directly overhead, and fly flat, parallel to the ground. At this point a kite may enter a power dive. Depending on the bridling, an overhead kite may suddenly nose-dive, rushing at the ground with just a little tug on the line. This is innocent amusement if the kite has sufficient altitude to recover from the negative flight angle. But if too close to the ground, a power dive (caused when drag overcomes lift) may prove fatal to the kite. Looping is only safe at high altitudes.

A kite is flying well when it lies at the proper angle to the wind (as bridled and tailed), does not exert excessive pull on the line, and responds promptly to tugs (rising several feet on a short pull downward on the line). Perhaps the most miserable of flights occurs when a kite refuses to rise more than a few feet off the ground. In this instance, consider adjusting the bridle angle or tail, or else save the kite for a windier day.

The best conditions for putting up a high-altitude kite are when the weather is warm, a little humid, with partially cloudy skies—the prime condition for finding thermals. A thermal is a rising body of warm air. If a kite finds a thermal, it can climb speedily for hundreds of feet. The thermals are usually found above broad areas with good sun reflection (parking lots, lakes, and other bodies of water).

But whether looking for high-flying thermals or not, *where* to fly must be considered quite seriously before you fly. Choose a field where there are no trees. The modern kite cliché is a Peanuts cartoon of bowl-headed Charlie Brown covering his eyes at the sight

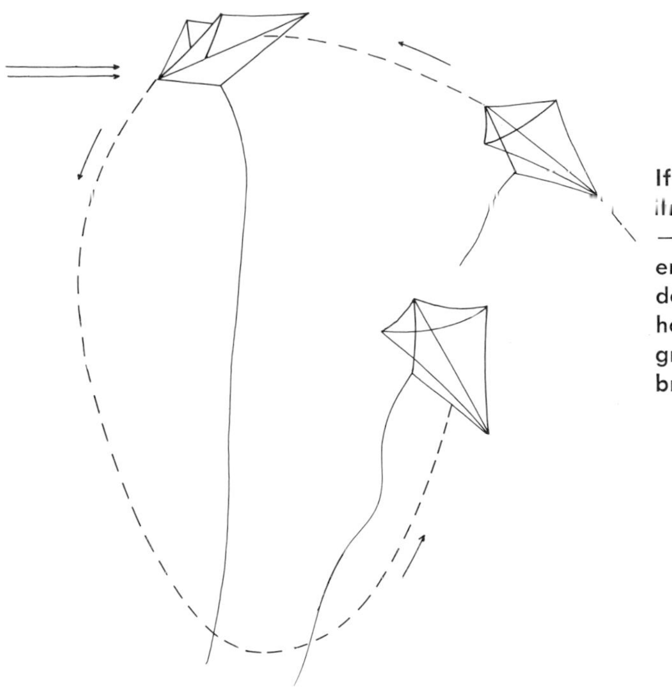

If a kite climbs too far overhead, beware! Past its flying apex, as the flying angle approaches −1°, a kite is most likely to tip nose down and enter a "power dive." The kite will soar straight downward, and only if it is high enough will it have time to right itself. Flying close to the ground? Too bad. Next time look for a better bridling and flying angle.

of a "kite-eating tree." Avoid areas with telephone poles and high-tension wires. Never fly on a street or over a road where the kite might distract drivers. There are Federal Aeronautics Administration regulations about flying kites in the vicinity of an airport. A beach is often an excellent place to launch and fly a kite, utilizing the shore breezes. Terrain usually affects the currents of air, as can temperature, thereby creating thermals. And while this terrain effect may be hard to detect from the ground, once the kite is up you will eventually get a "feel" for flight in that area.

The presence of wires and trees and other high obstructions is most markedly felt when you are in the process of launching or landing a kite. On a clear field and with correct handling, the skilled kiteflier can land his kite exactly where he wants it. In a steady wind, bring it in directly, along a straight line, winding the kite string at a steady gentle pace. In stronger winds, a flat kite will tend to keep rising and must be played with to be brought in. Reel it in as it briefly loops, drifts, or sags. If it begins to climb, hold it steady. Pay out line only when necessary (when you think the cord might break under the strain). At this stage, you will do well to wear a glove on one hand, so that you can handle the line, keeping a sensitive touch on it, and not allowing it to cut your hand.

Do not let the kite loop at low altitudes when reeling it in. If it tends to loop, walk it in by having a friend continue the reeling while you (with gloved hands) walk toward the kite, the line under your arm. This way you can shorten the kite line without actually reeling it all the way in. It will eventually come to your hand, if handled correctly. Always, when launching or landing, remember not to drag the kite across the ground. This obviously tears the kite surface, crushes spars, and snags and knots lines.

KITE TRAINS

In the kiteman's quest for height, he soon learned that a chain of connected kites, or kite train, could achieve the greatest lift. Kite trains were used to lift men, banners, meteorological instruments, fireworks, military scouts, and even to draw carriages like Pocock's Charvolant. Jalbert's parafoils, when flown in train, can reach altitudes of 17,000 feet, compared with an individual parafoil's limit of about 9,000 feet. A group of several kites, all attached to a common line, is particularly effective in gaining height. For many years the United States Weather Bureau lifted instruments on a series of kites to heights of several miles, and reported that the train's advantage is in maximally utilizing lifting power on several surfaces without having to expose the entire lifting surface to sudden changes in wind conditions. Pressure, temperature, and heights may affect one or two kites in the train, but along a line of thousands of feet, all the kites will not be affected in the same adverse way, permitting the instruments to continue to rise and to maintain altitude. Some of the Weather Bureau kites reportedly maintained altitude and retained stability in 80 mph winds over a mile above Earth.

Any type of durable kite may be used in train flying, including the traditional Hargrave box kite, tetrahedral, and Conyne kite (French military kite). It is advisable to keep all the kites in one train of the same kite family, however. To form a train you need at least two people. Using a strong flying line, put up your first kite. Let it out several hundred feet. In the meantime, your assistant should launch the second kite and let it out to about half the distance of the first. With the two in the air, tie the ends of both lines to-

The kite train has its rewards in allowing kites to reach maximum altitude. Start the train with your most reliable and stable kite. It is usually best to use the same type of kite consistently in the train. Since kites in train generate more lift than individual kites, be certain to anchor the flying line on the ground.

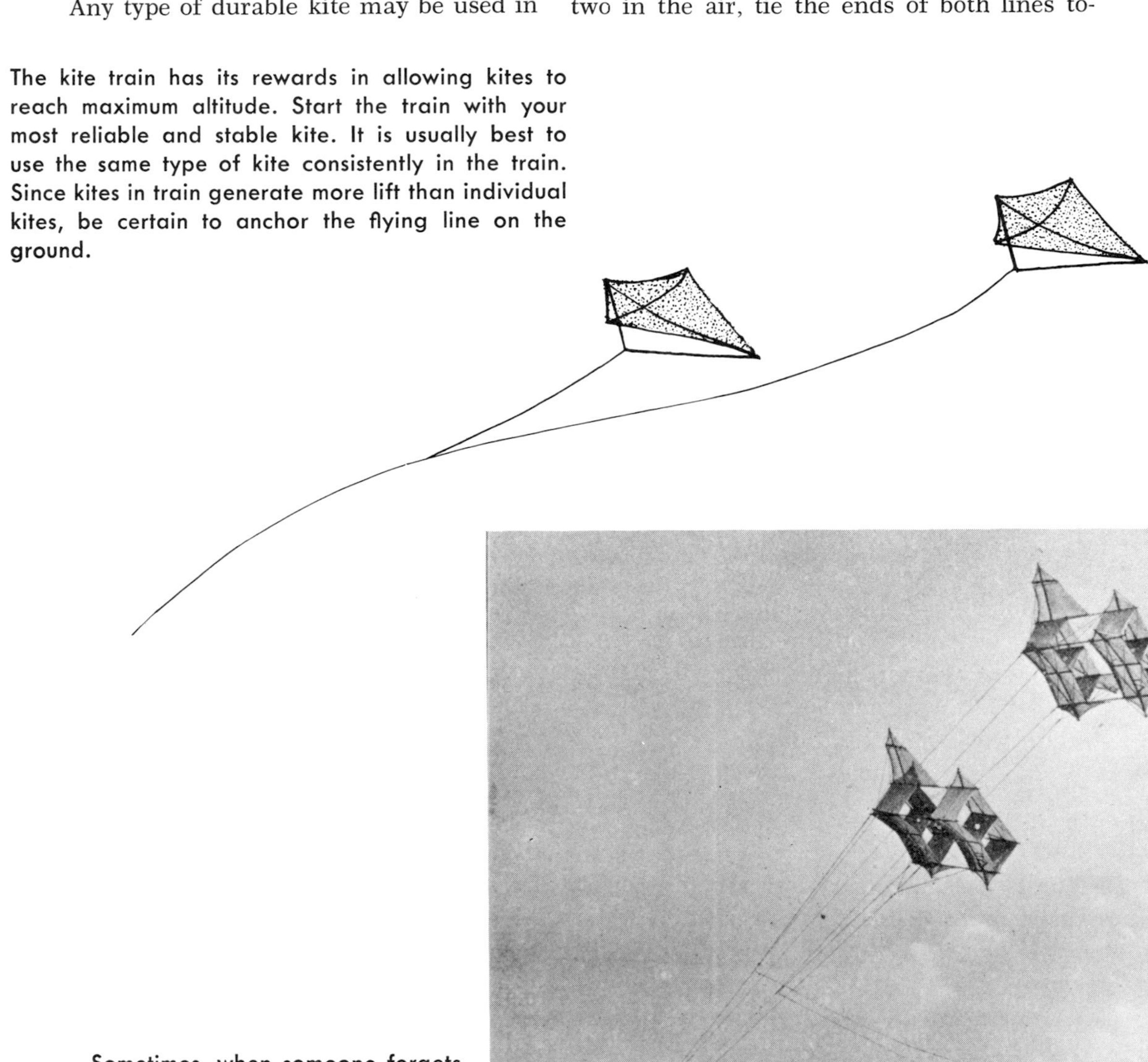

Sometimes, when someone forgets to anchor a train of kites he can get a free ride like this daredevil. Courtesy: Smithsonian Institution.

gether so that the remaining line on the second kite's spool becomes the main flying line. Pay out two hundred more feet or so. Launch a third kite, attach it to the second kite's line so that the third kite's line becomes the new main line. Continue this process to extend the train even farther. But beware, your kite string needs to be strong enough for the combined pull.

A KITEFLIER'S CLINIC

Most of the problems kitefliers face can be solved by adjustments in bridling (the angle), bowing, and ruddering. The following brief list of common ailments and suggested possible remedies may clarify the place of some aerodynamic considerations for tethered flight, and should, at any rate, get the kiteman thinking in terms of his kite's requisites for good flight.

AILMENT	*REASON/SOLUTIONS WORTH CONSIDERING*
Kite flies at too flat an angle but still can fly in a gentle breeze.	Bridle is probably too high. Lower it gradually, recheck by flying again, then readjust if needed.
Kite appears to be topheavy (nose-dives, flies like fishtail, responds erratically, etc.).	Bridle may be too low—bring it closer to leading edge. Bow may be too deep—lessen the tension of the bow slightly. May need a change in aspect ratio if wingspan is too great at top end—increase the length and weight of tail or ruddering device.
Kite darts side to side.	Needs greater directional (lateral) stability—adjust bridle with possible addition of more shroud lines; check that bridle lines are of equal, taut length; consider addition of a keel to the kite.
Kite darts to one side.	Correct balance by adding weight to one side of the kite, or by readjusting bridle legs along one edge of the kite.
Kite makes quick loops.	It isn't right for the wind conditions—try deepening bow, again checking bridling for imbalance, or lengthen tail.
Kite moves in broad circles.	Tighten lower bridle lines but without altering the angle of tow. Experiment with variations in tail material to offer greater flexibility in added length (the tail should swing like a pendulum to correct swaying before circling becomes chronic).
Kite lacks lift, is sluggish.	Problem could be too much drag or else too heavy a kite for the day's wind conditions. Reduce length of tail, lessen bow (to increase size of lift surface), wait for a heavier wind.
Kite is gamey, skittish, a fickle flier.	Bridle may be too short—add length to shroud lines for better control leverage than before. Add more shroud lines to better distribute the responsibility for lift and control. Wind may be too heavy—try adding to the tail.

BASIC CONSTRUCTION TECHNIQUES

Chapter 3

The essential materials for constructing kites have remained the same for centuries: bamboo or wood, cloth or paper, and string. The techniques, too, have endured. The frame is still cut and lashed and glued. The covering is still glued or sewn to the frame, and the kite is still bridled and flown with string. Today, however, modern materials offer many more solutions for kite designs than were possible when the first kite was sent aloft two millennia ago. Plastic films and cloths, modern lightweight papers, plastic and aluminum rods, and some of the newer glue compounds should all be considered part of your designing vocabulary.

No matter what materials are used in kite building, the objective must be the same: to build a kite with the lightest materials that will be structurally stable for that design. The operative words here are *for that design*, because your choice of wood, covering, and string should always be dictated by the needs of the structure. Where a tiny diamond kite might be framed with toothpicks, a very large kite could require thick bamboo or aluminum tubing. Form should follow function.

A "Flying Red Line" being made by sculptor Tal Streeter at his studio in Shizuoka, Japan. Courtesy: Tal Streeter, *The Art of the Japanese Kite.*

Master kitemaker Matsutaro Yanase amid the materials and products of his art. There are approximately 135 kitemakers in Japan. Courtesy: Tal Streeter, *The Art of the Japanese Kite.*

TOOLS

Most of the tools for kitemaking are readily available. Straightedges, a ruler, sharp pencils, and a compass will aid in ruling the correct lines. Scissors, a razor knife, sandpaper, and a small file should meet the needs of most situations. A needle and thread (or optionally, a sewing machine for some designs) will meet other demands. As you can see, the tools are fairly traditional; they cover the basic ruling and cutting operations that are central to this craft. Any conveniences which you care to introduce are, clearly, to your advantage, but the basic equipment will serve admirably.

THE KITE FRAME

In the Orient, where the first kites were flown, the traditional framing materials have remained the same to this day: bamboo and cypress wood. Each has the virtue of being strong and lightweight. The weight of the kite frame is an important consideration, especially in a light wind where small amounts of extra weight may substantially affect flight potential. The kitemaker should always attempt to build the lightest possible frame, but once again, this is totally within the constraint of seeking the best possible materials for a given design and size of kite. Never confuse heavy wind kites with heavy kites. Most often, kites that fly well in heavy wind are light, strongly built, and fly at low profile—thereby developing less drag.

The most versatile kite-framing material is bamboo. It is extremely light and flexible and very easy to work with. Presplit bamboo is available from many craft suppliers and from the Go Fly a Kite Store in New York. A very good source is an old bamboo shade—most contain enough strips for many kites. You can also split your own bamboo from a pole or an old cane; the technique is shown in detail below. No special tools are necessary for forming this material. A sharp knife and some sandpaper will suffice for most cutting and shaping operations. Bending bamboo into the intricate shapes required for many oriental kites (see Chapter 5) can be accomplished either by soaking in water or by heating the strip slowly in a candle flame.

Of the variety of woods and doweling available, application must be your guide. Balsa wood, for instance, will provide ample support for only a light, small kite. Balsa strips will also serve well as spines for Scott Sleds where their function is primarily to give shape rather than to withstand pressure or stress. Many kites are still made only with

Tal Streeter uses traditional materials to construct his Flying Red Line kite/sculptures. Here he lashes bamboo. He covers the kites with Japanese paper and paints them. Courtesy: Tal Streeter, *The Art of the Japanese Kite*.

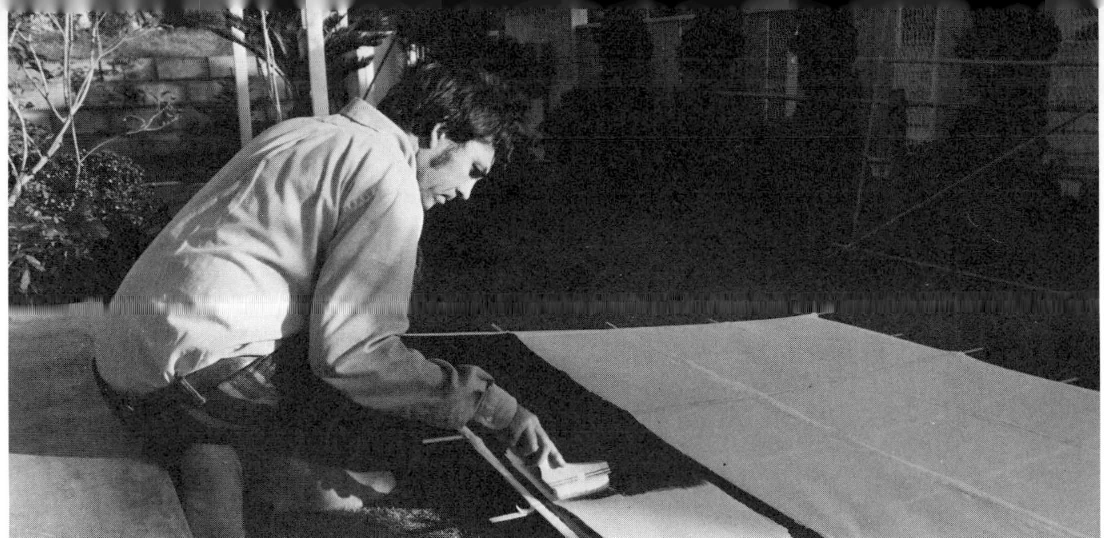

reeds or rattan to support them. Other kites demand more structural support. Cypress wood, because of its straight grain, is a good choice. In northern Japan, where it gets too cold for bamboo to grow, cypress has been used for centuries. Spruce strips, although sometimes expensive, are also strong, lightweight, and good for kites that require solid or intricate construction. White pine has many applications, provided that it is not cut too thin, and cedar is useful, too.

Application will ultimately determine which framing material works best. Very large kites—like the Hamamatsu kites and the giant delta wings—use bamboo and aluminum poles respectively. Because they are large, develop a great deal of lift, and require strong support, those "heavy" kite frames are necessary and not excessive.

The newest material for kite framing is the fiber glass rod. Sculptor Charles Henry's innovative designs suggest that fiber glass will open an entirely new design vocabulary to kite craftsmen if they follow this lead. Although fiber glass rod is still an expensive material, there is no denying that it is the very strongest, most flexible, and resilient material in relation to its weight and strength. We consider this to offer the most exciting potential and strongly urge experimentation.

NOTCHING FRAMES

In cases where string guidelines must be attached to wooden frames, the sticks are usually notched to allow the string to rest securely. Since notching may cause a split in the spar if pressure is applied, it is wise to lash the stick just below the notch. Once the string has been inserted, the stick end may be lashed to hold the string in place. An alternate method to the notch is to drill a hole in the wood and pass the string through it. Once again, it is advisable to lash the stick to avoid splitting.

THE KITE COVERING

The earliest kites were undoubtedly covered with silk. Known in China as early as 2600 B.C., silk cloth was the obvious choice for kite construction. Even today kites are constructed with this material. Not only is silk strong and dense (allowing little air to pass through it), it is also very expensive, unfortunately. Consequently many other materials are used.

The suggestion of paper as a kite covering has early precedents as well. From the Caroline Islanders, who used leaves and plaited straw as kite coverings, to the Japanese, early and late, paper has a very traditional and respectable history in this craft. To be sure, it meets our most important demands: it is light, easy to work with, can be very strong, is inexpensive, and can be decorated in hundreds of different ways.

Almost any paper can be used as a kite covering. Some use brown kraft paper. Bermudian kitemakers have long fancied tissue paper as have craftsmen in India. The Japanese are partial to fine bark paper. In the West, where our paper traditions are not as highly developed, we tend to take an eclectic approach to paper selection. There is nothing wrong with this. It can, in fact, lead to interesting design solutions. See

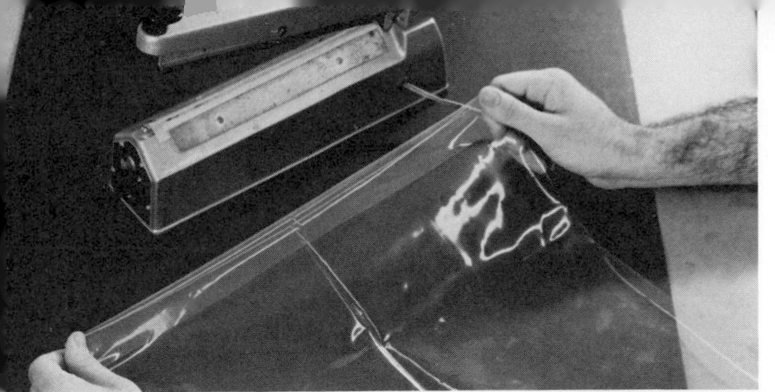

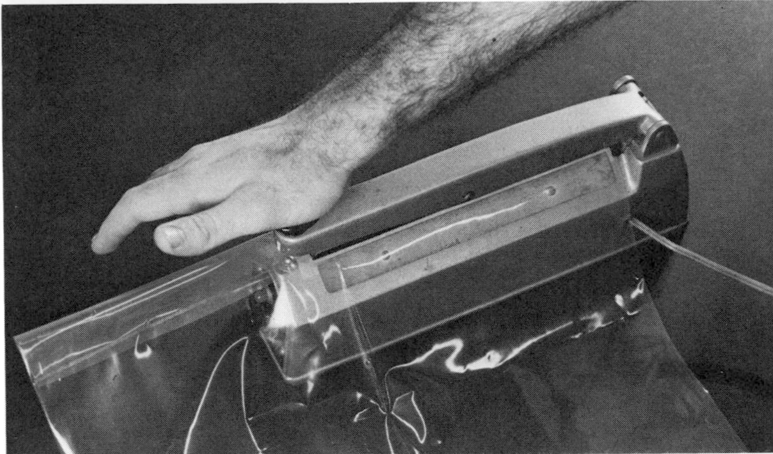

Plastic film, the most modern material for covering kites, responds to new techniques as well. While all films can be taped, the polyethylenes can also be heat sealed. The film is folded, placed over the element of a heat sealer, pressed briefly, and a sleeve/hem is created. Spars can be held in place easily, and the process is quick and clean. Many commercial kites are made with this technique.

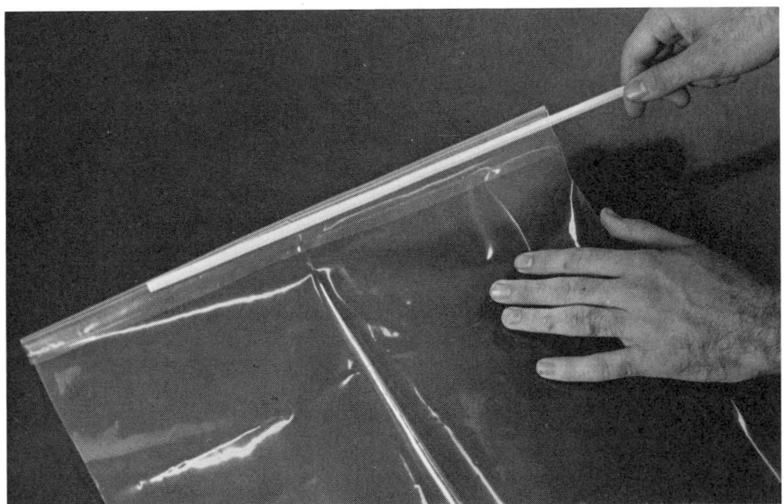

Chapter 4 for some ideas on many of the basic paper (and cloth) decorating techniques.

Your choice of paper should range as far or near as your whim dictates. Only bear in mind the size and strength limitations which will be placed on the covering. For instance, a thin paper on a large kite may not be suitable; the covering may not be durable under wind pressure, and the paper may tear. Conversely, heavy paper might weigh down a small kite unnecessarily.

COVERING MATERIAL	*TEAR STRENGTH*	*ADHESIVES*	*DECORATIVE TECHNIQUES*	*RANGE OF WEIGHTS AVAILABLE*
Papers	low to medium	white glues, rubber cement, adhesive tapes	nearly any imaginable technique	lightest (tissue) to heavy (nearly cardboard)
Silk and cotton cloth	medium to high	fabric glue, sewable duct tape	dye, print, batik	light to medium
Zephyrlite and Stabilkote (and other synthetic fabrics)	medium to high	should be sewn or taped	come in a range of colors	light to heavy, a full range
Mylar	high	Mylar tapes, other adhesive tapes	solvent-based marking pens	lightest to heavy
Polyethylene film	low to medium	adhesive tapes, cloth tape, heat sealing	solvent-based marking pens	lightest to heavy
Tyvek	very high	rubber cement, leather cement, sewable, some contact cements (use test strips with adhesives to be certain)	some inks, some paints, dyes, most techniques (again, use test strips)	light to heavy, full range available

As mentioned above, silk is still used strikingly on some very special kites, though it is more difficult to handle than other materials. Many other fabrics have come into use as well. Sailcloth and cotton cloth are both used very successfully in kite craft. Of the synthetic fabrics available, two weights of spinnaker cloth produced by Howe and Bainbridge, Inc., exhibit qualities particularly suitable to kite covering. Zephyrlite® and Stabilkote® are both extremely strong. The former is lightweight and has low porosity. The latter, while slightly heavier, is even stronger and has zero porosity. Both have high tear strength, too. The same company has a full range of cloth in other weights which are suitable for extralarge kites and for hang gliders.

The plastics, which have affected so much of modern living, cannot be excluded here either. Plastic films of polyethylene and Mylar® both make excellent kite coverings.

Polyethylene films come in a variety of weights and colorings. They are easy to attach with tapes, and they can also be heat sealed. The commercially manufactured Puffer Kite® is constructed of a light plastic film which has been sealed with heat to create a balloon kite. An advantage of polyethylene is that it is very inexpensive. In the thinner sheets it may tear or stretch, but it can be easily patched and tightened with adhesive or cloth tapes. Most plastic films—Mylar and polyethylene—can be decorated with solvent-type marking pens.

Mylar, manufactured by Du Pont, has all the qualities of a good kite covering. It is an extremely thin, light polyester film, it is easy to cut and attach (adhesive tapes work best), and it is amazingly strong. Mylar is available in different thicknesses and colors at many hobby and plastics stores.

A new product which has met with a very enthusiastic reception in the commercial kite industry is another Du Pont product, Tyvek®. This is a spun-bonded olefin. It has the consistency of paper, can be cut, colored, adhered, and sewn, but quite unlike most papers we have seen, it is virtually impossible to tear!

Another consideration in choice of covering is the porosity of the paper, plastic, or cloth. The two extremes of porosity are obvious: materials which will allow all air to pass through completely (namely air itself) and materials which will allow no air to pass through (solid objects, plastic films, etc.). Your choice of covering will influence the kite's flight. If, for example, you choose to fly a kite covered in Mylar in a high wind, the nature of this material (zero porosity) will affect your bridling and venting needs. On the other hand, if you were to fly the same kite in the same wind with a covering of perforated paper, the bridling and venting could and should be different. Clearly this factor is compensated for by bridling, in many cases, but it is wise to know how the choice of materials can affect flight and structure.

THE KITE LINE

The first kite lines were, most likely, silk. Until very recently, many oriental kite lines were still silk, and a great prize to the winner of a kite fight was the capture of the opponent's line as well as his kite. Silk, while quite strong, is very expensive, and other materials have become much more popular and efficient.

String, cord, twine, fishing line, seine line, twisted or braided nylon or dacron, monofilament nylon, button thread, or even ordinary thread may serve as a flying line. (A note of caution: *never* use wire as a flying line. Franklin's experiment was as foolhardy as it was interesting.) The important consideration in choosing line, of course, is its strength in relation to expected pull of the kite. Some insist that the line strength should be three to four times the expected pull. Without delving into the scientific derivation of this relationship, I quote a simple rule of thumb suggested by Wyatt Brummitt. The flying line should have a test strength (breaking strength) equal in pounds to three times the kite's frontal surface area in square feet. By this formula, a kite with a surface area of 4 square feet (2 feet by 2 feet) would require a line with a test strength of 12 pounds. A kite with surface area 9 square feet would need a line of 27-pound test strength, and so on.

Again, a pointed omission in the above is wire. Not only is there a danger to the kiteflier; there is a danger of fouling electric wires as well. With so many alternatives available, you should, with some experimentation, find a line which meets your needs.

One word of caution is due on knotting and splicing lines. No knot will be as strong as the line itself. Although reweaving is possible with thicker woven lines, this is often impractical—or impossible—with thin or monofilament lines. Wherever possible use a single length of line. When joining, tie a square knot or weaver's knot, and when attaching line to bridle, tie it with a slip knot. Timber hitches and cloth knots also maintain line strength well.

MECHANICAL AND ADHESIVE JOINING

Attachments are of two types: adhesive and mechanical. In kite flying, attachments are used in two basic areas: frame construction and covering. In both areas large varieties of attachments are applicable.

The essential purpose of framing a kite is to assure that a certain structure will be maintained in the face of the wind. Toward that end, kitemakers seek to build frames that will keep their shape, and joints should be solidly tied and glued. In many cases it will be tempting to cut a notch or bevel to create a better footing, and this is clearly necessary in some instances, but remember that cuts and slices will weaken wood and should be used sparingly. When notching always use a sharp-bladed tool. A neat trick to keep wood from splitting around a notch is to bind the area with a few turns of thread, as mentioned earlier.

The best tying lines are cotton and linen thread. All tied joints should be reinforced after lashing with a white glue or contact cement for additional safety. The most desirable method is to tie the joint tightly and lash it with 6 to 8 inches of thread. Apply cement to the joint so that it will penetrate

1

2

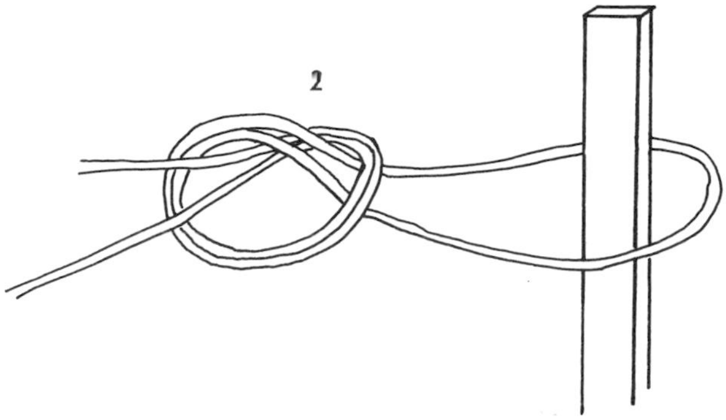

3

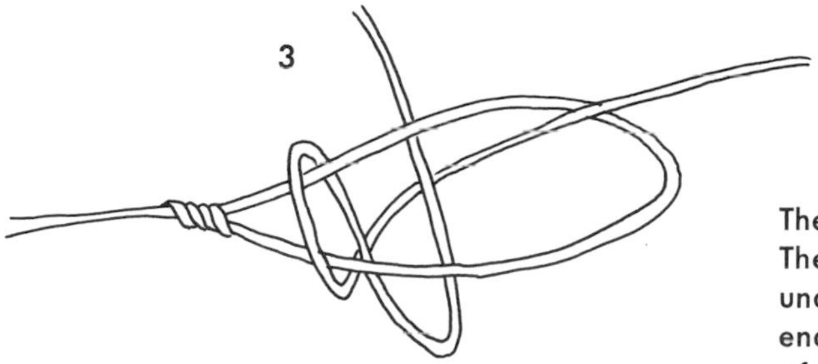

These three knots are useful in kitemaking. The square knot (1) maintains its strength under stress, making it a useful knot for ending lashings and for attaching lengths of line. The loop (2) makes a good end point for bridles, and the tiller hitch (3) eases attachment to bridles since, while it does form a firm knot, it can be released by just pulling on the loose end.

the bindings, and allow the joint to dry thoroughly. When dry, trim string ends and (optimally) coat the whole thing with waterproof cement. There are other alternatives as well. Many of the supersticky strapping tapes (often with a Mylar base) will provide as secure a bond as you could desire—especially on smaller kites.

Some commercially constructed kites employ metal staples which allow the sticks to be rotated to position. This, however, does not provide a great deal of support. Other commercial inventions promise to revolutionize kite construction, though. The use of plastic tubing—both flexible and rigid—has made the assembly of kites much faster. Craftsmen have shown increasing interest and ingenuity in applying tubings.

There are two basic types of plastic tubing: flexible and rigid, both of which are translucent or transparent. The two types have substantially different characteristics although their application is the same. The rigid tubing is most often some type of

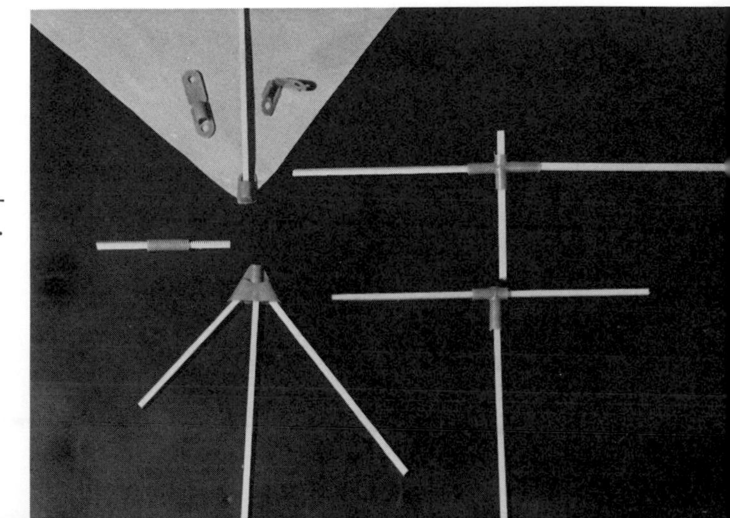

Commercially molded parts—if obtainable—make handy additions to a kitemaker's parts kit.

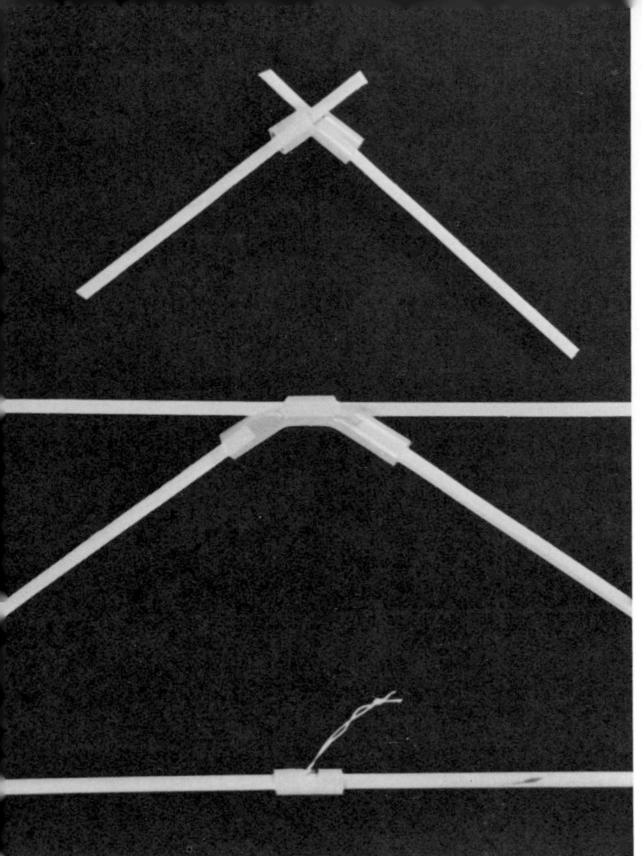

Polyethylene tubings can be easily cut, and the flexibility and strength of this material makes it ideal for joints of all kinds.

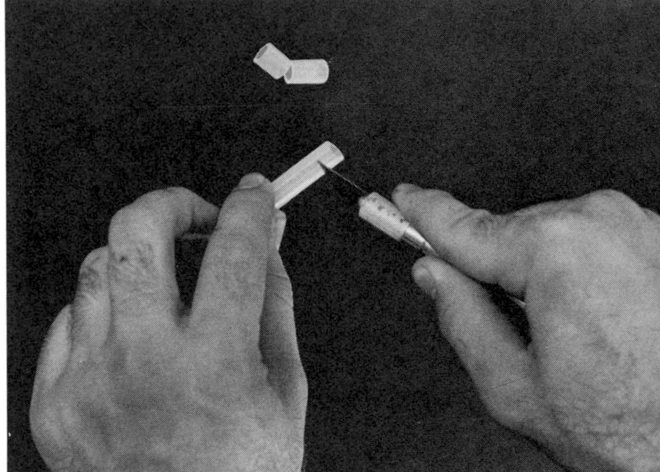

thermoplastic which means, essentially, that it can be heated and reshaped a number of times. This can become an important design tool. By inserting your spars into the end of a short length of tubing, you can then heat the tubing so that it will contract around those braces. At the same time, the tube may be given the proper dihedral angle, and when the plastic cools, not only will the frame elements be locked into the joint, but they will be locked in at the proper angle as well!

Flexible tubing offers other possibilities. Most often made of polyethylene, the flexible tubes are easily cut with a kitchen knife or razor (rigid tubing can be cut with most saws). And, as shown below, different configurations of slices into this material will provide different joints. Since this plastic will stretch, it is often possible to squeeze the spar into the tube in order to assure a firm fit.

Because only small lengths of these materials are necessary to provide solid joints, and since they are very light, the use of plastics as jointing mechanisms has become very popular—and practical. Where they are used, it is recommended that a dab of white liquid glue be applied to assure a firm attachment. This will still allow for dissassembly of the kite, an added bonus of this method of construction. If a permanent joint is desired, substitute a two-part epoxy cement for the white glue.

The use of fiber glass rods as kite-framing materials was mentioned earlier. The attachment methods for rods are somewhat

Charles Henry wrapped fiberglass cloth dipped in epoxy around this joint of fiberglass rod to secure it. The [illegible] painted with airplane dope to secure the stitching.

more specialized. Tying with string will not provide a satisfactory joint on fiber glass. There are several alternative methods of joining these rods. The easiest and the best for experimentation is just to use adhesive strapping tape. We specify strapping tape because this material, often on a Mylar base, is especially strong. A second technique is to use rigid or flexible tubing—once again with the reinforcement of an epoxy cement. The third solution for a permanent structure is to wrap the joints with fiber glass cloth strips saturated in epoxy or catalyzed polyester resin (boat resin). These materials are readily available in most hardware and craft stores (and see Supply Sources in this text).

Methods of attaching the covering to the frame can be divided into mechanical and adhesive devices as well. The adhesive techniques are quite obvious: for papers the white glues are very good, and rubber cement will provide a strong bond too. A traditional glue is made by mixing flour and water into a semiliquid paste. Cooking it just until it boils will allow it to dry almost clear. Cockroaches love it, but adding a little cayenne pepper to the mixture will keep them away.

For the plastic films an adhesive tape must be used: tapes of Mylar are best because they are the strongest and lightest, but they are slightly more expensive than other kinds. Mystik®'s cloth tape is another good choice for reinforcing and attaching plastic. Tyvek, while slightly problematical in this regard, seems to respond fairly well to rubber cement and leather glues. In the mechanical area the two basic methods are sewing and using grommets. Cloth coverings and coverings of Tyvek may be sewn either by hand or by machine. Dacron threads with widely separated stitches are recommended. Stitches which are too close might create a sort of perforated line susceptible to tearing in high winds.

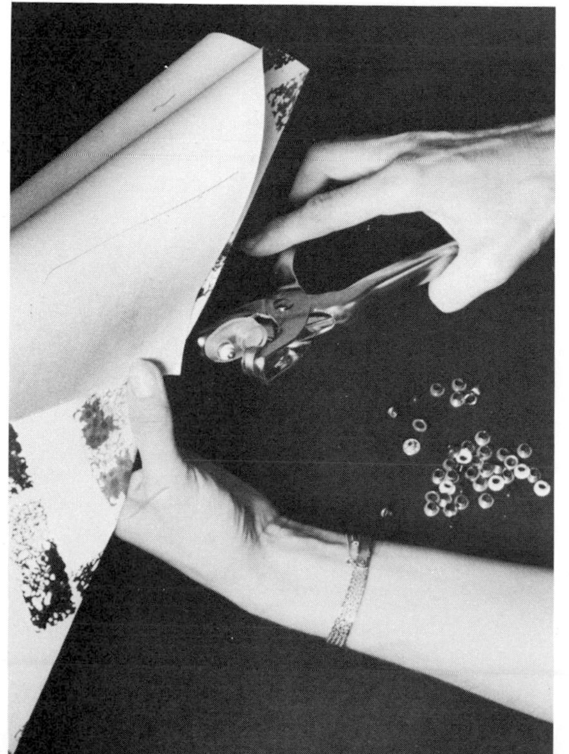

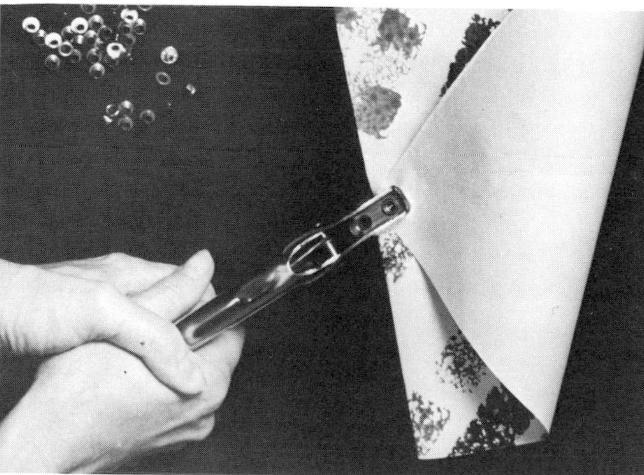

An inexpensive grommet puncher saves a great deal of time in attaching coverings and making holes for bow and bridle strings. The grommet also protects coverings from tearing by supporting the hole. In this example, a single grommet acts as mechanical bond and bridling point for a simple kite.

KITE BALANCE

If the essence of good kite craftsmanship had to be boiled down to one word it would have to be *symmetry*. Balance is an extremely important consideration for successful flight. Balanced construction should be kept in mind during any discussion of construction techniques, design, and materials. Test all spars to determine dimensions *exactly*. Check and recheck to approach perfection in this consideration.

BASIC KITE DESIGNS AND CONSTRUCTION TECHNIQUES

In this section, through step-by-step photographs, we have detailed the processes involved in the construction of several different representative types of kites. They are different in design and origin and in materials used. Our attempt is to present something of the range available to kite craftsmen and, at the same time, to present sound construction techniques and practices.

THE DIAMOND KITE

The most popular kite in North America and most of the Western world today is the diamond-shaped kite. Made with sticks of wood or plastic rather than bamboo, this American classic is particularly simple in design. Because of its size and shape it is not as maneuverable as many other kites, but it can stand up to high winds at relatively great heights.

The kite frame is made of two sticks. Spruce or pine is most often used. The spine is 34″ long, the crosspiece 28″ long × 1/8″ × 3/8″. Before joining the sticks together a notch is made in each of the four ends. These notches will accommodate a string guideline. The joint is made 8″ from the top of the spine and at the center of the crosspiece. First lash it with string; then use glue to bond the sticks securely together. To complete the framework use a strong cotton or linen thread or string as guideline; insert the string into the notches at each end of the sticks, pull it taut, and knot it. This should create a solid frame on which to mount the paper covering.

Cut a piece of paper so that it is the exact shape of the diamond framework, but with a 1/2″ margin all around. This margin will be folded back over the string guideline and glued down. The paper should be slightly smaller than the actual framework where the stick ends will protrude.

With the paper cut to size, one side is painted with water-thinned acrylic colors. These paints dry very quickly, and they are very light and flexible.

When the paints have dried, line up the paper with the framework. Crease the covering sheet along the line that corresponds to the string guides. Be certain that the crosspiece lies against the paper and that the spine is on top.

Then apply glue to the flaps and fold the paper back onto itself. Glue it down firmly, sealing the string in between. Glue all four sides. Work slowly, making as few wrinkles as possible.

To bow the kite, the two ends of the crosspiece are drawn together so that the front painted surface is convex. Wind conditions will determine how deep or shallow the bow needs to be, but always store the kite flat.

Because the kite may have dried or have been glued unevenly, you might want to eliminate wrinkles after construction. To do this, spray the back of the paper lightly with water from an atomizer to soften any wrinkles or pockets. Place the dampened (but not wet) kite where it will dry evenly.

The diamond kite may be bridled for flight in one of two primary ways. You may pass a string through the front of the kite through a pair of holes made at the point where the frame sticks intersect. To make certain that these holes will not widen or rip in the wind you should place a looseleaf reinforcer around each before threading the line through.

An alternate method of bridling is a two-legged bridle attached at the top and bottom of the spine and meeting at the level of the crosspiece.

A tail is a necessity for stabilizing this heavy-boned kite. A general rule of thumb is to make the tail 1½ times the length of the spine. Use a thin strip of cloth, with short strips knotted around it at 6″ intervals. Tie the tail end to the spine bottom, and it's ready to fly.

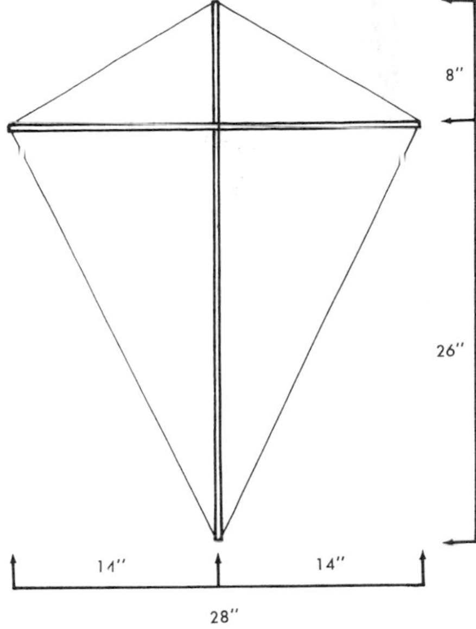

The spine of the diamond kite is 34″ long. The crosspiece is 28″. The thin solid lines indicate the string guideline which is slipped into notches at the ends of the wood strips. Pull the string taut; the covering will be glued over it. Lash the sticks with string and then secure the joint with glue.

Choose a lightweight, strong paper or cloth for the covering. The paper was cut to shape with an extra ½″ margin all the way around for gluing. Painting with fast-drying acrylics speeds the decorating process. First thin the paints with a few drops of water; paint that is too thick will make the paper inflexible and interfere with balance. Sometimes, if paint is too thick, it can crack off the blown kite surface after only a short time.

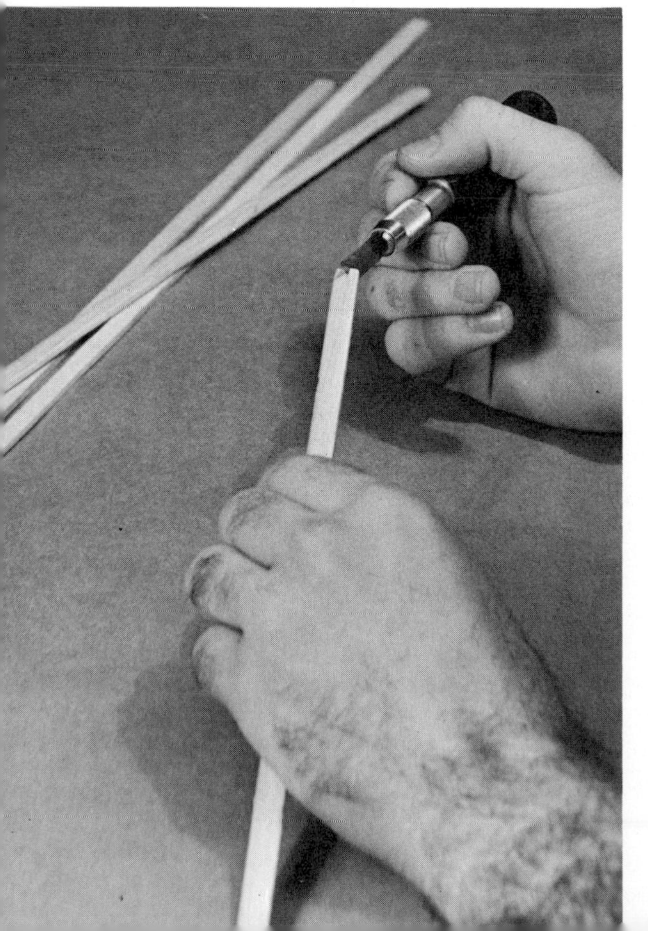

Notch the ends of the wood sticks with a sharp knife, and, later, pass the string through. To avoid splitting, lash the wood just below the end of the notch. To hold the string in place firmly you may want to lash the end *after* the kite has already been strung, too.

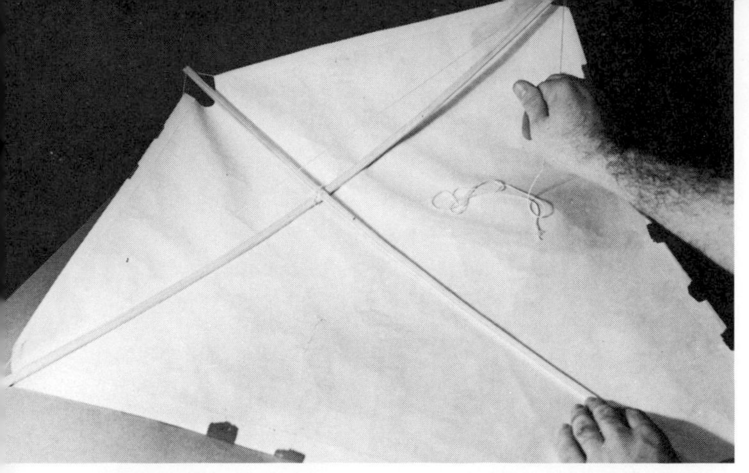

After gluing the margin of paper around the string guideline, you can eliminate any wrinkles in the paper by spraying it with water from an atomizer. Do not soak the paper, however; when the water dries the paper will have stretched taut like a drumhead. To bow the kite, tie a piece of string to both ends of the crosspiece; tighten the string until it is bowed. Use a deep bow for heavy winds, a shallow bow for light breezes, and release it entirely when the kite is not in use. Always store bowed kites flat.

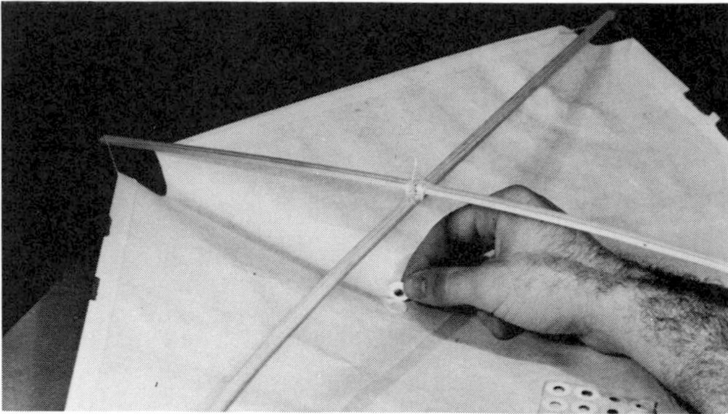

The kite may be strung for flying with a one or two-legged bridle. In the two-leg bridle one begins at each end of the spine, connecting a foot or two in front of the kite on line with the intersection of the wood sticks. The single-leg bridle requires that a hole be punched through the paper at the point where the ribs intersect. To keep this hole from enlarging, secure it with looseleaf paper reinforcers or tape. Pass the end of string through this hole from the front of the kite and tie the string to the intersection.

Affix a cloth tail to the base of the spine; bow the diamond kite according to the wind, and let 'er go.

Diamond kites come in all sizes. William Bigge's kite of thinnest wood and plastic film is so light that when released in a still room it floats to the floor slowly.

This cutaway diamond (so called because the covering is cut away from the string guideline in some areas) shows some possibilities. Courtesy: Benn Blinn.

THE EDDY KITE

Patented by William Eddy in 1897, the Eddy kite took its inspiration from Malay kites of similar design. As high as it is wide, the Eddy makes use of a shallow dihedral to give it stability. So well conceived are the proportions of this kite that no tail is necessary.

The kite is simple to construct, although care should be given to precise cutting and joining. When the wings are bowed you should allow for some pocketing of the covering material. For this reason, the Eddy is best suited to a cloth covering, which is more flexible. To make assembly easy, hem each side of the fabric so that the guide string can be inserted. Notch the ends of the stick to accommodate the guide string. Fit on the covering, and the kite is complete. The length of the bridle should be slightly longer than the spine—in this case about 75″.

Because of the stress placed on the spar stick, it is wise to reinforce it at the center. To do this, cut a strip of wood of the same dimensions as the spar but only a third as long, and lash this piece to the spar over the center area. This will give it added strength.

The Eddy, like many kites, can be built in very large sizes. Because it flies well, the only constraints on increased size are strength of materials and strength of the flier. For larger kites you will need heavier frames and stronger flying line.

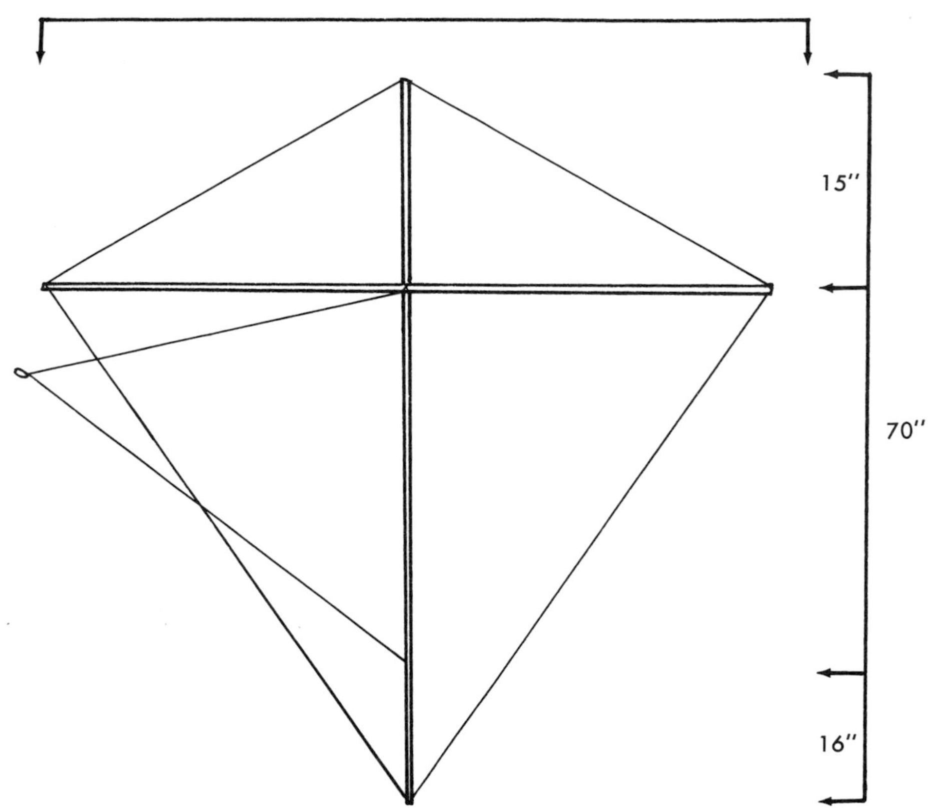

The Eddy kite, based on a Malaysian design, is similar in appearance to the diamond, but it flies quite differently. Spine and crosspiece are the same length. They are joined at a point 80 percent up the spine. The kite is flown bowed but tailless, with bridling as shown.

THE BERMUDA THREE-STICK KITE

Legend has it that kites were introduced to Bermuda by a schoolteacher who sought an effective way to describe the Ascension. Kites have been a popular local recreation ever since. Each year Bermuda is host to an endurance contest for kitefliers from all over the world. A Bermudian, Vincent Tuzo, currently holds the record of 49 hours, 40 minutes, set in 1972.

The most popular kite in Bermuda is the three-stick kite. Covered most often with cut and pasted tissue papers, as many as twenty of these individual kites are sometimes grouped together to create a large, colorful kite which fills the sky. Variations of this basic design include hexagonal and octagonal kites.

The construction method is similar to that used on both diamond and Eddy kites. After the center joint has been lashed tight, a string guideline is drawn through notches in the end of each stick to create a tight frame. The kite is then papered, bridled, and flown. All Bermuda kites are flown with long tails (the heavier the breeze the longer the tail) which are attached to a loop strung from the two bottom spars. Part of the beauty of this design is seeing those tails streaming through the sky on a sunny, breezy day.

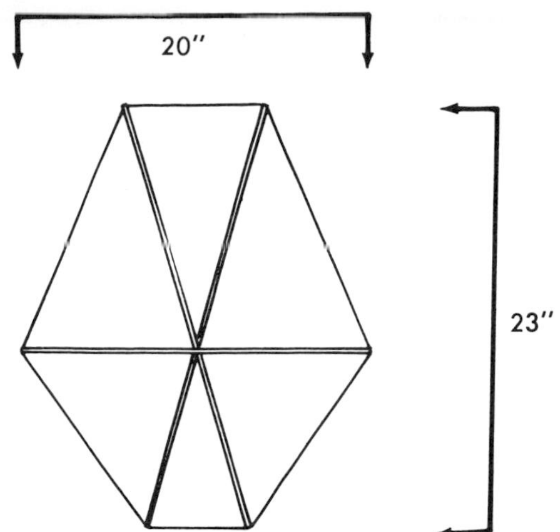

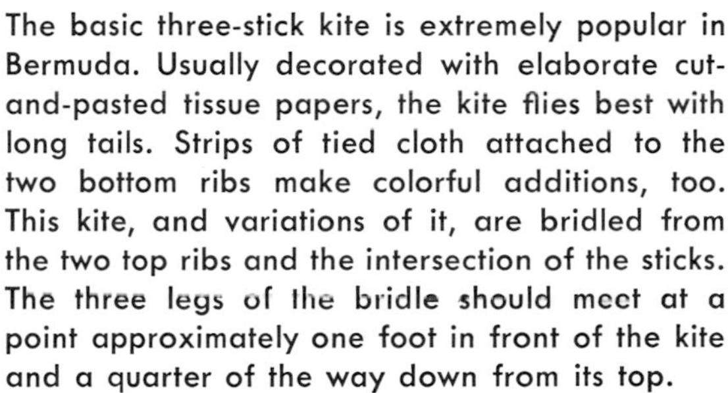
The basic three-stick kite is extremely popular in Bermuda. Usually decorated with elaborate cut-and-pasted tissue papers, the kite flies best with long tails. Strips of tied cloth attached to the two bottom ribs make colorful additions, too. This kite, and variations of it, are bridled from the two top ribs and the intersection of the sticks. The three legs of the bridle should meet at a point approximately one foot in front of the kite and a quarter of the way down from its top.

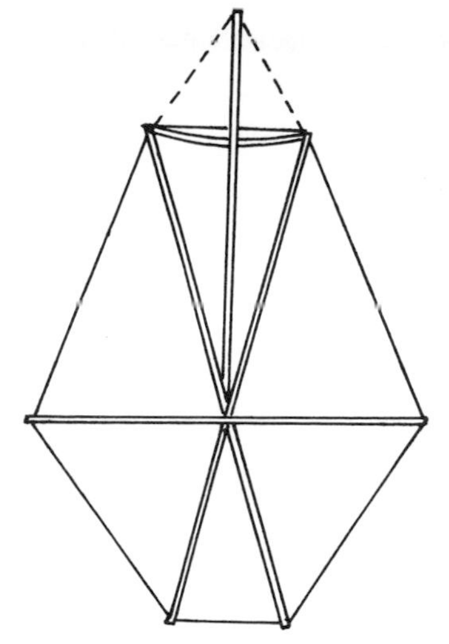

The head-stick kite involves the addition of two bowed sticks and hummers to the three-stick kite. The center stick is attached at the intersection, and its top is bowed back to the same intersection. The head bow attaches to the two top ribs; it is also bowed. Lash both bows together. Dotted lines indicate string. Do not cover the string, but make flapping paper buzzers. The buzzers are visible in accompanying photographs; they are also discussed in the Appendix.

Vincent Tuzo, master Bermudian kiteflier, holds two of his designs. The kite on the left is a combination of three head-stick kites and one octagonal kite, also with a head-stick. The right-hand kite combines a single head-stick three-sticker with a four-stick octagonal kite. Both kites display Bermudian kite designs and decorations.

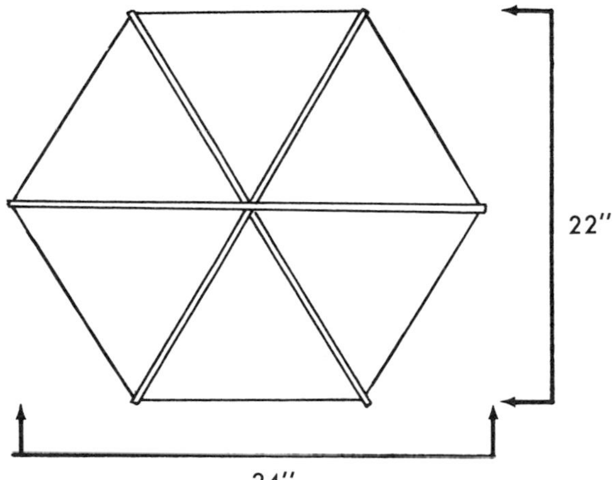

The hexagonal kite, employing three sticks of equal lengths, is another traditional design.

A complicated variation of the hexagonal kite uses venting to delineate a star in the center of the kite. The paper strips around the top of the kite are purely for decoration.

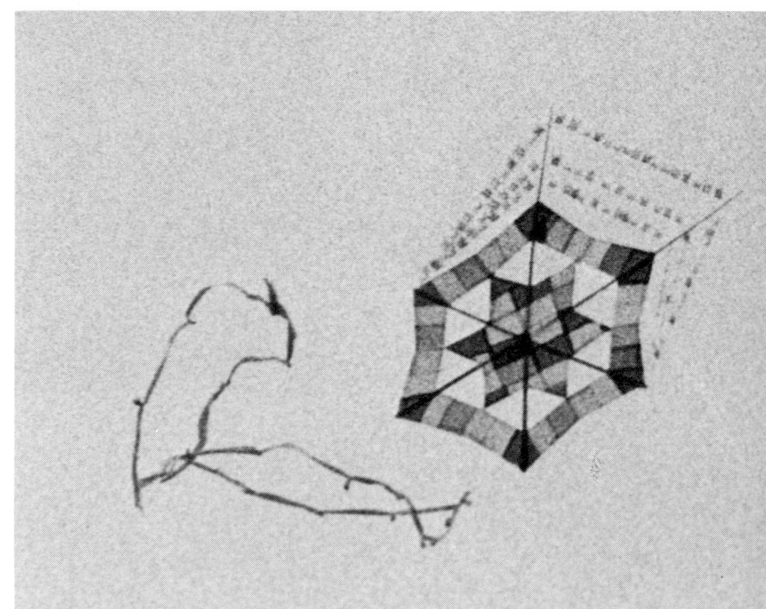

In flight, a long tail sashays through the sky.

A regular hexagon flies beautifully with a fringed tissue paper tail.

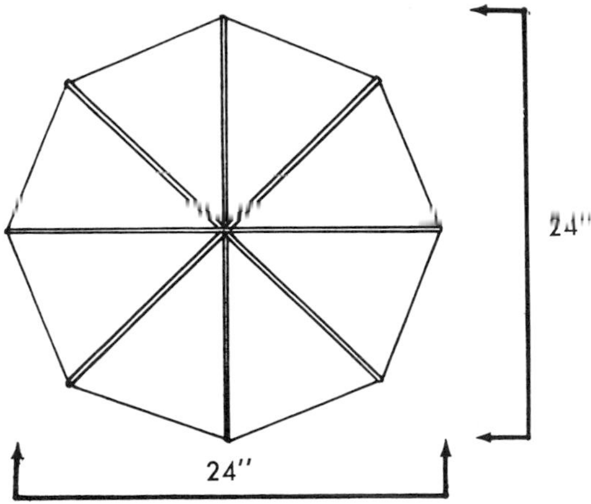

Yet another popular configuration employs four sticks to create a regular octagon.

Vincent Tuzo has a special attachment to both his kite design and this kite: it was with this kite that he set an endurance record for kiteflying of 49 hours and 40 minutes in 1972.

THE RECTANGULAR KITE

The rectangular frame is employed in many oriental kites, most commonly in northern Japan. This kite design is made with a more elaborate framework than the diamond kite. Bamboo or a thin spruce or cypress is best suited.

Construct the frame according to the diagram. String guidelines along each side of the kite frame are attached by tying one end of the line to a corner where the horizontal and diagonal strips meet. Keeping the string taut, simply hook it once around the next rib's end. Repeat this process for each successive rib until you reach the next corner of the kite where you again tie the string. Run the guideline about ½″ to 1″ inside of the end of the shorter ribs so that the rib ends can stick out of the kite paper later.

Repeat this process for each side of the kite to complete framework assembly. If you are using wood strips for the frame you may find that the four-stick intersection at the center of the kite is rather thick and awkward. The sticks cannot be notched because of the substantial weakening that results, but it is wise to file a groove slightly to make the joint more solid. In Japan a thin nail or two is driven through the framework at such bulky joints, too. Glue the sticks at the intersection, lash them, and apply more glue to the lashing to secure it.

Cut the paper covering to the shape shown in the diagram. Calculate for an additional margin which may then be glued back. Holes should be cut to accommodate frame sticks.

After decorating the paper and allowing it to dry, pass the rib ends through the holes cut for them. The two diagonal supports should be closest to the paper. Glue back the margins with rubber cement, white glue, or paste. When the glue has dried, spray the paper with water from an atomizer to smooth wrinkles.

For the kite to fly well, bridling must be done carefully. Measure and balance the kite to determine the exact center and quarter points. Attach a five-leg bridle to the points illustrated. These five legs should meet at a point at least the length of the kite away from the kite face. Before knotting or attaching the legs, be certain that they are lined up so that the kite will be well balanced. The five lines, when stretched taut, should meet at a point level with the second horizontal rib and at dead center.

This angle of bridle is more or less the norm for this type of kite. However, on windy days or calm days you will undoubtedly want to modify this angle to conform better to wind conditions.

Tails of straight paper 2″ to 3″ wide should be attached to the bottom corners of the kite. Once again, the norm calls for lengths equal to two or three times the kite's *diagonal length*. Adjust this for wind conditions as well.

The last step before flight is the bowing of the kite. Bow the rectangular kite at top and bottom. Heavy bows are for heavier winds. Light bows are recommended for lighter less aggressive air currents. Always release the bow when storing the kite; this helps to preserve the flexibility of the frame materials and structure.

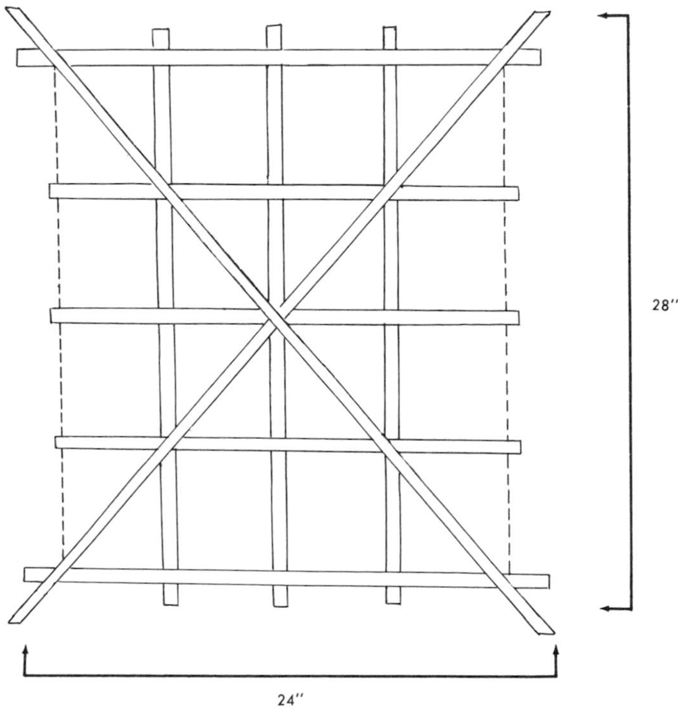

Glue and tie the frame in this configuration. Dotted lines indicate placement of string guidelines.

Sticks should never be notched at the center point—this weakens them at a point of stress. In order to achieve a better joint, however, sand or file each one so that they will fit together more snugly.

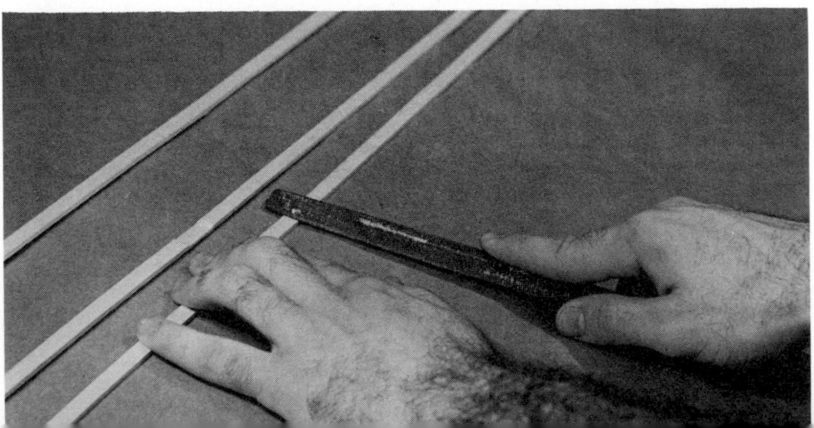

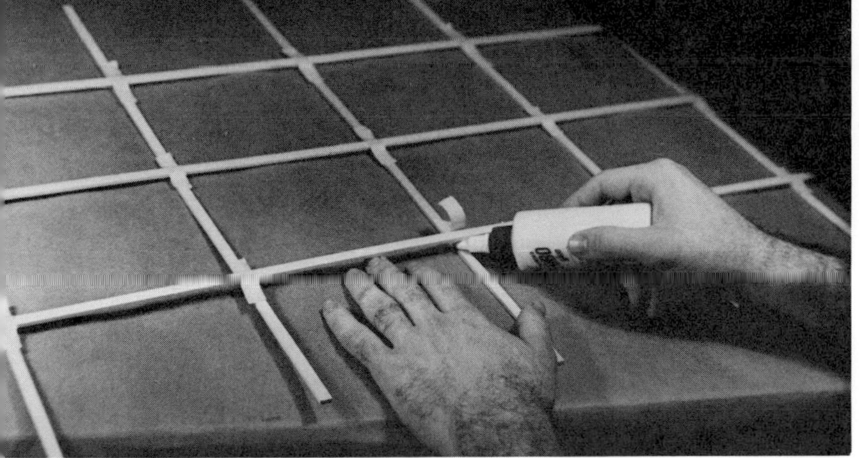

To build a strong frame, use white glue and string lashings. Here strips were held in place with masking tape so that gluing and lashing operations could be carried on uninterrupted.

Tie joints with linen or cotton string.

Run guidelines from one end to the other, as the diagram shows. Tie the string at one end, pull it taut, and loop it around the next rib. Continue to loop it around each spar and tie the string to the other corner.

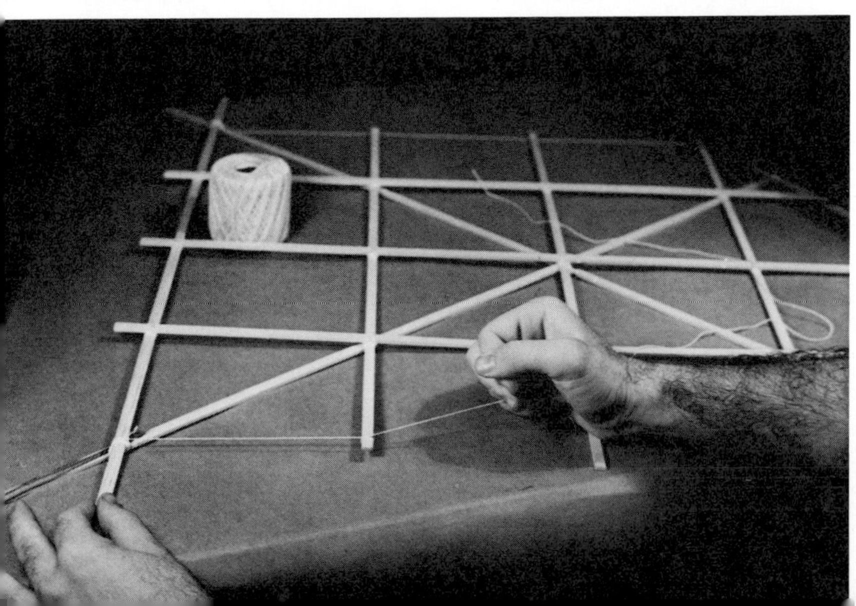

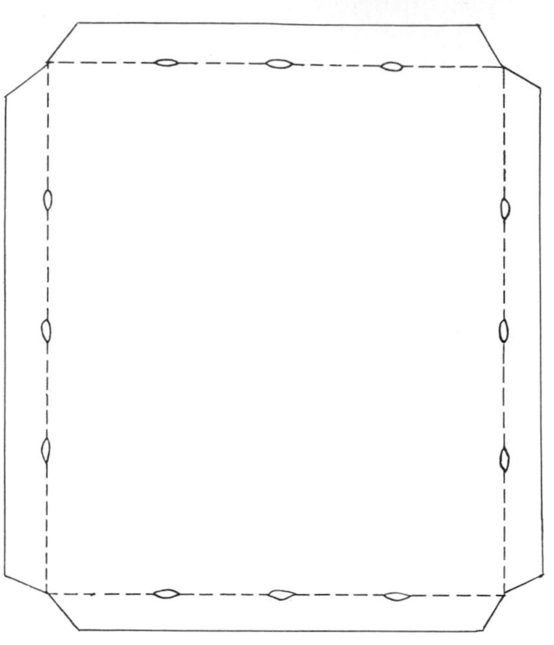

Using a strong, thin paper, possibly Japanese, cut the shape of the kite including an extra margin which will be glued back.

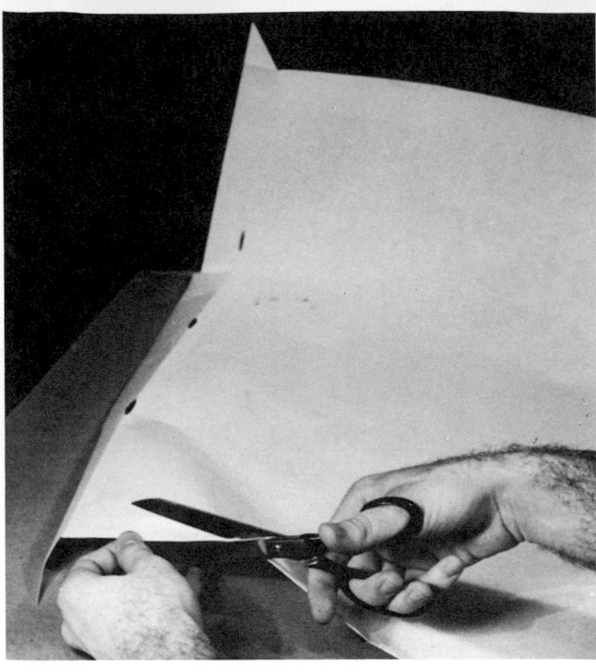

Cut holes at points where the ribs will protrude, and decorate the paper.

Slip the ribs through the proper holes, thereby mounting the paper on the frame. The diagonal ribs should be closest to the paper. Paste back the flaps over the string guides.

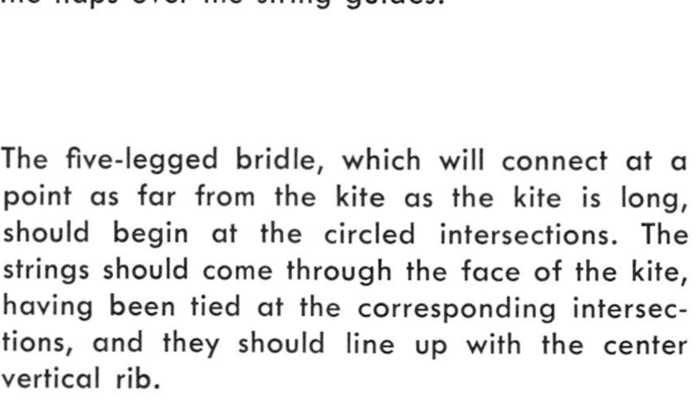

The five-legged bridle, which will connect at a point as far from the kite as the kite is long, should begin at the circled intersections. The strings should come through the face of the kite, having been tied at the corresponding intersections, and they should line up with the center vertical rib.

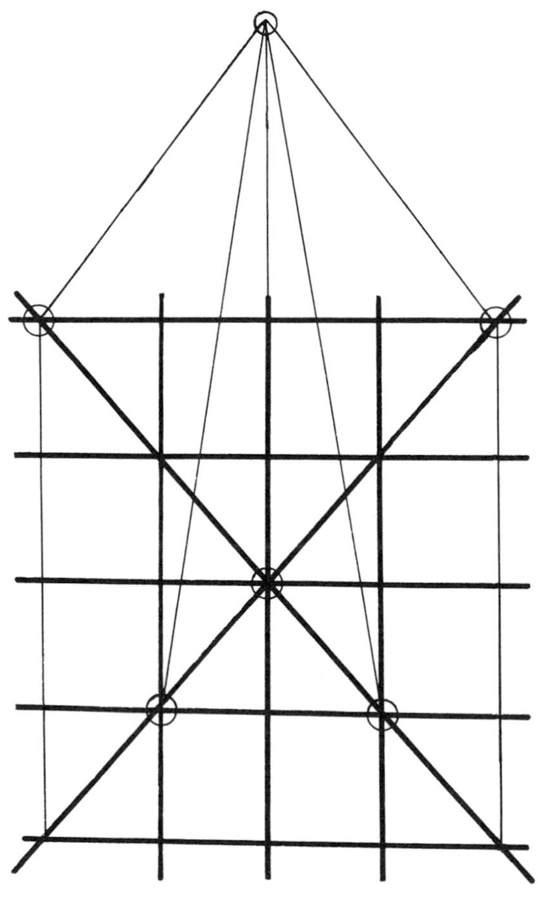

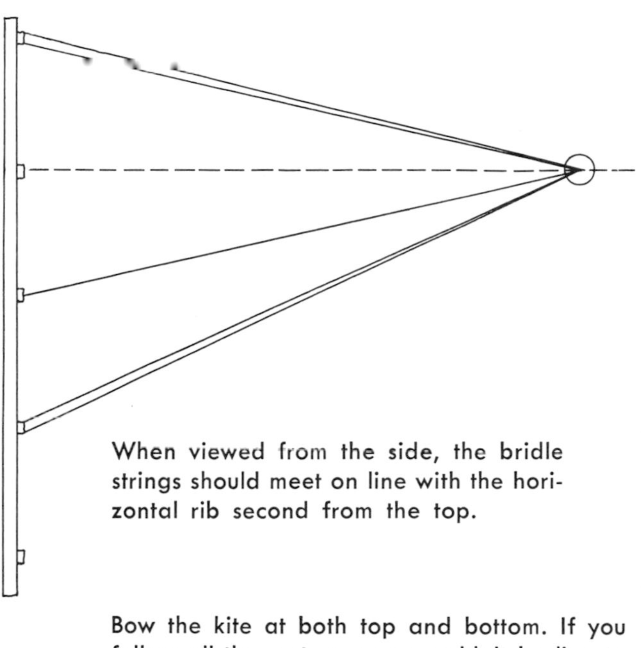

When viewed from the side, the bridle strings should meet on line with the horizontal rib second from the top.

Bow the kite at both top and bottom. If you follow all these steps, you wouldn't be lion to say you made this kite yourself.

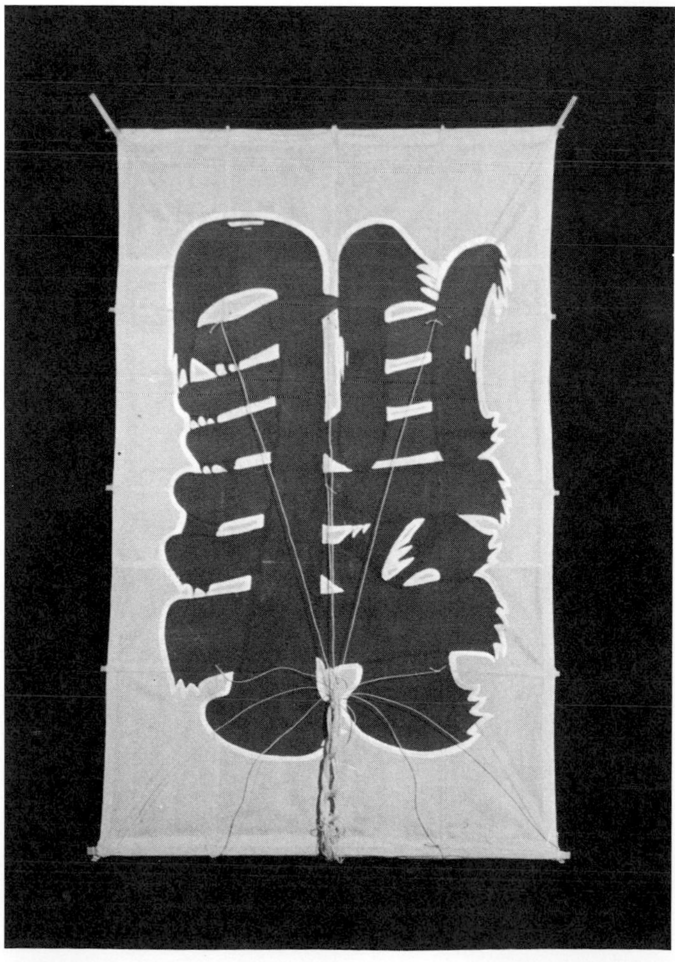

A modern Japanese rectangular kite with ideograph as decoration.

BIRD KITES

So much of man's desire to fly stems from the sight of soaring birds that it seems only natural for kite craftsmen to mimic the bird's form as well as function. So realistic are many bird kites that eagles and hawks have occasionally been deceived by high-flying impersonations.

Keith Shields has modified a Columbian *Buyeos* kite design which had the hawk as its basis. Shields's design uses a squat diamond-shaped guideline of #20 braided nylon line supported by two spars (32″) and a spine (30″) of ¼″ diameter maple dowels. The covering, here of kraft paper (brown wrapping paper), can also be made of cloth or plastic film.

The key to the kite frame is a unique strut affixed to the back of the kite across the two spars. This joining method imparts a gentle dihedral angle without using any bowstrings. The strut, a flat strip of pine 5⁄16″ × ⅛″ × 9″, is attached to the spars with two thin nails. The nails fit through fiberboard, sockets glued to the spars with two-part epoxy cement. In the cloth version, scraps of material are used as reinforcement for making sleeves for spars and spine. In the paper version use strapping or Mystik tape.

Other planar, bowed bird kites are manufactured commercially. They employ the same principle of guide string supporting the cutaway covering. The supporting strut in manufactured kites is usually replaced by a molded plastic joint which imparts the necessary dihedral angle to the spars. The way in which these commercial and the Shields kites use the guide string is a clever way of retaining strength while altering shape. In flight the exposed guide strings are invisible and these kites appear to be hovering birds.

Another technique of building bird kites calls for a much more realistic approach to design. Although the frames are often principally the same, some craftsmen use papier-mâché and tissue paper coverings to construct kites which are scale models—sometimes full size—of certain birds. Since, in some cases, this involves completely covering both sides of the wing, an actual airfoil shape is created—and this makes for very efficient, low-angle flight. These kites, which often duplicate the coloring and texture of the bird, can really be deceiving—especially to birds of a feather.

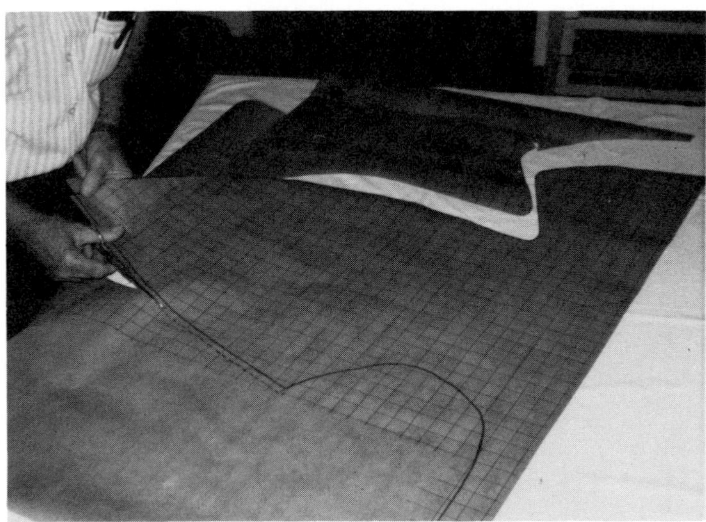

To construct a soaring hawk kite, Keith Shields begins by making a template. He draws a grid of one-inch squares on a piece of kraft paper and then draws one half of the bird outline on the grids. This series of process photos courtesy Keith A. Shields.

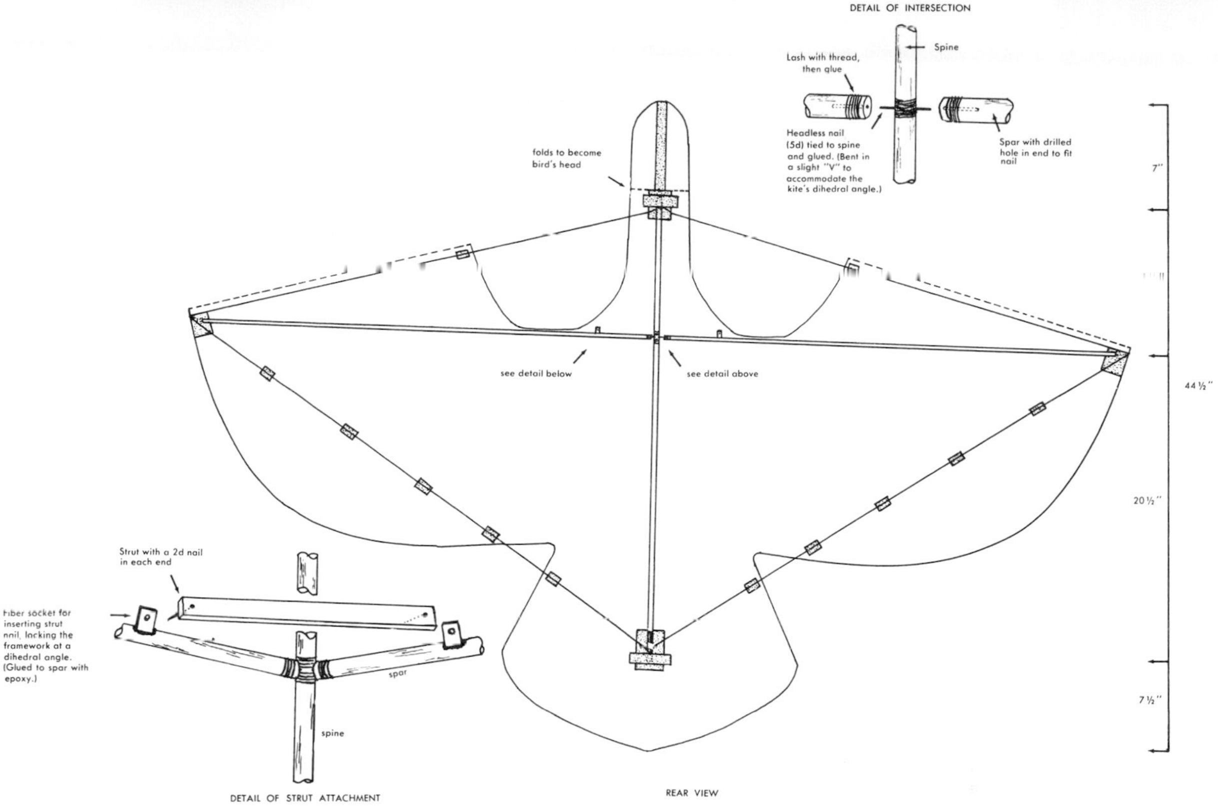

DETAIL OF INTERSECTION

Spine

Lash with thread, then glue

Headless nail (5d) tied to spine and glued. (Bent in a slight "V" to accommodate the kite's dihedral angle.)

Spar with drilled hole in end to fit nail

folds to become bird's head

7"

see detail below

see detail above

44 ½"

20 ½"

Strut with a 2d nail in each end

Fiber socket for inserting strut nail, locking the framework at a dihedral angle. (Glued to spar with epoxy.)

spar

spine

7 ½"

DETAIL OF STRUT ATTACHMENT

REAR VIEW

In the plan for this kite, gray areas indicate the use of cloth tape for reinforcement. The tape is used to form sleeves for the spars and spine, as well. The combination of strut (detail at lower left) and V-shaped nail at the spar/spine intersection (detail at upper right) gives this kite its dihedral angle in flight. Dotted lines along the top of the wing indicate excess paper which is rubber-cemented onto itself around the guideline. Where spine ends (near the top end of the kite) the extra paper (reinforced with cloth tape) is folded over to become both bird head and part of the bridle. Plan courtesy Keith A. Shields.

Shields bows the spine to slip it into the upper sleeve.

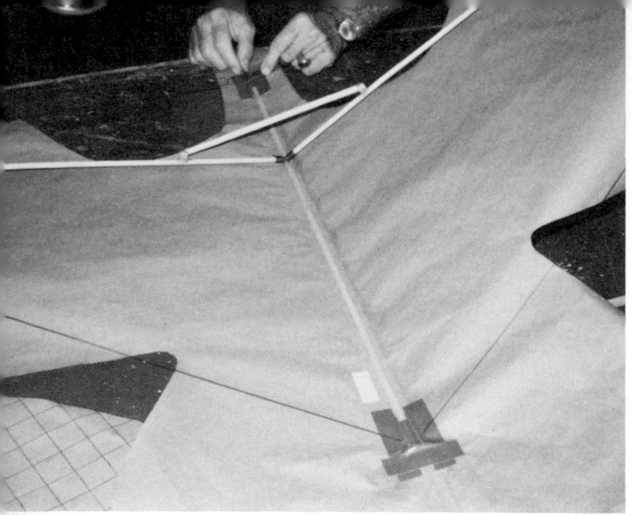

Place the wing spars into the wing pockets and snap on the central strut to give the kite its positive dihedral. The peripheral guide strings (which were threaded as shown in the diagram) are now tied together at the head.

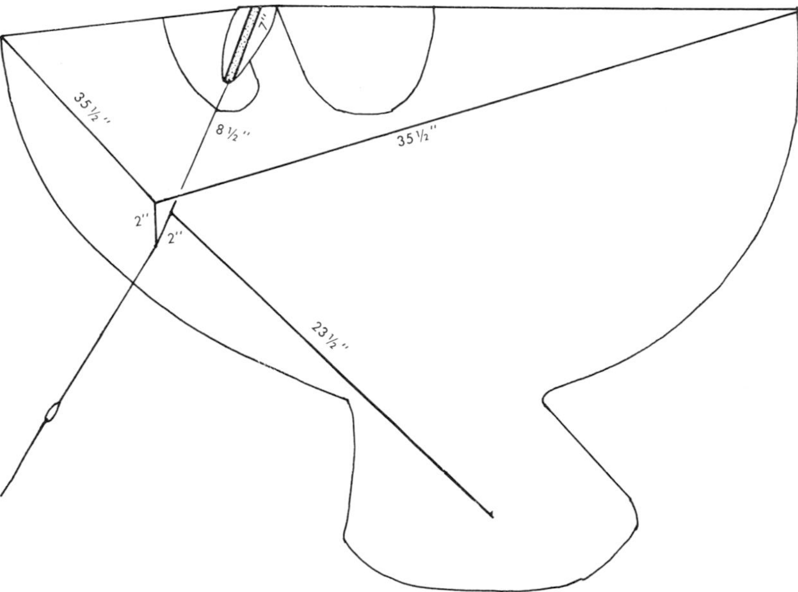

Shields recommends the use of a type of double bridle. One connects the nose and tail and one connects the two wings. He also advises that bowknots be used at all bridle/spar points to facilitate adjustments.

After checking the bridling, the soaring hawk is ready for flight. It requires no tail, is easily disassembled, and rolls up for easy carrying.

Primarily a light wind kite and a thermal flier Shields warns that these kites should not be flown on long lengths of line because "they then lose their identity. Five to six hundred feet of line is enough to have fun and attract plenty of attention."

The Airplane Kite Co. manufactures a variety of bird kites built along lines similar to the Shields adaptation of a Columbian bird kite. These cloth, paper, and Tyvek kites have very broad spines and fly in most winds. Courtesy: Airplane Kite Co.

A train of bird kites designed and built by Hod Taylor. They may look small here, but when they land, watch out! One has a 20-foot wingspan, and the other two are only 18 feet wide and still growing. The birds are built of heavy-gauge polyethylene and use lightweight aluminum tubing as spars and spines.

Bevan Brown has also been working in the bird kite genre. This pair of Jonathan Livingston Seagulls fly in formation and received special recognition at a Smithsonian-sponsored kitefly.

Brown rigged a special set of connecting rods and tubes to the wings to effect the tandem flight. The kites are built around sprucewood frameworks covered with paper.

There are two simple techniques for making heads for bird kites. Here crumpled paper is covered with a thin layer of instant papier-mâché.

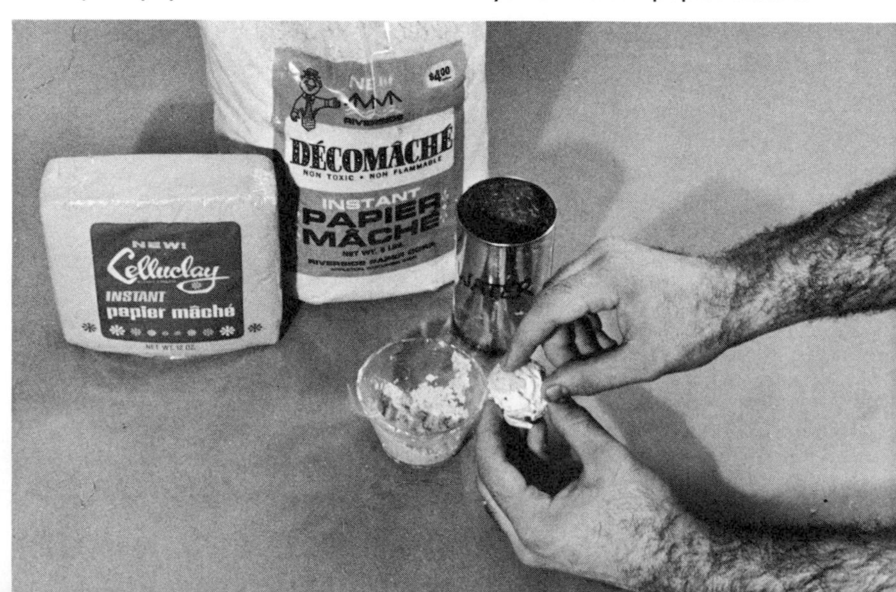

The papier-mâché mash is easily molded. It can be sanded and filed when dry. Apply it thinly to keep weight down.

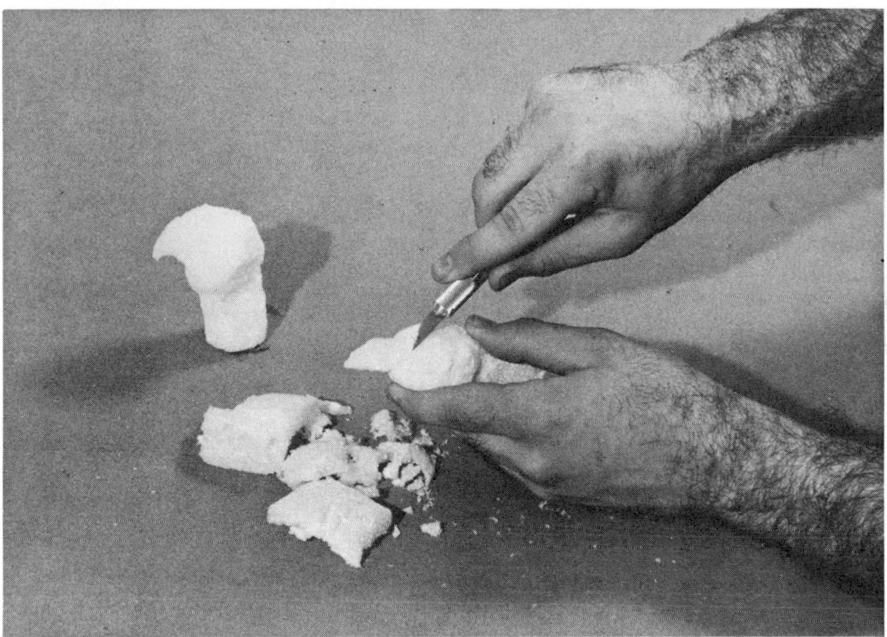

An alternative method of forming a bird's head or other light accessories for kites is to carve Styrofoam® brand plastic foam.

Strips of paper toweling are then dipped into a vinyl paste . . .

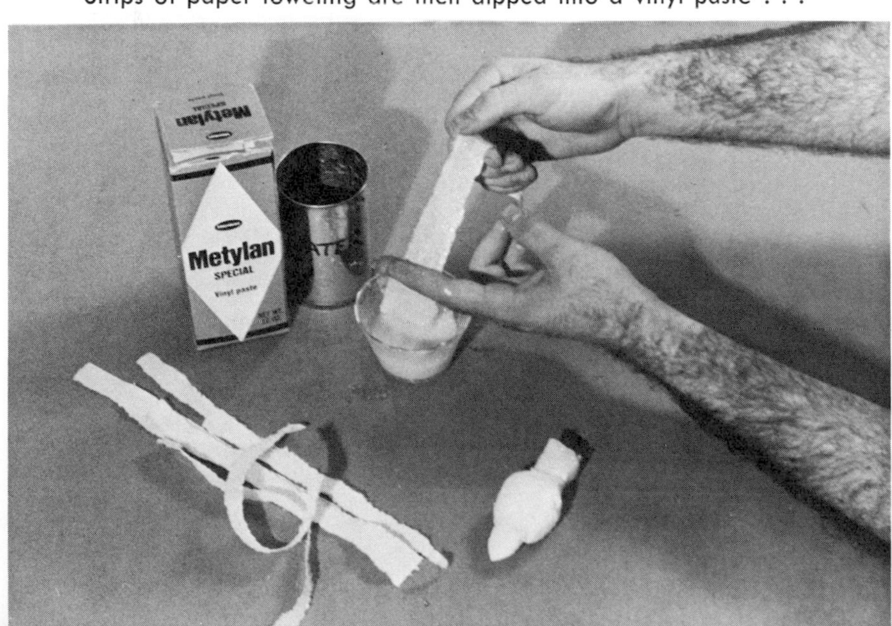

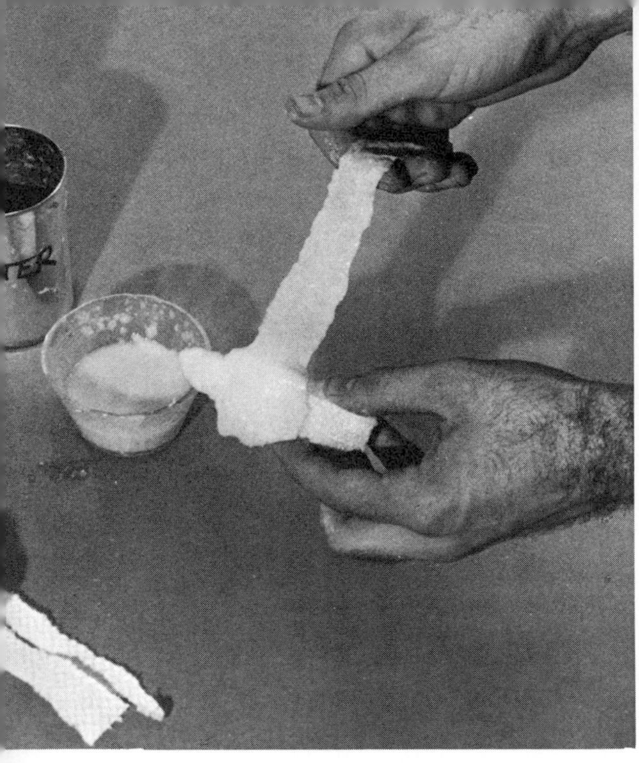

. . . and wrapped around the Styrofoam.

When dry, sand rough spots, and decorate. First paint the entire form with watered acrylic paints. Let this dry. This head was completed with feathered tissue paper adhered with white glue. (The glue can be made nearly the same color as the painted head by just adding a touch of acrylic paint to the adhesive.)

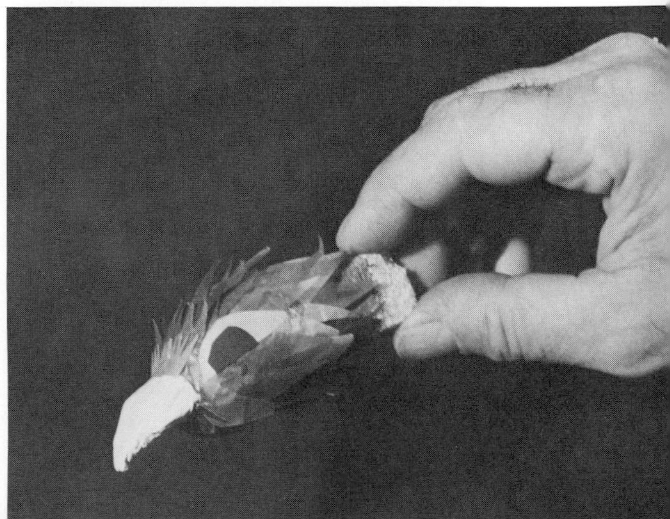

Another bird kite, this one made by Ezekiel Contreras, [illegible] ered with simulated feathers. Courtesy: Ted Norton.

But speaking of realism, this is a full-scale replica bald eagle with a five-foot wingspan. Courtesy: Ted Norton.

Another creation by Californian Contreras, the bald eagle really borrows both form and function from the birds. The feathers were simulated with polyethylene sheet. Courtesy: Ted Norton.

BOX KITES

Invented in 1892 by Lawrence Hargrave of Australia, the box kite was one of the first modern innovations in kite design; it was the first cellular kite. In its original three-dimensional form, the box kite incorporated two cells of different size, and it flew with the cells parallel to the horizon. The fashion today, however, is to construct both square cells the same size and to fly the kite vertically.

In the early twentieth century, the box kite was used extensively by meteorologists. They sent many kites aloft with measuring instruments and cameras. Other novelty applications included sending up men, fireworks, flags, and other heavy loads—both for entertainment and for practical purposes. The reason that this kite is so strong is that it has a doubled dihedral wing surface with venting between.

There are many ways to construct a box kite. Two general categories of the kite are rigid and collapsible. Each has its advantages. Rigid kites are stronger, but they are also bulky and difficult to transport. Collapsible kites, on the other hand, are easy to carry, but they present additional problems in construction.

No matter which type you build, all box kites are essentially the same structurally. All are built with longerons (spars and spines), paper-, cloth-, or plastic-covered cells, and most have some sort of inner supports to help the cells maintain their shape.

Box kites have been designed with triangular cells as well as rectangular ones. The idea and construction of triangular box kites is the same. The design was invented and patented in 1902 by an American, Silas J. Conyne. But, while it is still known as the Conyne kite, it is more popularly recognized as a French military kite, since the French early recognized its value and put it to use.

The box kite which is discussed here has some of the advantages of both the collapsible and the rigid varieties. Since it is made of four separate panels, it can be assembled and disassembled. And since the panels are all rigid, it has added structural stability. Internal support is provided by stringing the corners tautly at four levels, crisscrossing at the kite center. The counter-tension of the strings creates a firmness in the cells. The covering, made of indestructible Tyvek, promises to last a very long time.

The dimensions we have chosen for this kite are by no means the size limit. There are no hard-and-fast dimension and size rules when it comes to box kites—only that the materials used and the technique applied suit the design. The larger ones employ bamboo or aluminum poles. A 6-foot box kite is not unusual or unmanageable. It is a very reliable kite to fly. Slight variations in design can make this kite even more practical.

The stub-winged box kite—one healthy variation—has even traversed the Atlantic Ocean from New England to Ireland. Several years ago Walter "Scotty" Scott and Benn Blinn, two well-known Ohio kitefliers, launched 18 stub-winged box kites into the prevailing westerlies. Because no flier could practically accompany those kites, weights were added to the line to achieve proper drag. That at least one kite did arrive is a testament to both the conception and the stability of the design.

Although Hargrave originally flew his box kites with a line attached to a single point, bridling has been accepted as a more effective tool in flying these kites. Several types of bridles, both two-leg and four-leg, are described and illustrated in Chapter 2. Both the Conyne and stub-wing box kites are discussed in Chapter 6 on cellular kites.

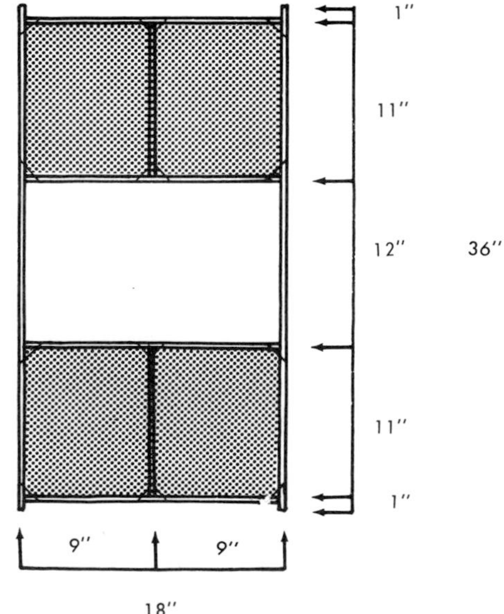

This box kite is constructed in four congruent panels which are lashed together.

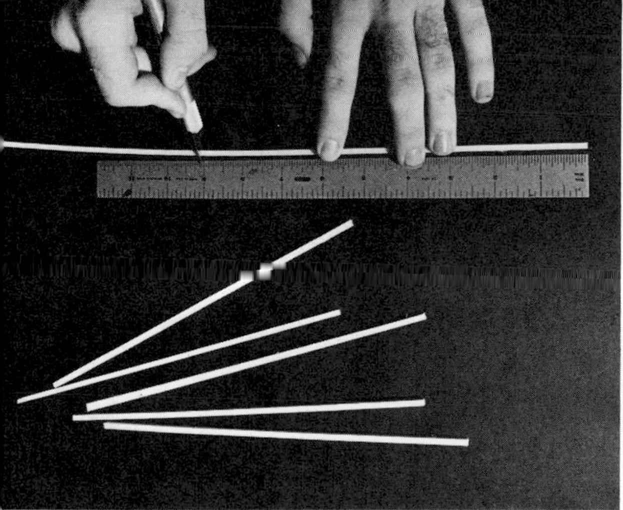

Cut sticks for the frame from 3/16″ square spruce sticks. Other woods will work well too.

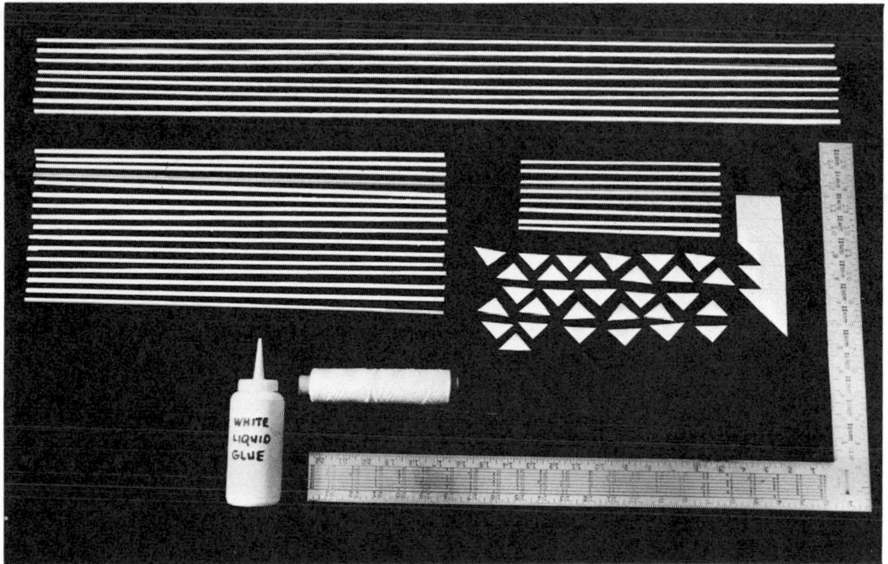

The materials for one box kite include: eight 36″ sticks, sixteen 18″ sticks, eight 11″ sticks, triangular reinforcements cut from white posterboard, string for lashing, a straightedge right angle, and white glue.

Take care in assembling the frame so that the angles are true right angles. Attach wood and paper reinforcements with white glue or contact cement.

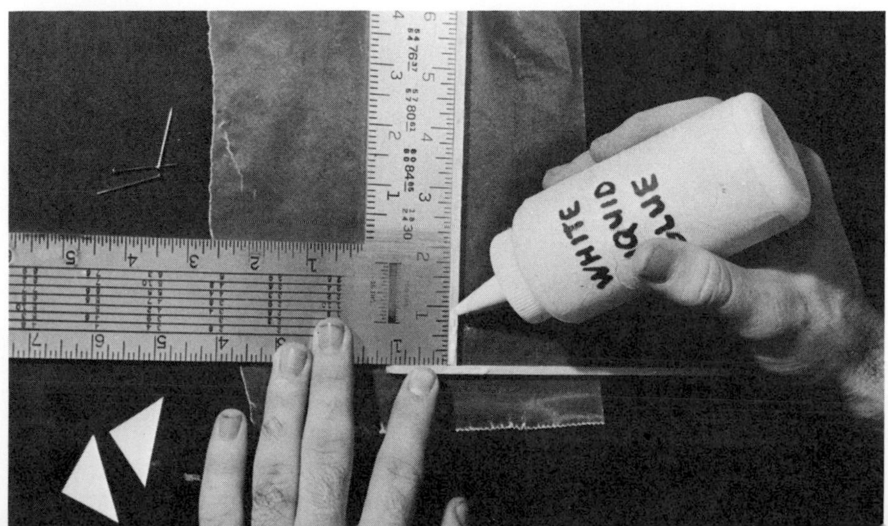

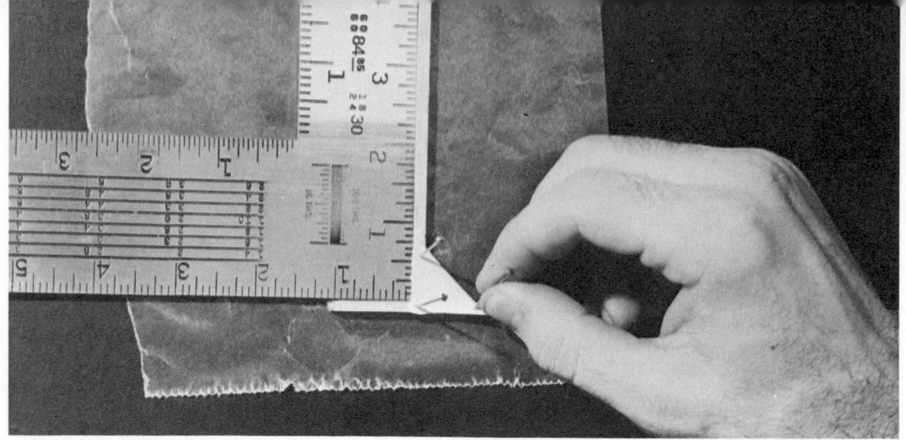

Use pins to keep the reinforcements aligned while the glue dries.

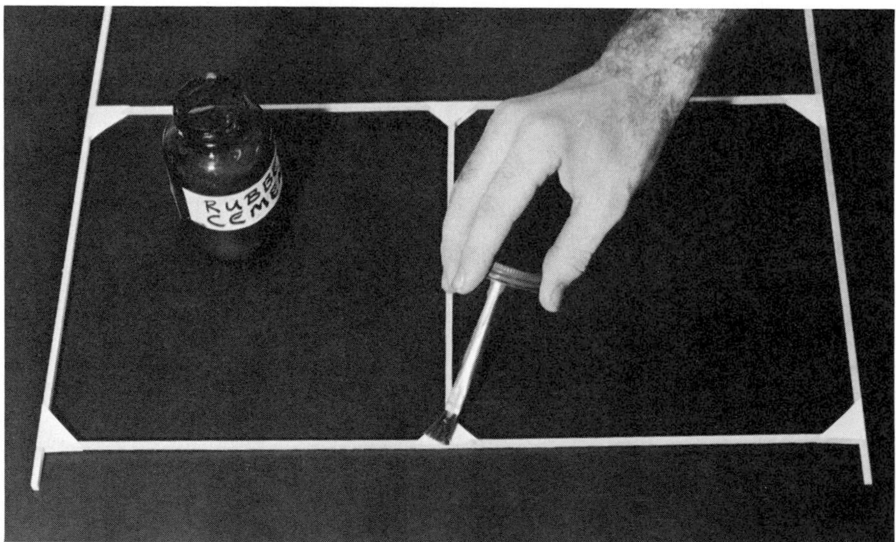

Tyvek is adhered to the frame as covering material with rubber cement. Coat both the frame and Tyvek with rubber cement. Allow the cement to dry.

Then press frame and Tyvek together. This is the best way to use rubber cement since it creates a permanent bond.

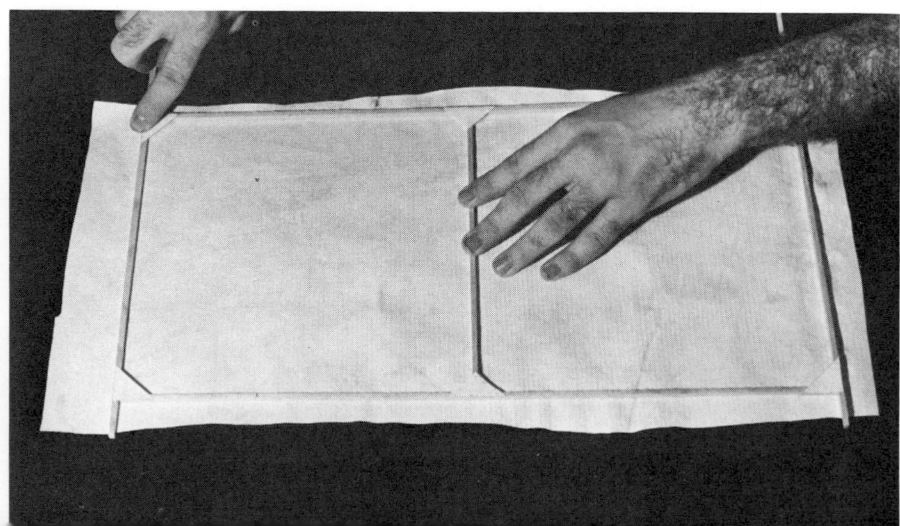

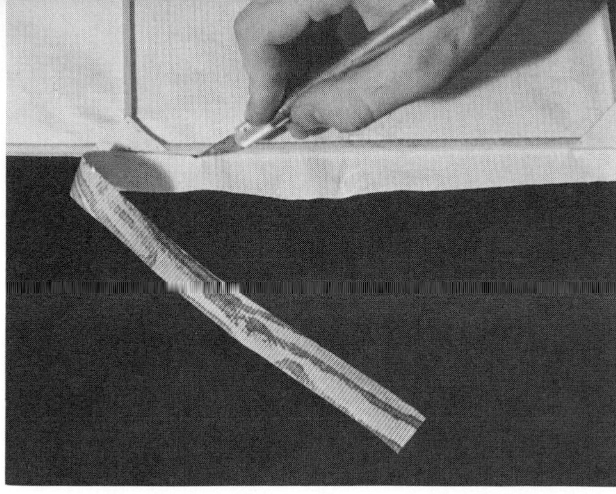

Trim away excess material with a knife.

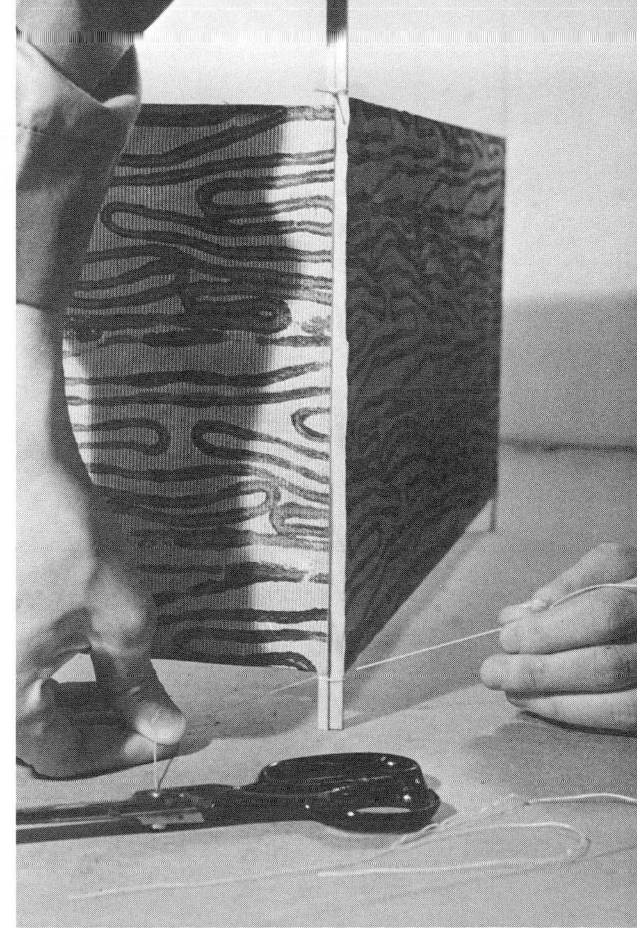

The four completed panels are tied together at four points, above and below each panel.

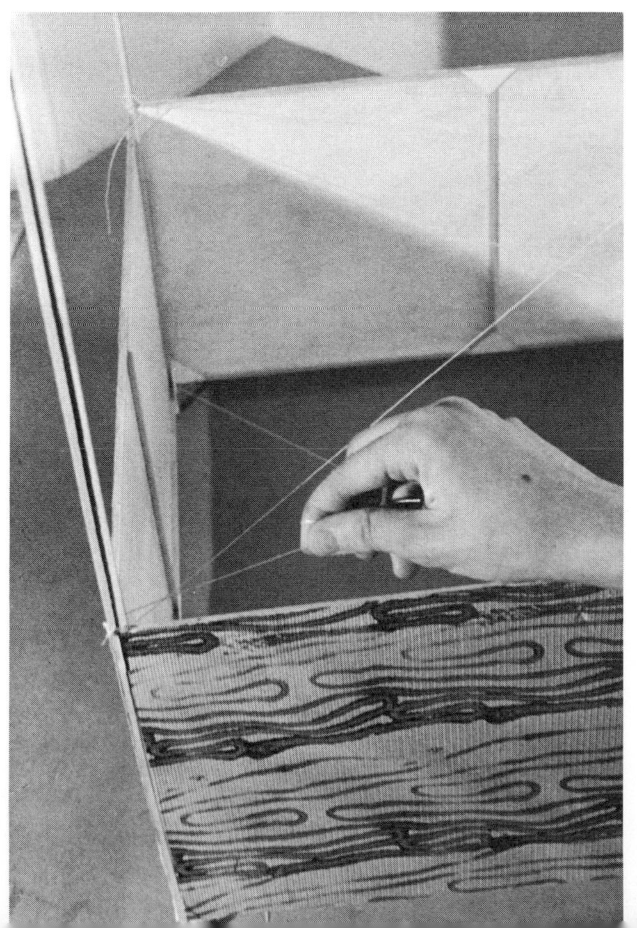

The kite is reinforced by tying cross strings at the same four points at which the panels are tied together. Make certain that the kite is square.

The finished kite can be flown flat or on an edge, as you prefer.

AIRPLANE KITES

Kites proved to be the inspiration for the airplane, and experiments with kites by Hargrave, Bell, the Wright brothers and others certainly helped to advance airplane design. But as much as kites provided inspiration to those inventors, the airplane has provided inspiration for modern kitemakers.

For many, kites which conform to airplane design are the only kind to build. Many intriguing designs have certainly evolved from their efforts. Stratton Air Engineering sells plans and materials for a series of very enjoyable single, double, and triple-winged kites. They are easy to assemble and they fly well. More importantly, they provide an excellent starting point for those who would experiment with this type of design but do not know where to begin.

William Bigge, on the other hand, began by building model airplanes. He is a physicist whose experiments with airplane/glider kites are the most scientific that we have yet encountered among kitemen. His structures, which act as kites when heading into the wind, will also fly backward as gliders when released. Masterfully engineered and painstakingly constructed, Bigge's kites have won awards at many kite festivals.

He uses spruce, Styrofoam® (polystyrene foam), and polyethylene film for his structures. Spruce for the wings and fuselage provides maximal strength with minimal weight. The Styrofoam wing supports are very light as well, and the polyethylene wing coverings provide the necessary strength and tension too. Because many of his kites use transparent films, once a kite has been launched it seems to disappear—only the thin frame is visible in the sky.

Yet another of William Bigge's designs is the small airplane kite also pictured here. Constructed entirely of very thin plastic foam, this kite is literally as light as a feather. It will fly in the lightest breezes. A third Bigge kite, shown earlier in this chapter, is a diamond kite which is so small and light that it can be flown indoors with the wind resistance created only by gentle tugs on the line.

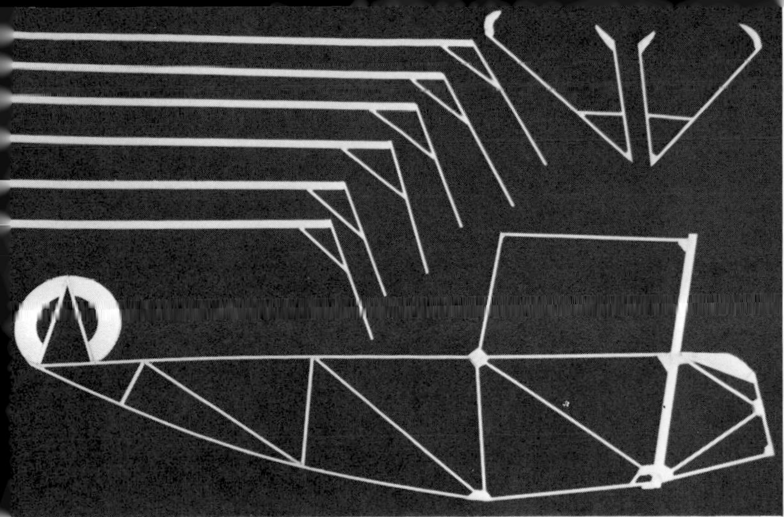

Stratton Air Engineering packages a kite with wood and covering for airplanes in different designs.

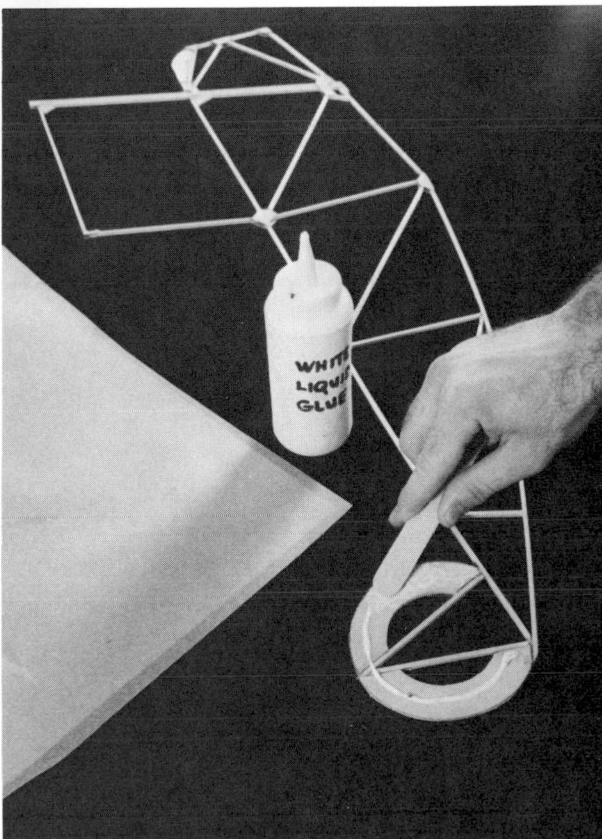

The frame is assembled with white glue or contact cement. The tissue paper covering is also adhered with a white glue.

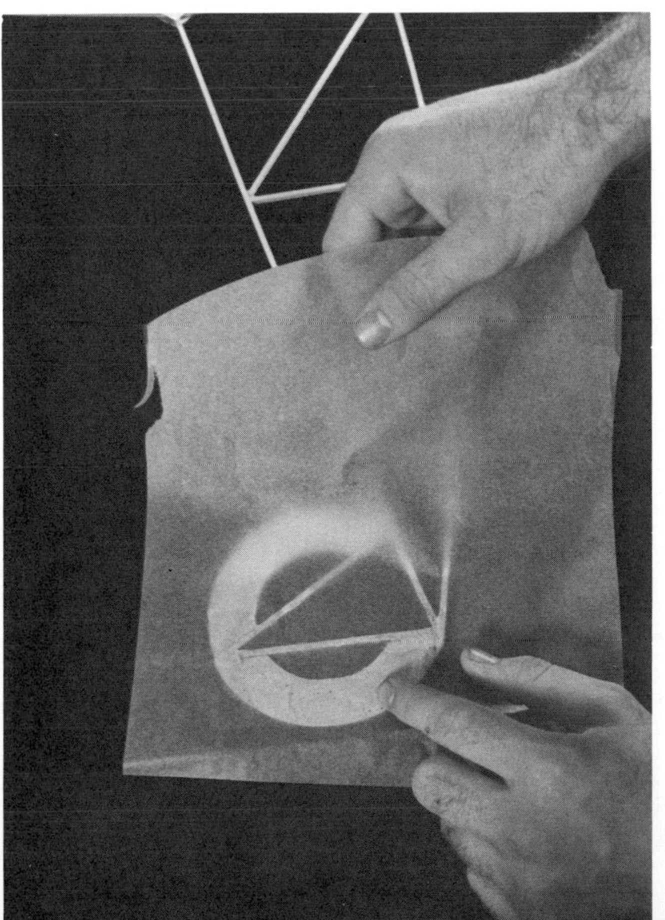

Be careful to apply the tissue paper slowly so that it does not wrinkle.

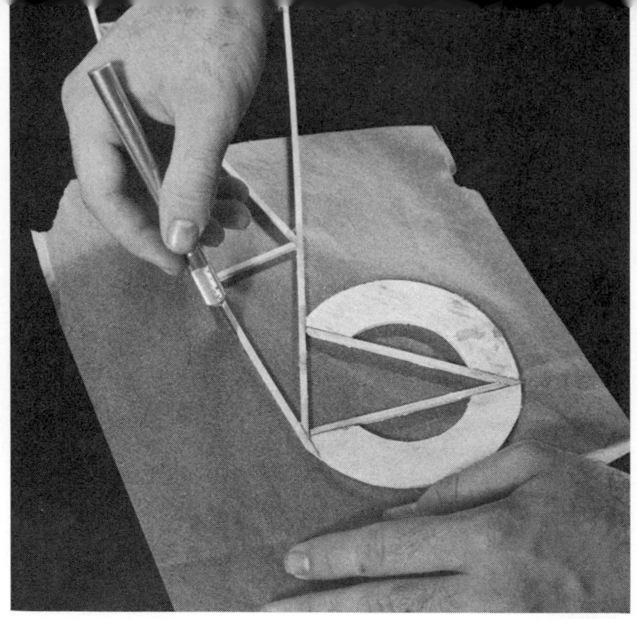

Excess should be trimmed away with a sharp knife. A dull blade might tear the paper.

Molded plastic wing mounts maintain proper wing angle.

William Bigge soaks spruce strips overnight in water with a dash of ammonia to soften them for forming. His recommendation is to bend them around a form smaller than the projected final size in order to make them more pliant and responsive.

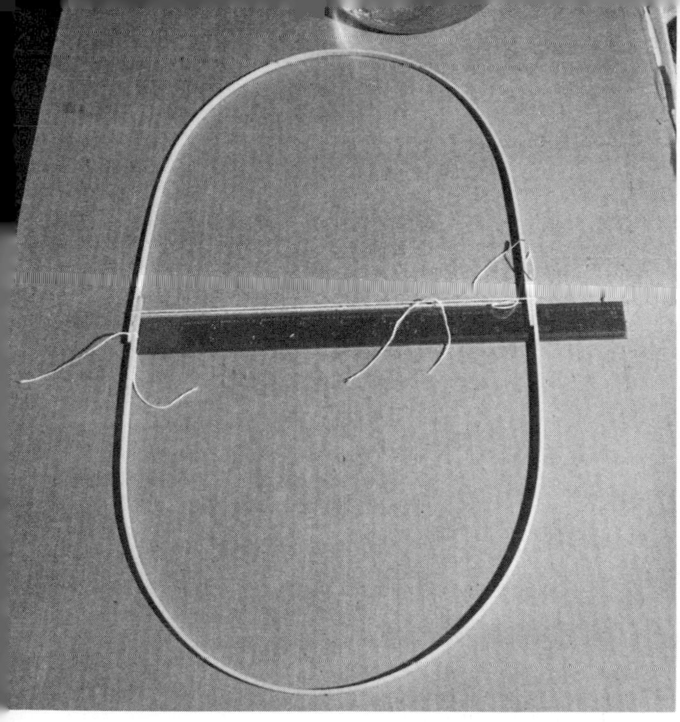

The strips are strung to the proper curve for wing tips and allowed to dry to shape.

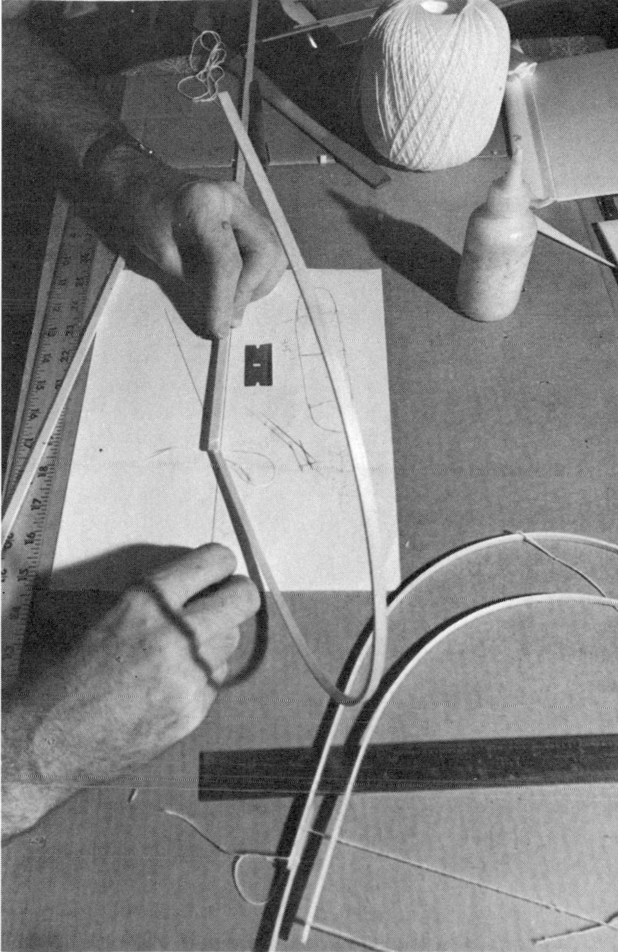

They are then tied and glued to the frame with contact cement. Here Bigge adjusts the joint for the proper dihedral.

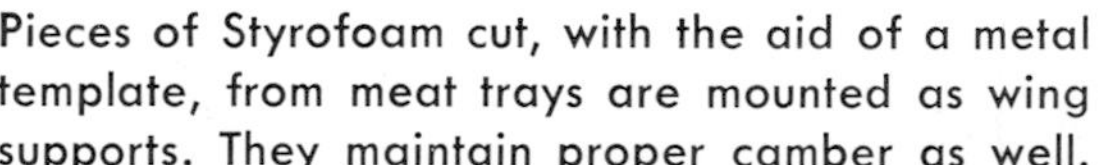

Pieces of Styrofoam cut, with the aid of a metal template, from meat trays are mounted as wing supports. They maintain proper camber as well.

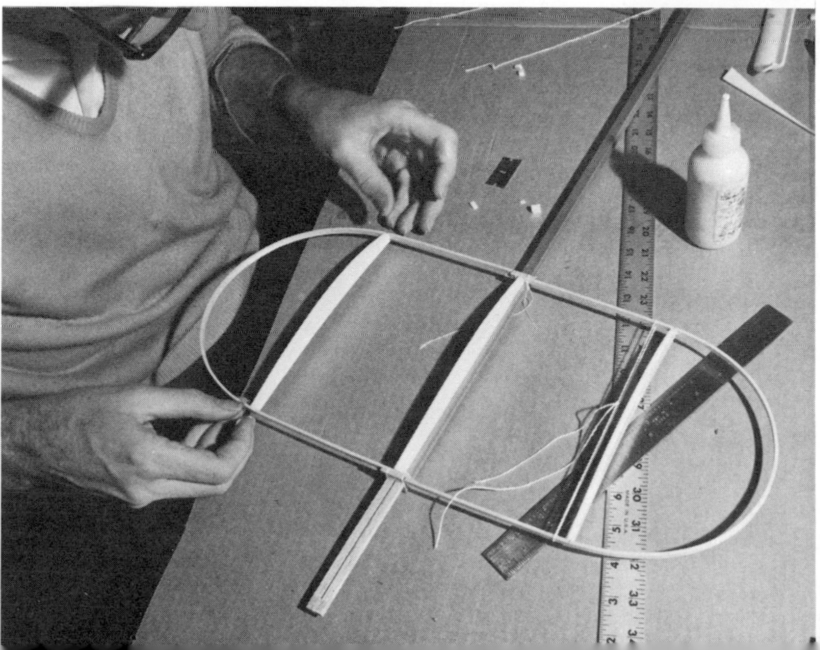

The keel, with point of attachment for the bridle, is mounted and supported by four lines which are adjusted to make the keel remain perfectly centered.

The rudder assembly allows for adjustment of angle and depth.

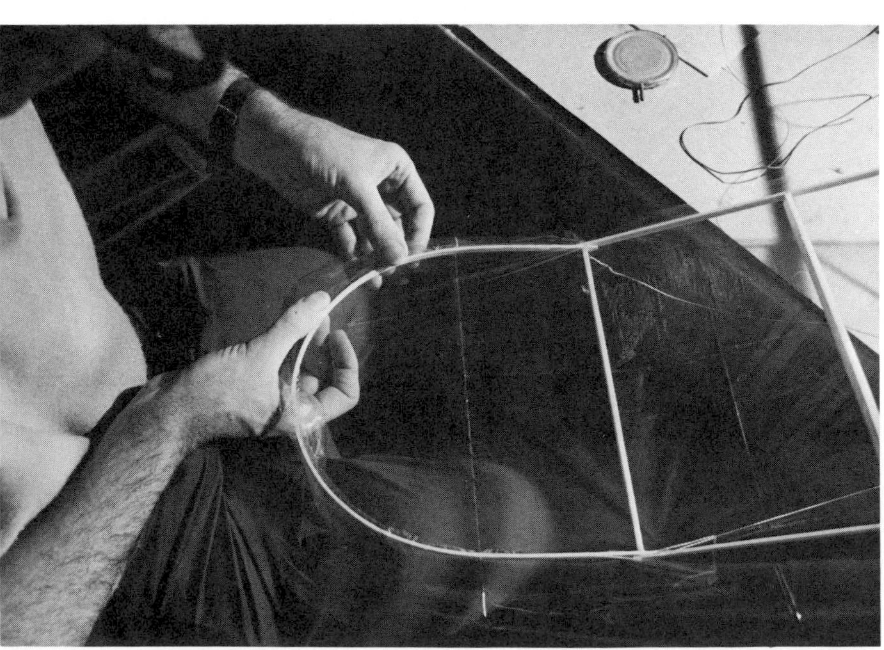

Bigge covers the airplane kite's wings with clear, thin polyethylene film. Excess is trimmed away after the cement has dried thoroughly.

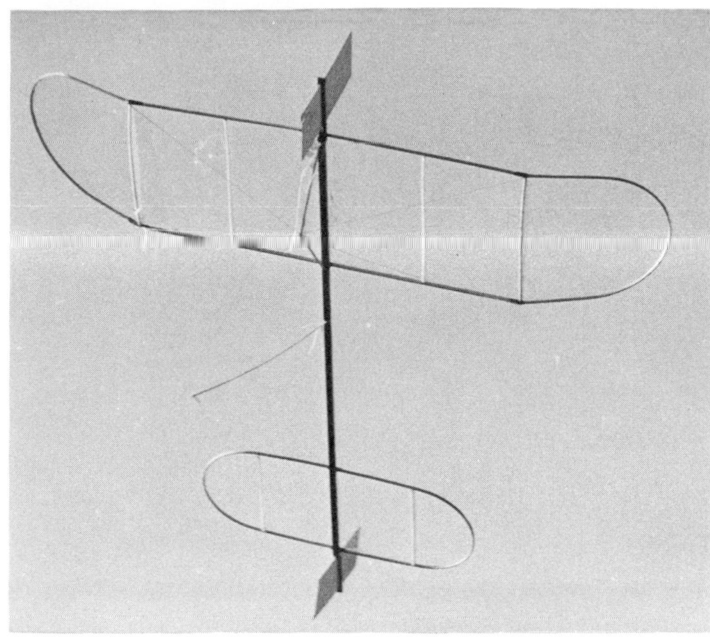

In flight the kite appears to be a floating frame of thin wood strips. The design is so carefully conceived and executed that the kite flies easily in most breezes and, when given slack, acts as a glider and floats gracefully backward.

Physicist William Bigge adjusts a larger version of the same kite covered in opaque plastic film. Courtesy: William Bigge.

Another Bigge design employs exceptionally thin plastic foam sheet. Not only are the wings very flexible—the kite is virtually weightless.

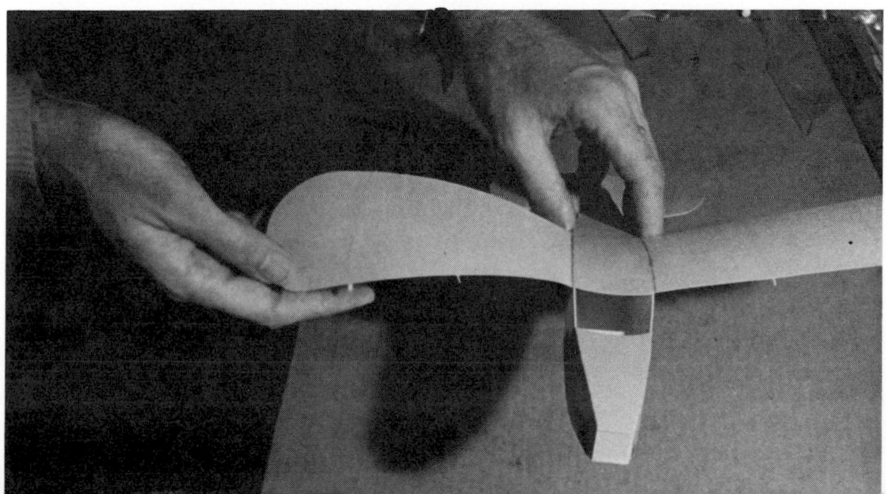

Built to fly in a whisper of a wind.

STRIPPING BAMBOO

Bamboo, which was probably the original framing material for kites, is still one of the best. It is available from many craft suppliers in a presplit form or in slats from old shades. A bamboo pole or cane serves admirably. Both can be readily used in different thicknesses and lengths.

Frank Rodriguez demonstrates bamboo splitting form. The pole is first cut to a workable size—be certain that it is long enough for your spine, spar, or bow and allow leeway for trimming. Then split the pole roughly in half with a sharp-bladed knife or a bladed tool and hammer. The same technique is then used to split off a thinner piece of bamboo which will then be trimmed and shaped to become the spar or kite hummer bow.

For shaping bamboo, a sharp knife and sandpaper are necessary. Use the knife to shape the strip of bamboo roughly. Trim the knuckles down slightly; they will require more work later. Where you are ready for the smoothing operations, keep the knife perpendicular to the bamboo and use a back and forth motion to scrape away rough areas. Sandpaper (hand held or wrapped around a wooden block) should also be used to form the bamboo into a smooth, sheer stick.

For a simple spine or spar, of course, little work will be necessary. As long as the bamboo is roughly symmetrical (or can be made so easily) you need not go to great lengths to sand it smooth. Most planar oriental kites use thin bamboo strips just as they are split from the pole. In this case, however, Rodriguez is making the bow for an Indian Fighter kite, and the bow must not only be smooth and flexible; it must be absolutely symmetrical as well. Greater caution and skill in cutting bamboo is also called for in making some oriental kite designs which use a variety of thicknesses in a single kite. Combinations of thicknesses usually run from the use of a solid (albeit small diameter) bamboo shaft for the spine; the use of normal strips (untapered) for standard secondary spars and spines; occasional use of broader, thicker slats of bamboo used as center spines or as spars near the leading edge; and the use of especially thin reedlike strips to serve as guide strings along the outside edges.

From a bamboo pole or cane, cut a workable length.

Split the bamboo roughly in half with a knife. You might need a chisel and hammer to begin the split—bamboo is a strong material.

From the half bamboo, use a sharp knife (and perhaps a hammer) to split off a strip of the thickness you will need. For the bow of a fighter, a ¼″ piece will be fine.

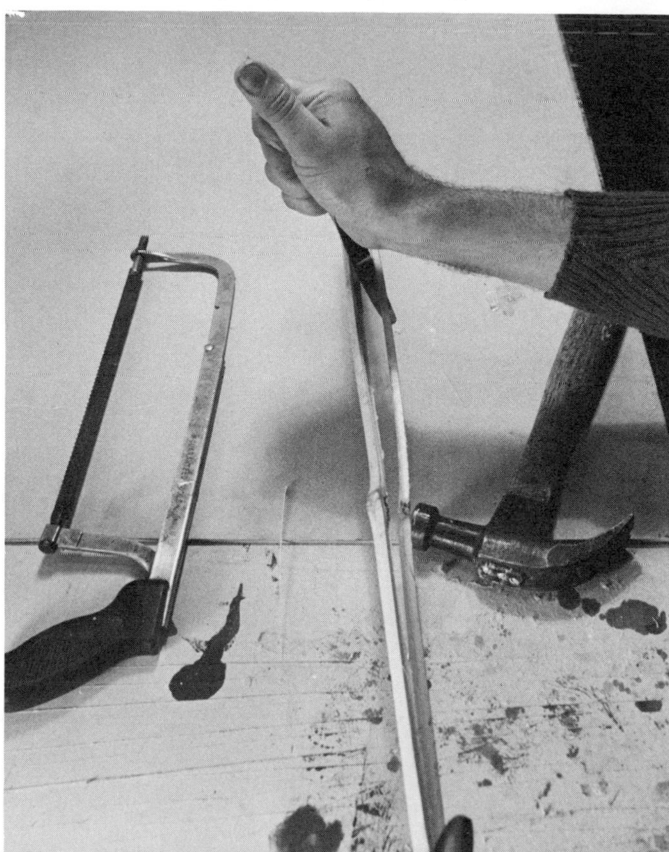

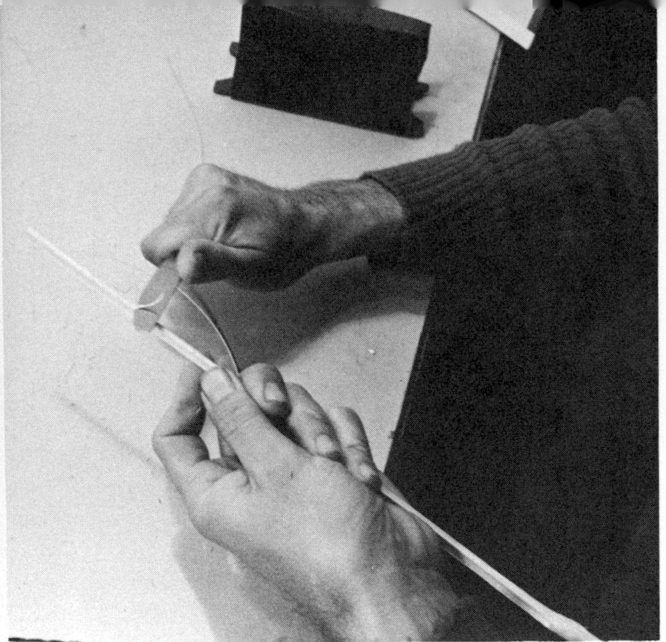

Trim all rough edges from the bamboo and taper the ends slightly.

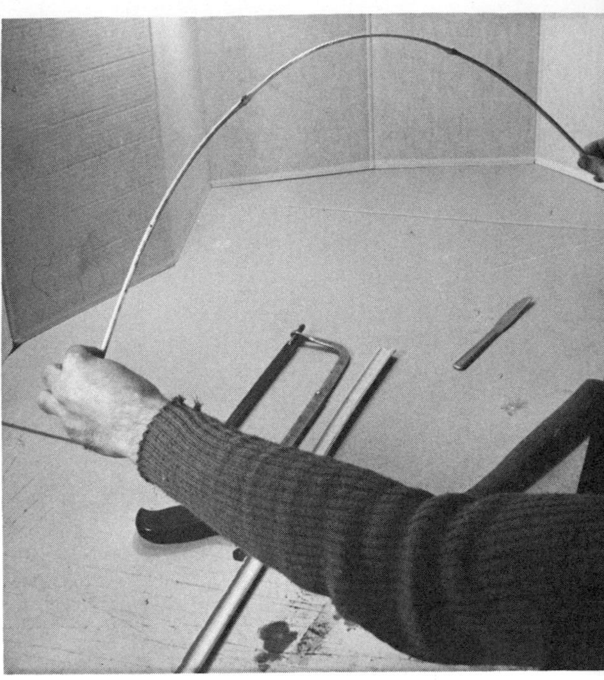

Frank Rodriguez then bows the strip to see where the irregularities are.

Sections that are too thick, such as the knuckles, are pared down with a knife. Remove small amounts of excess at a time, and you will eliminate the risk of overcutting.

Moving the knife blade back and forth quickly shaves small slivers from the bamboo, further refining the bow.

During the cutting and shaving processes, Rodriguez continually checks the bow to make certain that he is cutting the proper areas. The goal is to make the curve symmetrical. The bow is the key to a good fighter kite. One of the last steps is to sand the bamboo to make it completely smooth.

The finished bow is a work of art, in a way.

INDIAN FIGHTER KITE

Although a version of the fighting kite is constructed in most Asian countries, the Indian Fighter kite is particularly notable because of its sensitivity and maneuverability. The keen flier can direct his Fighter to swoop, attack, retreat, rise, fall—all with the flick of a finger. With the traditionally treated string—dipped in crushed glass—the kite becomes a tactical weapon with which to set loose and maybe even capture an opponent's kite.

When the Fighter kites go into the air and start moving toward each other you know the challenge has been set and accepted. Invariably neither kiteflier's tool is without its sharp edge of glazed string. By rolling the flying line in sticky gum or egg white and then in ground glass, the string is prepared to sever an opponent's. The aircraft swoop, dip, jockey above and beneath, each seeking the optimal approach, kite orientation, and string position for sawing through the other's line. Then, one kite (and sometimes both) floats helplessly untethered. But for the skillful kiteman there are spoils still to come. The victor is, in some countries, free to entrap the floating severed kite, bring it back to earth, and claim it as his own.

As is obvious from just this brief description of the custom of Fighter kites, they are a completely unique genre within the kite world and should be built, launched, flown, and fought with that special quality in mind.

Because it must be constructed of the lightest and most resilient materials, bamboo and strong light papers are traditionally used. Frank Rodriguez, New York City's professional kitemaker, makes Fighters with bamboo or fiber glass rod and Mylar. Mylar is an ideal material for covering the Fighter kite: light, very strong, and responsive.

Fighter kites are near the acme of kite craftsmanship, because they require a delicate balance in the bow and, later, in the entire kite. Since a good Fighter must respond quickly and accurately to the gentle pull and release of flying line, bamboo (and now fiber glass) makes an ideal bow. Rodriguez demonstrates here how to properly taper and shape a bow in bamboo. Great care is taken to form this element. The bow is always thinner at the ends than at its middle and the key is symmetry. Once the bow has been completed, the covering is attached with Mylar-based strapping tape. Covering is as much a part of the delicate construction process as shaping the spar.

A Fighter variation, the Nagasaki-hata kite, comes from Japan. The major difference between the two is that the hata uses a string guideline rather than an unprotected edge. Tension in the Japanese version is maintained by the string rather than the paper alone. The decoration of the hata is traditional. In some ways it resembles the decoration on the Indian kites, since both are of cut and pasted paper. Performance, sensitivity, and cultural histories are similar as well. Quite possibly they were born of the same design hundreds of years ago during the sweep of kites through the Orient.

To best launch the Fighter kite, let another person hold it fifty feet or more downwind. The following instruction for kite fighting and control are based on Surhendra Bahadur's *Indian Fighter Kites*. The kite should be held for launch by the top of the crosspiece with the leading edge facing straight up. Bring the line taut. At the word Go, your launcher should release as you quickly draw the line in by the arm-length for ten or twenty feet. Let the excess drop by your feet—it will soon be fed out again. The tugging creates extra wind pressure on the lift surface, giving extra lift power. When you feel the breeze pressure on the kite, stop drawing in line and instead give the line quick jerks (done by stretching the line-holding hand forward and then snapping that hand back to your chest). Let more and more line slip out slowly. With a well-made Fighter kite you can generally stop feeding line and maintain a consistent altitude beyond two hundred feet.

Great. The kite is flying, but now how do you pick and win a fight? If the kite is standing relatively stable in the lower stratum, let out about three feet of line very quickly. The kite will start to turn. When the leading edge turns slightly in the direction that you want the kite to move, start drawing back on the line at a medium pace. The kite will follow your lead and go in that direction. (No, it doesn't *always* help to talk to the kite.)

The most difficult aspect of kite fighting is developing a sense of touch through the line, wrote the master kiteflier, the late Surhendra Bahadur. There is a unique way of holding the line in hand to facilitate this sensitivity. Hold the string between thumb and forefinger with the thumb touching the forefinger ¾″ from the fingertip (at the last joint of the finger). This point of contact generally affords you the best opportunity to feel string contact. Now for the battle plan: when your line touches your opponent's, immediately play out string, as slowly as you can. *Never* let the string flow stop for more than a fraction of a second. With practice you should be able to keep the flow smooth and tensely slow, never losing the tautness, never losing control.

There are several ways of approaching the opponent's line to sever it. The key in any approach is keeping your kite in a position conducive to certain requisite motions. For instance, if you touch his line with your line on top, the kite should be prepared to roll out rapidly while simultaneously moving farther out. Slowly feed out string from the thumb and forefinger while making small movements with the fingertip—this will make the kite revolve or roll out while it moves farther out. If you touch the opponent's line from underneath, keep the leading tip of your kite straight up. Feed out string so that the kite rises rapidly. If your opponent isn't quick about it, this tactic will momentarily "hang" his kite string across your taut razor's edge line—the prime opportunity.

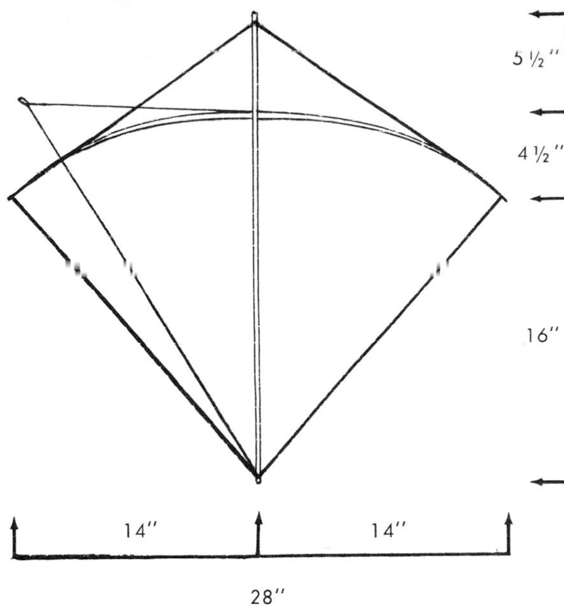

Classic fighter kites are constructed of bamboo: a bow and a spine.

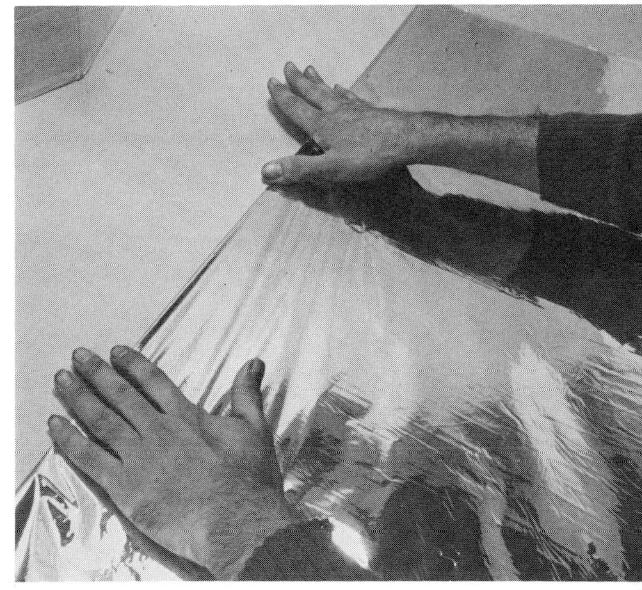

Frank Rodriguez lays out a sheet of .25 mil Mylar folded in half. Mylar, manufactured by Du Pont, is a polyester film which has a very high tensile strength for its weight and thickness.

Lay the template for half the desired covering on the folded Mylar, and cut with a very sharp razor knife. When unfolded, the doubled sheet should be the correct size and shape. Doubling assures symmetry.

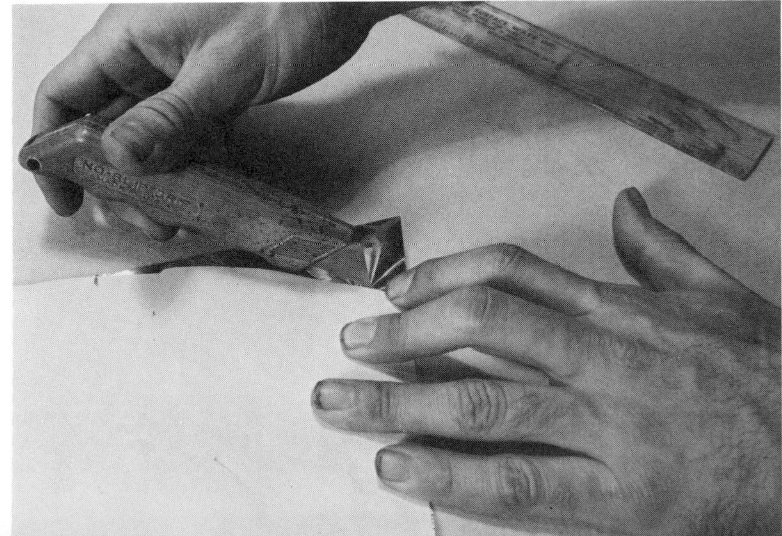

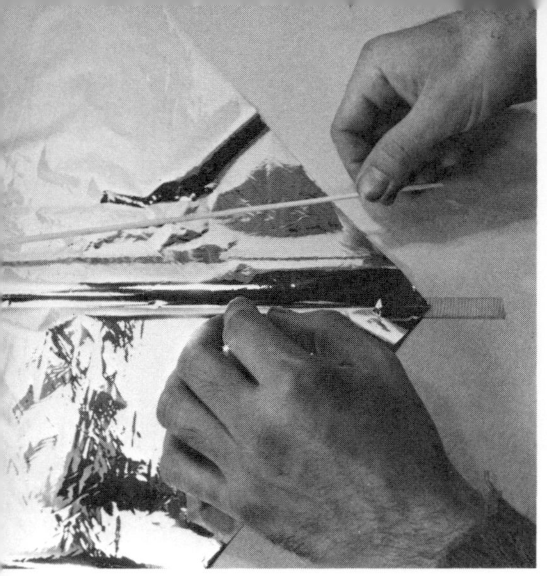

The spine is held in place with two pieces of Mylar-based strapping tape. The tape is wrapped around both sides of the kite as shown. The spine must hold the Mylar taut.

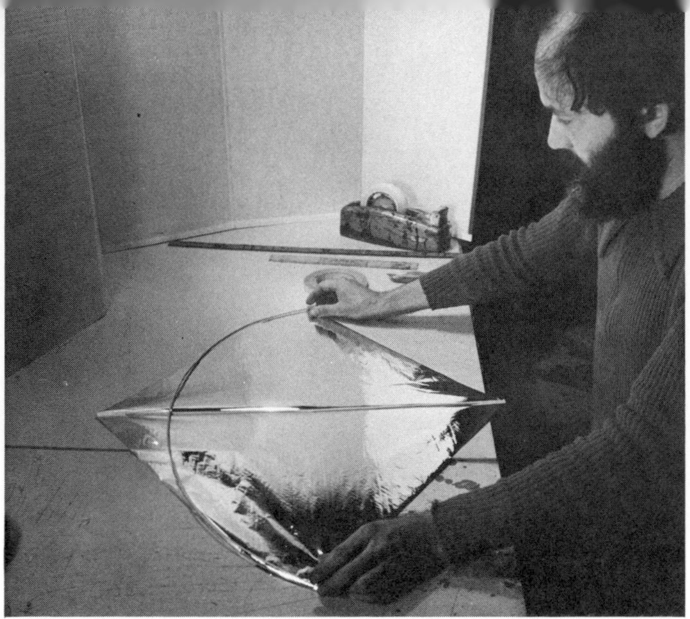

Rodriguez then tests the bow once more for curvature and size.

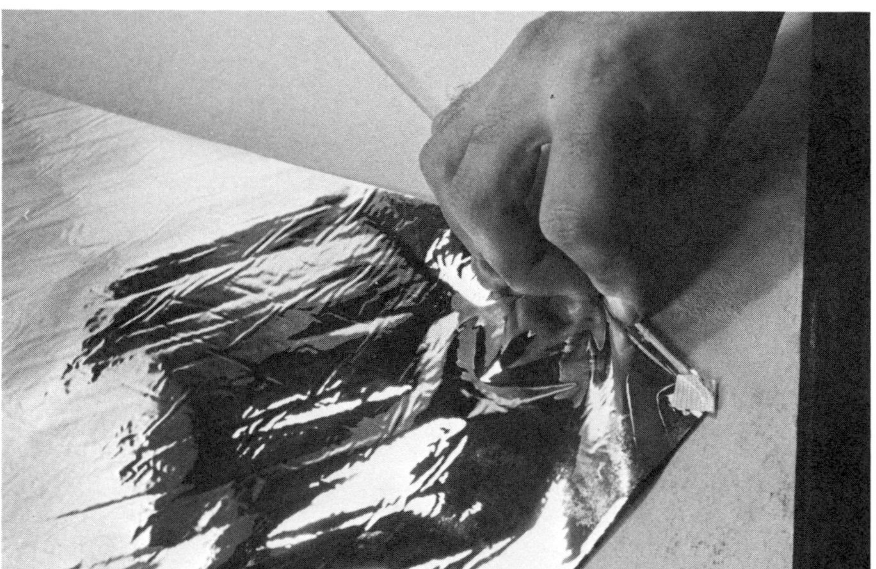

The bamboo bow is first attached at the corners. The shiny part of the bamboo should face down, or inside the bow. With the corners attached, tape down the Mylar over the bow up to the point where the bow diverges from the kite edge. Work both sides of the bow at the same time to make certain that they remain symmetrical.

Attach spine and bow with a single piece of tape.

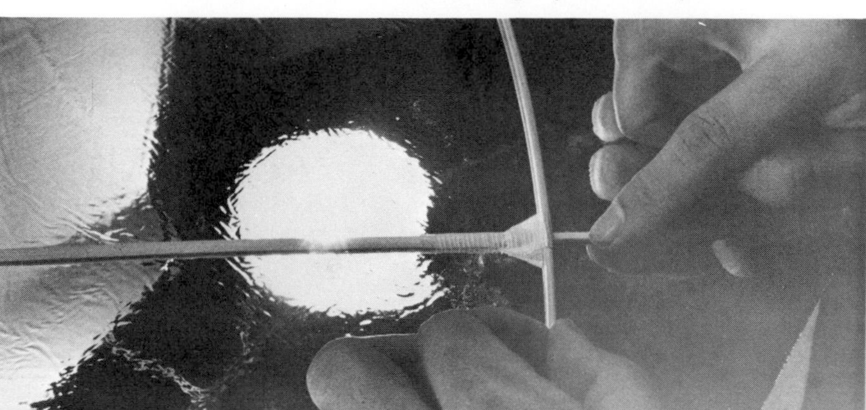

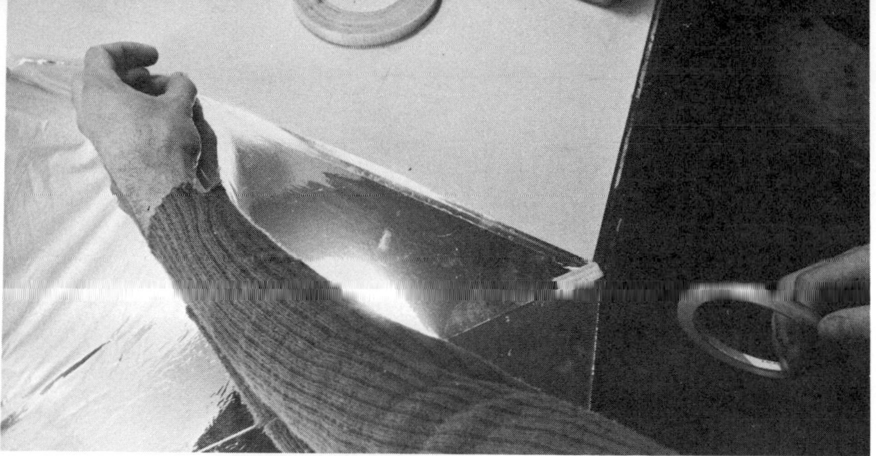

The trailing edge of the kite must be supported by a strip of tape. Otherwise it will be ripped to shreds after a few flights.

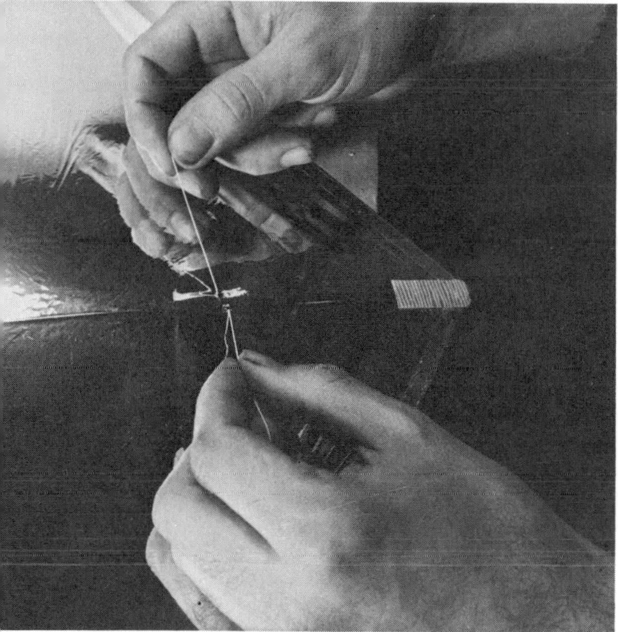

The bridle is threaded with a needle and thread. Reinforce the holes with another small piece of tape to prevent tearing.

A tail, thin strips of plastic film, is added at the bottom. Note that, at the left, the spine is further attached to the covering with a piece of tape.

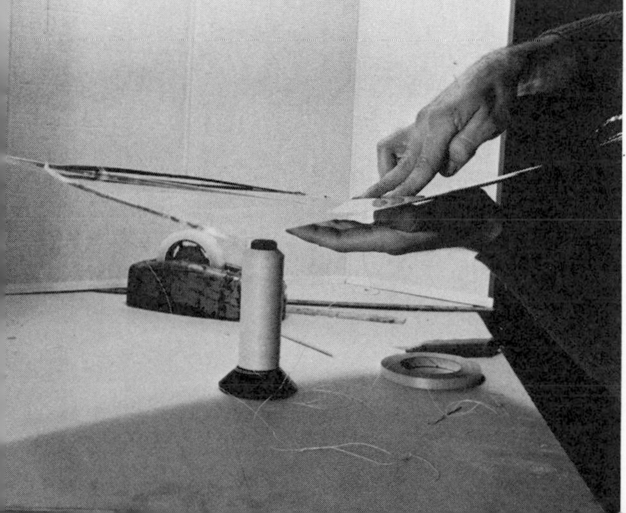

Frank Rodriguez then gently curves the spine in the palm of his hand—do not bend it too much!

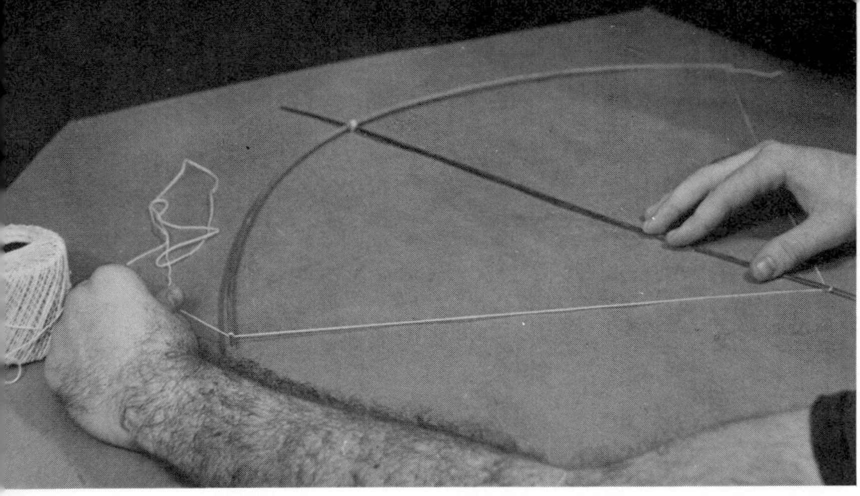

Other fighter kites of similar design use different construction techniques. The Nagasaki-hata kite, for example, employs a string guideline to maintain the bow and to support the covering (usually of paper).

Although the string guideline is not an Indian technique, the use of cut tissue paper designs is. Place a piece of paper slightly larger than the frame below the frame and cut out designs with a knife.

Paper of a different color is placed over the open spaces and adhered with rubber cement.

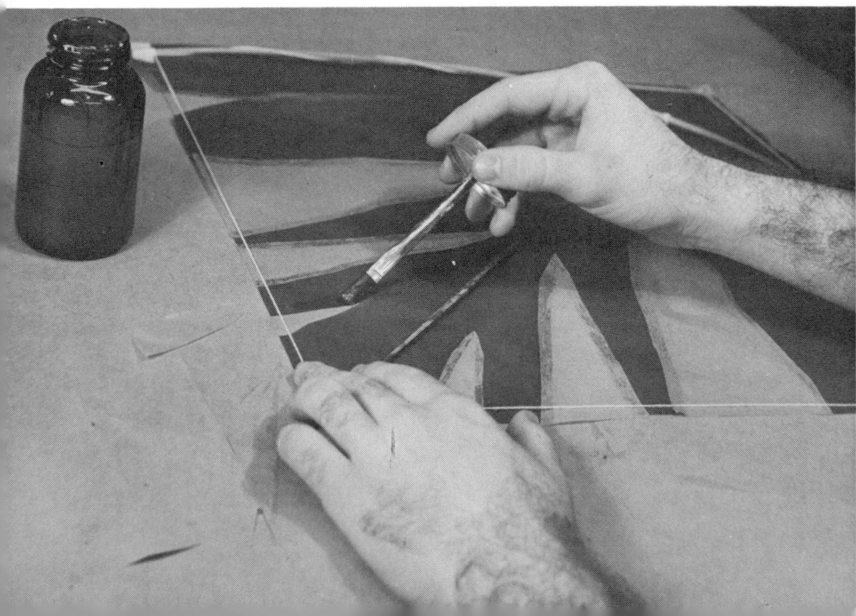

Attach tissue paper fringe tails to the ends of the bow, and the kite is ready to be bridled and flown. Happy fighting!

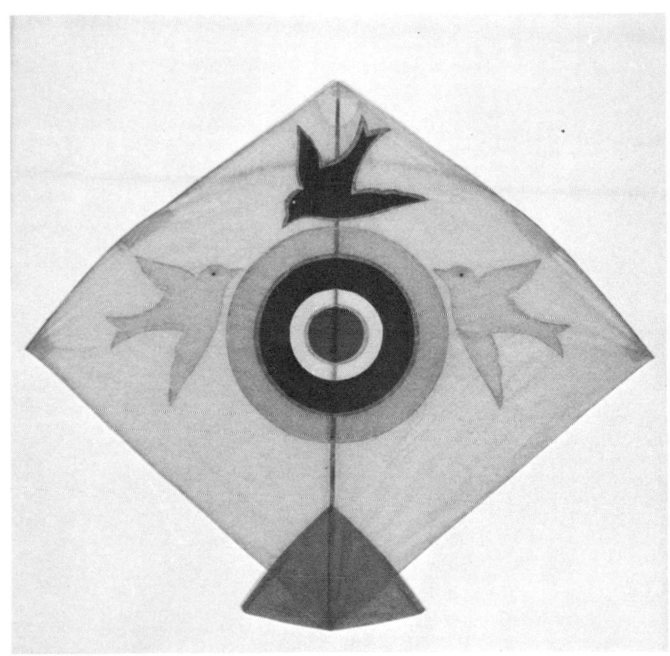

An example of a traditional Indian Fighter kite with cut and pasted tissue paper covering.

This close-up shows the use of paper tapes.

HEAT-FORMING BAMBOO

While bamboo can be shaped by cutting and scraping, it can also be easily formed by either soaking or heating.

To soak bamboo, place it overnight in a solution of water with a dash of ammonia. The next day, tie the bamboo to the desired shape around a form or over a jig. When it dries it will have assumed the shape of your mold.

Although the soak method is used with bamboo, this technique is more popular in shaping woods—like pine, spruce, cypress—because bamboo can be formed more quickly and easily with the application of heat.

To shape bamboo by heat, apply tension to the strip in the direction that you would ultimately like to shape it; simultaneously, draw it back and forth through a candle flame. Never allow the bamboo to stay in the same place under the flame—it may burn. To learn the limits of this material and technique, experiment with a few pieces. You will find bamboo remarkably responsive.

When shaping bamboo, the object is not to bend it to the exact shape. This would eliminate structural tension from the frame—which is not at all desirable. Frame tension maintains kite shape and provides "spring" which helps the kite adjust to minor changes in wind direction and intensity during flight. Also, bamboo that has been overheated tends to become brittle. A frame made with bamboo thus weakened makes a flaccid and fragile flier.

CIRCLE KITE

The circle kite is another of oriental design. Based on four circular sections joined over crosspiece and spine, this kite takes advantage of bamboo's flexibility and formability.

Each circle was constructed with two 36″ pieces of bamboo (you may choose to halve this measurement and make each circle from a single strand—making the kite half this one's size). Bamboo of this length is nearly flexible enough to make the 20″ diameter circles required, but it was heated slightly to make certain that each strip bent evenly along its entire length. Because of knuckles and irregularities in every piece of bamboo, it is wise to test the strips and make certain that the bamboo will conform to the desired shape under tension. Even in the simple case of a circle, bamboo that does not accept the proper shape could cause annoying irregularities in flight.

The ends of each strip are notched shallowly to make gluing and lashing easier. All joints are glued first, tied, and reinforced with more white glue.

Each circle's covering of Tyvek is then stretched tautly over the frames. The adhesive is a strong rubber cement; the cement is applied to both surfaces to be glued, allowed to dry, and then the surfaces are pressed firmly together. Tyvek, which will not respond to most white glues, needs special attention where gluing is concerned. Even better than gluing Tyvek would be to sew it onto the frame either by hand or machine.

The completed circles are lashed together, and crosspiece and spine are lashed on as well. Before flying, attach a tail to the bottom of the center pole. Determine the length by wind conditions.

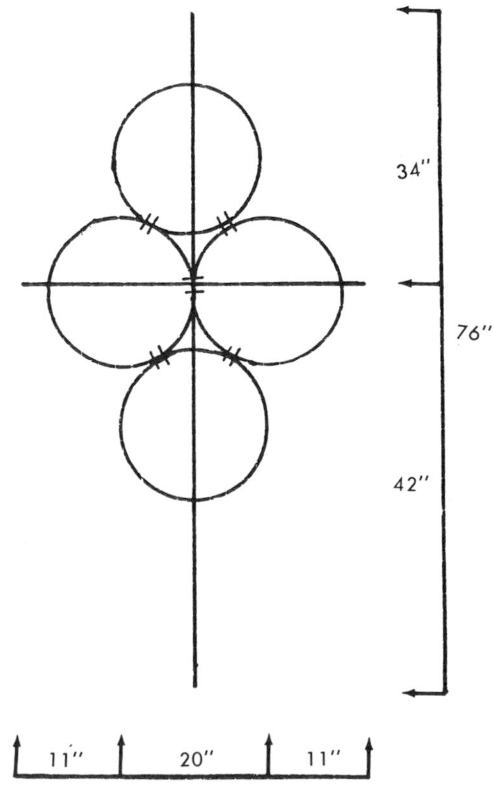

The large circle kite, of oriental origin, makes use of bamboo's easy formability.

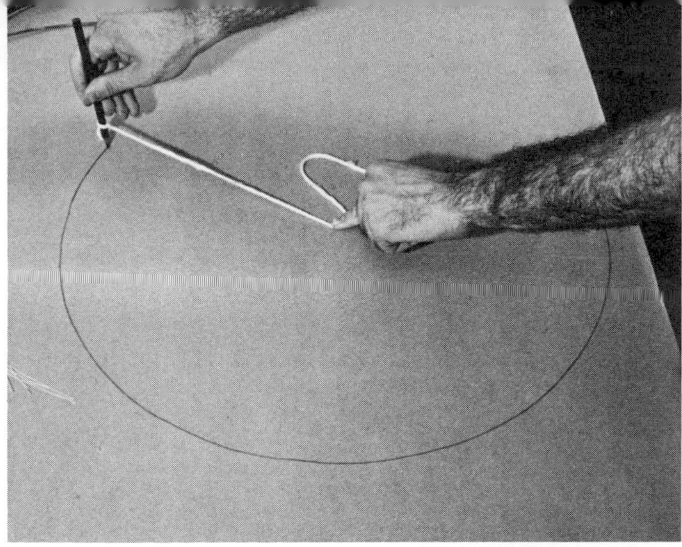

The guide for shaping the bamboo is drawn on paper. This will help in shaping the bamboo so that it is symmetrical and bends evenly.

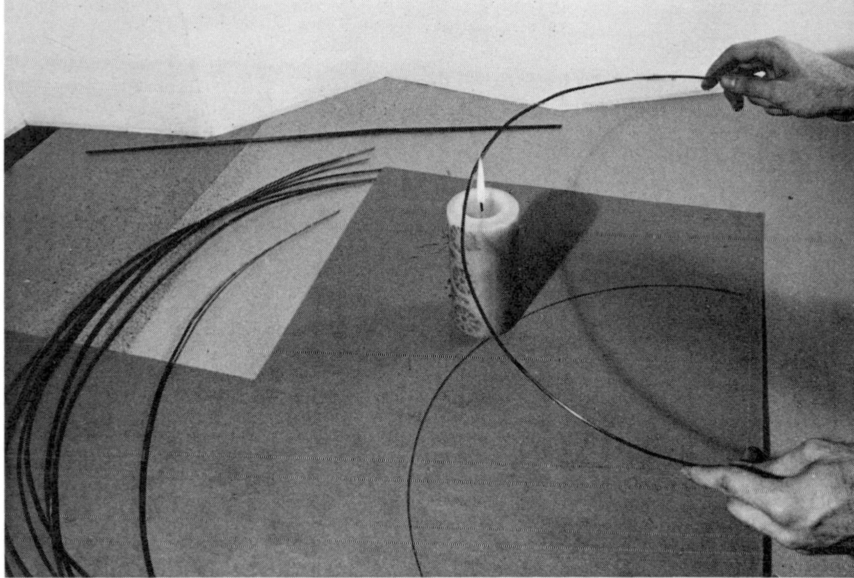

Heat bamboo by moving it through the candle flame. Never allow it to rest in one place too long or the strip will become deformed —or even burn. When shaping bamboo, the object is never to force it to assume the exact shape. Rather it is to relax certain sections that are stiffer or thicker so that the bamboo has spring and bends evenly.

Two pieces of bamboo were used for each circle. In order to obtain a firm joint, the ends of the strips were shaved slightly flat so that they would meet solidly.

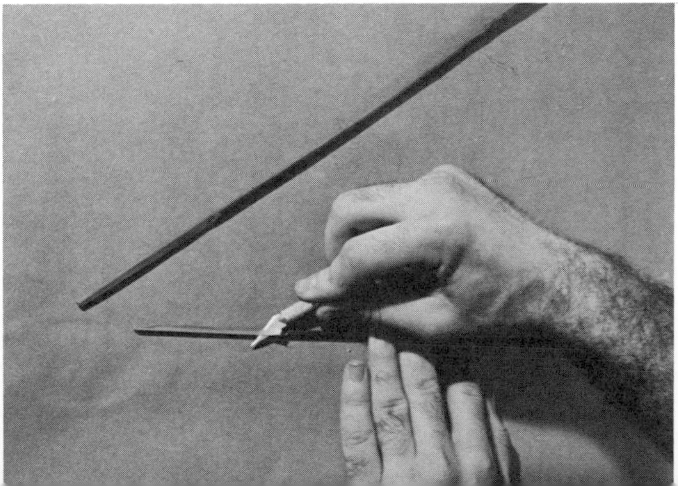

Every joint is glued, tied, and glued again.

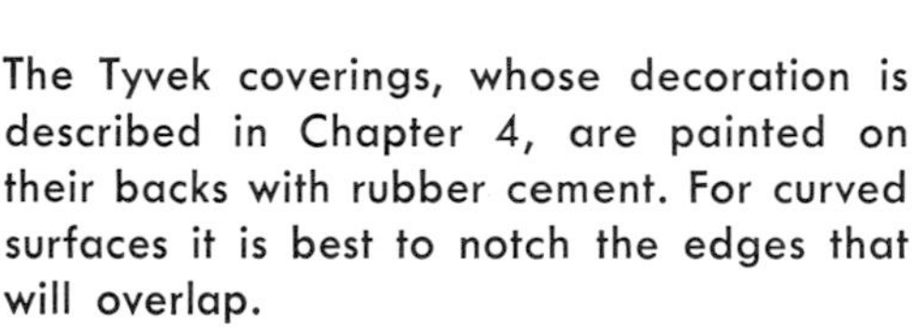

The Tyvek coverings, whose decoration is described in Chapter 4, are painted on their backs with rubber cement. For curved surfaces it is best to notch the edges that will overlap.

Bamboo frames are fitted into place, and the preglued tabs pressed down to complete the units.

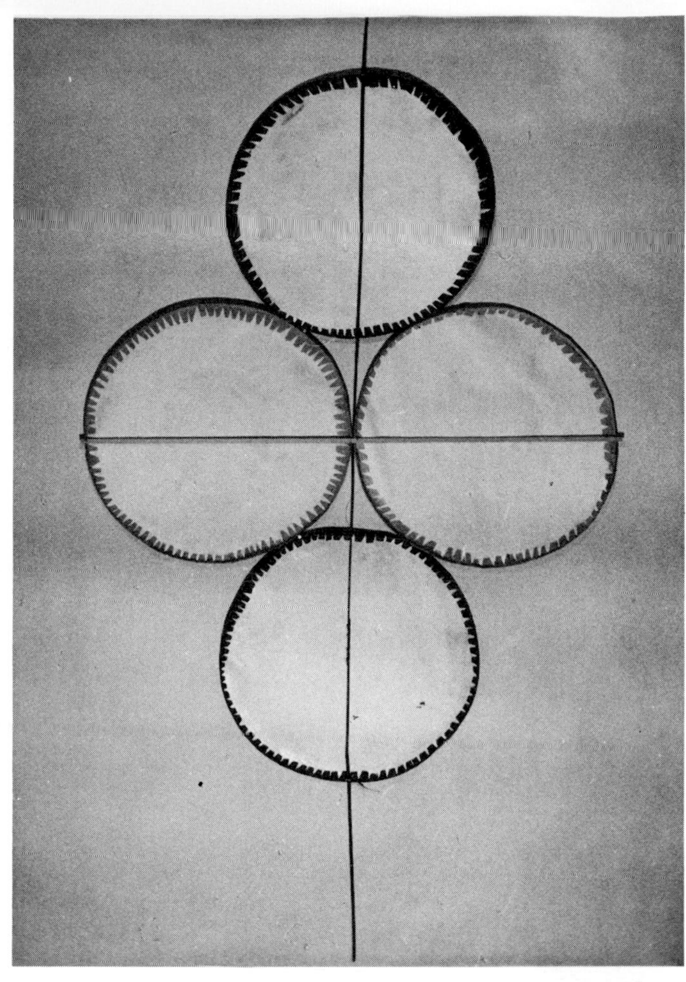

Lash the four circles to a spine and crosspiece of bamboo. The circles should be lashed to each other as well.

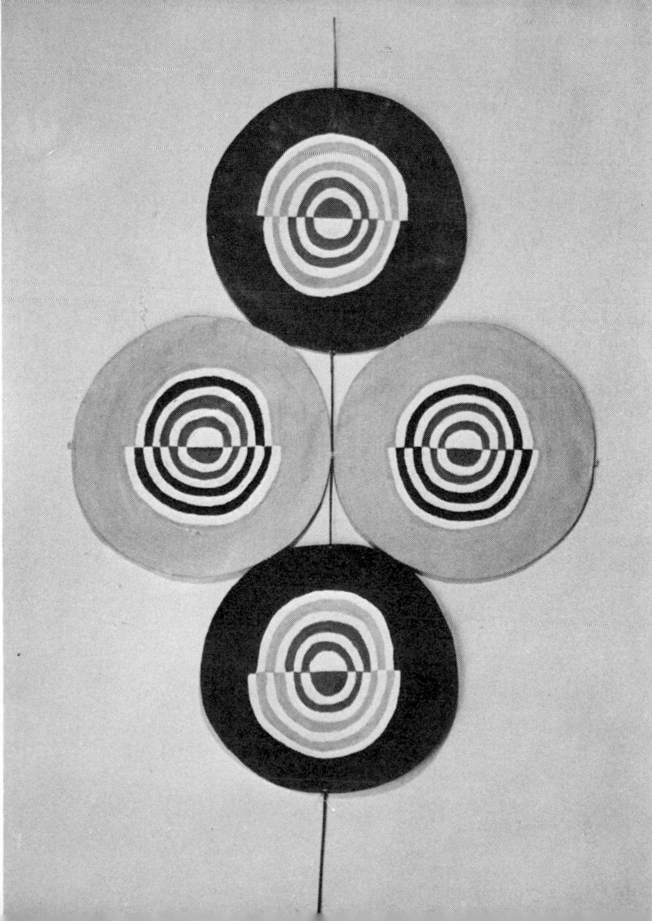

A LANTERN KITE

The lantern is a traditional Chinese kite design. Resembling festival lanterns, this kite was often launched during celebrations with candles burning brightly inside.

Because it is a three-dimensional kite, it is highly stable. Most kitemakers, when flying this kite for the first time, are amazed that the bridle consists of only the flying line tied to a single joint. In flight, this point of attachment becomes the top or leading edge. It flies beautifully, too!

The kite consists of three circles of bamboo constructed from three strips 36″ long. Heat forming is recommended—both to eliminate irregularities and to allow the strips to bend more easily. Three braces, one for each circle, should be made with six 11″ pieces of bamboo. The braces and circles, when lashed together, are assembled on four 30″ strips of wood or bamboo.

The covering, as with any kite illustrated here, is up to the maker. We chose a purple Zephyrlite because it would easily accommodate the circular form. The cloth was stitched around the frame with a dacron thread. The fabric should be drawn taut. If necessary, add an occasional tack to attach the covering firmly to the frame.

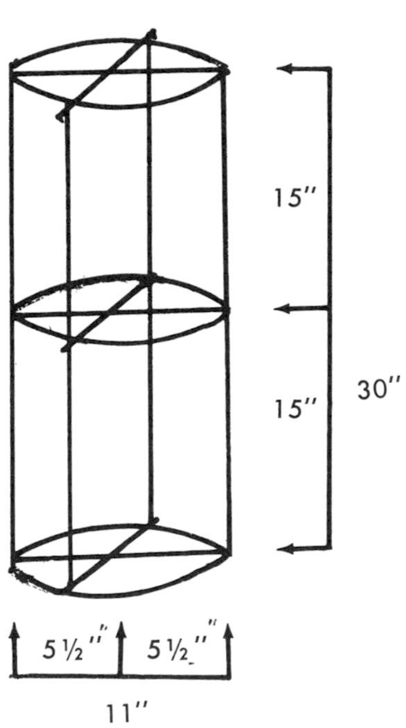

The lantern kite is constructed with three circles of bamboo supported by bamboo crosspieces and longerons. It is, in fact, a cellular kite. This form, although invented in China, was also experimented with during the early twentieth century.

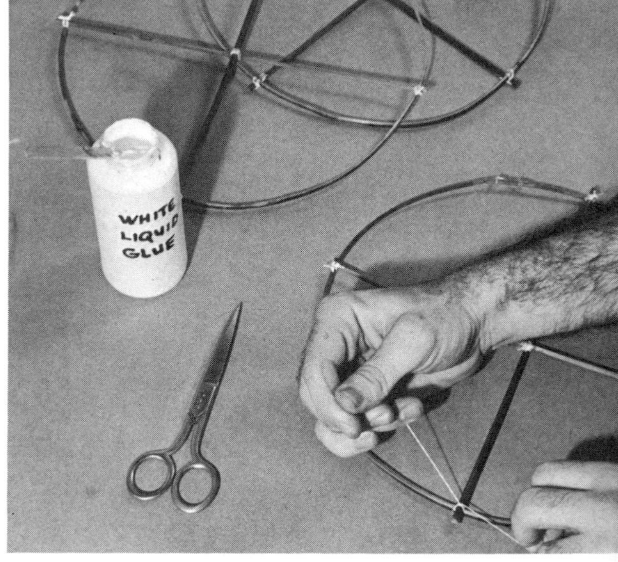

Tie supports and circles together securely and daub the joints with white glue to secure them.

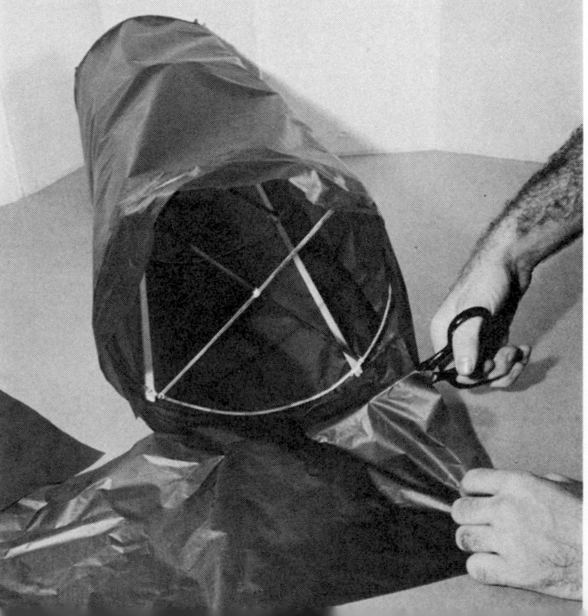

Zephyrlite, a synthetic cloth manufactured by Howe and Bainbridge, Inc., is wrapped around the kite frame and cut to size.

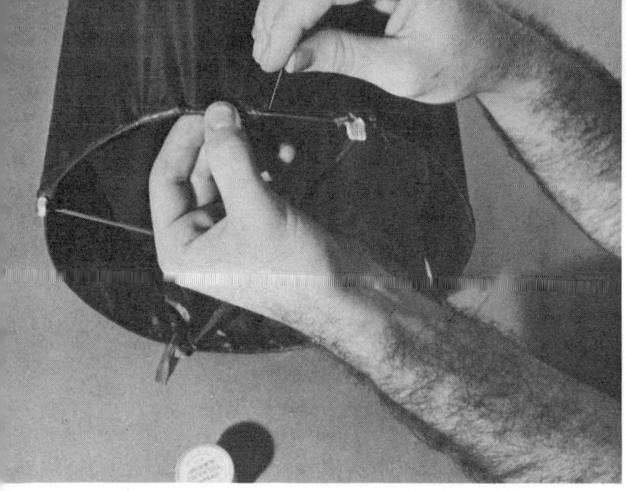

During sewing of any kite surface, stretch the fabric or paper taut. For this fabric we used Dacron thread.

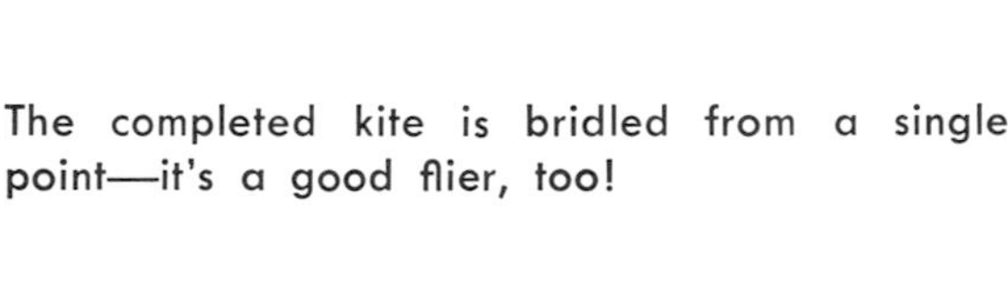

The completed kite is bridled from a single point—it's a good flier, too!

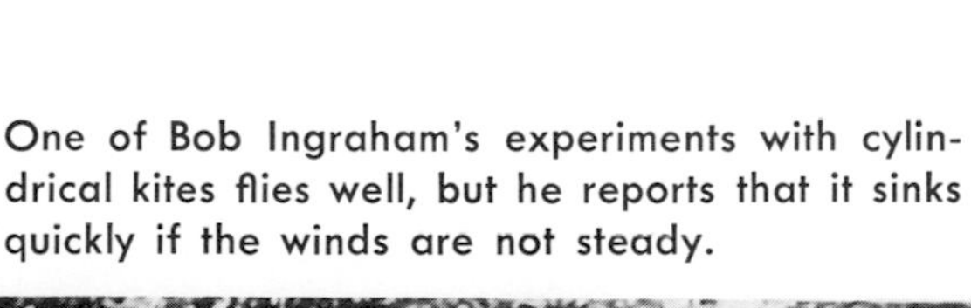

One of Bob Ingraham's experiments with cylindrical kites flies well, but he reports that it sinks quickly if the winds are not steady.

THREE-DIMENSIONAL BAMBOO BODIES

By far the most intricate bamboo structures are to be found in the three-dimensional bodies of modern Chinese kites built in the People's Republic of China.

Finely cut, drilled, and assembled, these bamboo bodies for birds are an art form in themselves. The wings which accompany most in this series of kites (also modeled after insects) are also finely constructed. Many fold at one or two points and have built-in wire braces which hold them rigid.

For the truly painstaking craftsman, this Chinese folkcraft will provide a worthy challenge and, no doubt, a great deal of pleasure as well.

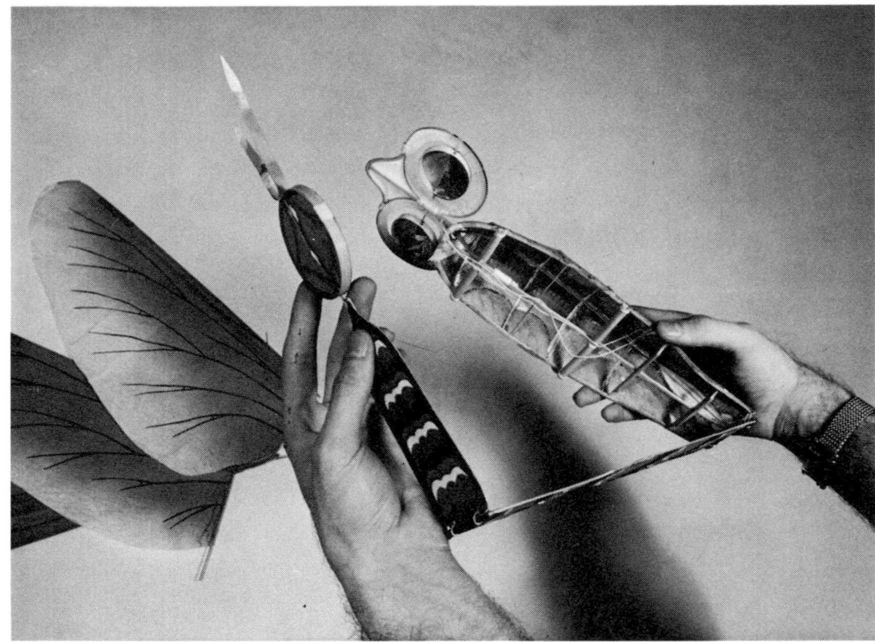

Crafting kites of bamboo is still a high art in China, where this marvelous three-dimensional body of bamboo is built. Fine pieces of bamboo were drilled and assembled. Reed tubes are used to hold the wings in place on the back side of the body.

KITE CRAFTSMANSHIP

The few kites illustrated in this chapter present basic techniques and guides in construction. As in any art or craft, the construction of kites offers infinite possibilities for combination and design. It is sometimes better to be less specific at the risk of omission than too specific and dogmatic. Kitemaking is a plastic art. It requires a certain degree of skill and experience, but the most important elements are perception and curiosity. Your own designs are potentially the best solutions ever devised.

DECORATING THE KITE FACE

Chapter 4

While one should never sacrifice aerodynamic qualities, kite aesthetics should still be a primary concern for the kite craftsman who takes real pride in his creations. Decorations on paper and cloth have existed almost as long as the paper and cloth itself. There are so many concepts for decorating paper and cloth that only a few are presented here, but these should serve as a starting point for improving your kites' appearance. Remember, kites are capable of aesthetic as well as aerodynamic lift.

Some of the ways that kite surfaces can

Kite painting is a traditional art in Japan. In a time of technological excesses it is dying out and only a few painters remain. Mr. Hashimoto, the last kitemaker in Tokyo, begins this kite portrait by painting the outline over a pencil sketch.

Outlines are filled in and accented with colors traditional to Japanese prints and paintings.

Kite paintings, like this one, are sometimes collected in their own right.

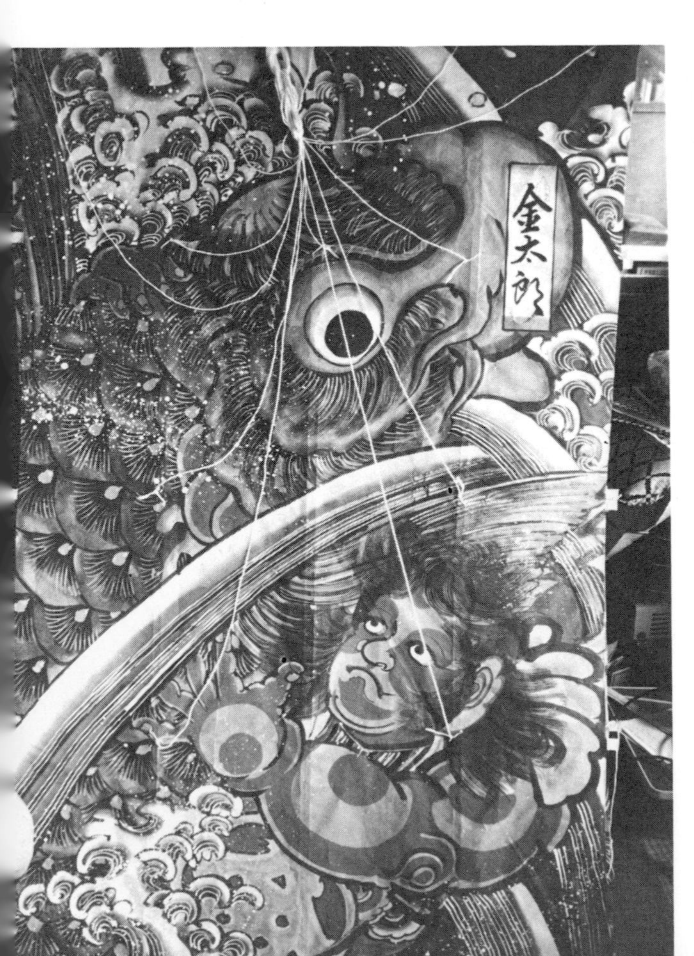

Hashimoto not only paints the kite coverings, but he and his wife make the kites and bridle them as well.

be decorated are by directly painting with acrylic, watercolor, or ink; stamping and printing, using resist materials such as tape, paste, or wax (batik); fold and dye; tie and dye; marbling; covering an area, painting and then uncovering the protected parts (stenciling); the list goes on and on.

Whatever decorating technique you use, be certain that it does not add excessive weight to the covering material. You will find that some paints, if not thinned, may buckle the paper and eventually crack. Before decorating massive pieces of kite facing, experiment with the technique. Just as you must understand some principles of flight before flying a kite well, so you must appreciate how certain paints and dyes react with particular papers and cloths. Repeat designs or designs which cover the entire kite facing in an even coating are recommended.

TAPE RESIST

Resist techniques are among the simplest methods of decorating paper or cloth. They easily permit simple, random, overall design patterns.

Masking tape is cut and pressed onto the paper or Tyvek in a linear design. Acrylic paint, which has been thinned with a little water, is then painted over the paper and tape and allowed to dry. Once the paint has dried, the tape is removed to reveal the natural areas of paper which were protected from the paint.

By using a single acrylic color as the main hue for the decoration, a second and third color can be used in a few spots to accent the dramatic linear design. For example, a green acrylic paint (which dries quite quickly) can be more exciting with additional touches of aquamarine blue.

In some areas where the tape has not been pressed down sufficiently, or else when using a cloth or paper in which the paint runs slightly, the sharpness of the original tape design may be softened with "leaks" of paint under the tape. This provides more of a "batik" look to the kite face.

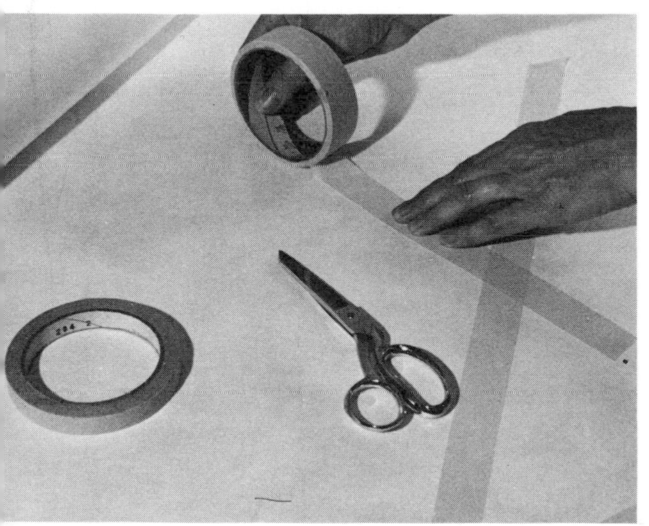

To make a linear tape resist pattern (here done on Tyvek) apply strips of adhesive masking tape to the flat surface. Press down firmly.

Paint on your choice of colors. Test the paint on a scrap first to be certain it will "take" to the fabric. Acrylic paints thinned with a little water are a good choice for Tyvek. Notice how the taped areas resist the paint.

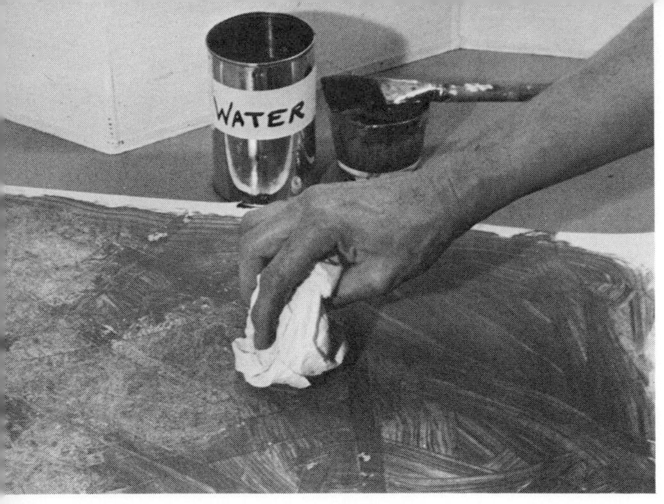

The texture of the Tyvek can be brought out through the thin paint by daubing the still wet surface with a paper towel.

After this daubing, repainting with another color or two can reinstate some accents and highlights in the design.

After the paint has dried, remove the tape to reveal the original untouched portions of Tyvek. We chose to accentuate the textural qualities of the material by not pressing the tape down too firmly, thereby allowing some paint to seep randomly under the taped lines.

The tape resist was done in a combination of green and blue. The white areas stand out well against this color combination. It looks like a rather confused airport viewed from a jet.

RUBBER CEMENT RESIST

Even more of the free-flowing batik look is achieved by using rubber cement as the paper's protective coating. Rubber cement cannot be used with cloth, however, since it will not rub out of the fabric later on in the process.

Smear the rubber cement onto the Tyvek or paper in whatever pattern you like. Let it dry. Paint the paper with acrylic diluted with a bit of water to thin it somewhat. (Straight acrylic paint is much too thick for kite faces, and might crack off later if not diluted slightly with water.) Let the acrylic dry. Now rub off the rubber cement. This can be facilitated by forming a rubber cement ball and rubbing it over the kite face. The rubber cement on the surface will be lifted up by the hardened rubber cement ball with the original paper surface showing through where the rubber cement protected it.

Another technique for decorating the kite face uses rubber cement as the resist material. Wherever the cement is brushed on, the surface will remain unpainted.

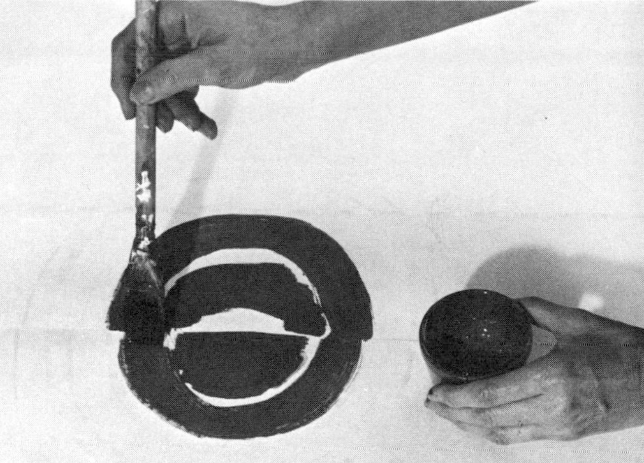

After spreading on the rubber cement, paint with acrylic or other medium. Acrylic is good because it dries fast, cleans off with water before it dries, and comes in a variety of colors. Never apply acrylic paint directly from the tube. If the coat on a kite face is too thick, it is likely to crack and cause imbalance in the kite because of excess weight.

When the paint dries, rub off the rubber cement. This is facilitated by making a ball out of the excess cement and using that ball to pick up the rest. Revealed is a batik-like design which is then trimmed and attached to the bamboo or wood framework.

BATIK

Batik is an old technique used for decorating fabric and paper. It achieved excellence in Java (Indonesia). Batik is a resist technique using wax to protect areas of color, and it is applicable to kite decoration since the wax is later removed.

To make a batiked design, melt paraffin safely in an electric frying pan, a double boiler, or a crayon melter. Wax can be applied to the paper or fabric with a brush (or tjanting—a miniature "watering can" with a fine spout that is difficult to control). Coloring should be liquid and transparent such as batik dyes, India ink, or food color. Transparent color mixes differently from opaque pigments. For instance, fuchsia and yellow make red; violet and green make blue; fuchsia and green make yellow-orange. When working with batik, it is best to start dyeing with light colors first and successively apply darker colors.

In batiking paper or fabric, start with a light or colored material. Paint with wax the area you want to remain the original color. Then brush your first color over the entire sheet. Allow the dye to dry. Then, with wax, draw the next design component, keeping in mind that this design will be the color you just dyed the paper. Then brush on your next dye color and, if you like, continue with waxing and dyeing. The wax maintains the last color used. When finished, sandwich the batiked paper between newspaper and press with a hot iron. The newspaper will absorb the wax, leaving the batiked color only.

Working with a brush (or tjanting) is a controlled approach to batik design. It is also possible to create very attractive random effects with dots and splashes of wax. Later, when the whole sheet has been waxed (and just before applying the last color), pop the whole paper or fabric sheet into the refrigerator or freezer for a minute. Then remove it and crumple the wax a little before adding the final dye coating. This gives a characteristic batik effect of random fine lines.

To batik paper or cloth, melt the wax (paraffin) safely. A crayon melter is used here, but a double boiler on a hot plate may be used instead. Brush the first pattern, in wax, onto the paper. Since the paper is white, these lines will be white in the finished kite surface.

Brush the first, lightest color dye over the areas that you want to be this color.

Dry the dye and then paint the second pattern with wax; dye the paper as shown here and repeat the process until the design is complete.

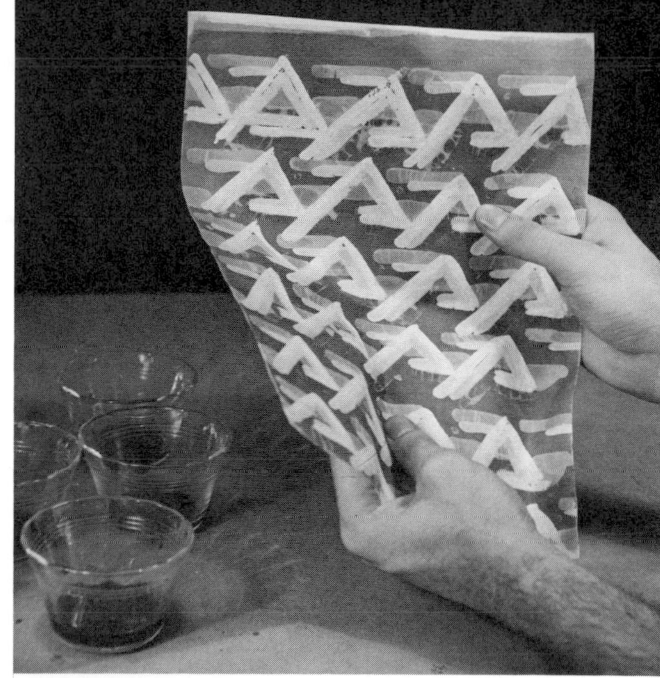

The almost finished piece is cracked to create a random dyeing effect with the last and darkest color.

The paper is placed between a sandwich of newspaper and pressed with a hot iron to melt all the wax. The wax is absorbed into the newspaper, bringing the weight of the paper or fabric back to normal.

The finished design.

Another batiked design using random splashing and dropping of wax.

SPATTERING INDIA INK

In another kind of masking technique, India inks can be sprinkled over the kite fabric.

Protect the design areas which are not to receive the sprinkling by using the tape, rubber cement, or just by laying down pieces of paper. Dip an old toothbrush into a pan of India ink (which comes now in many colors). With a tongue depressor or a knife, scrape across the bristles of the toothbrush so that they "fire" a spray of ink droplets onto the sheet. Continue this until your sheet has the intensity of color you desire. Make certain that you wear old clothes during this process —a toothbrush doesn't always place the drops exactly where you might expect them to go.

Let the ink dry, then remove the protective paper, tape, or rubber cement.

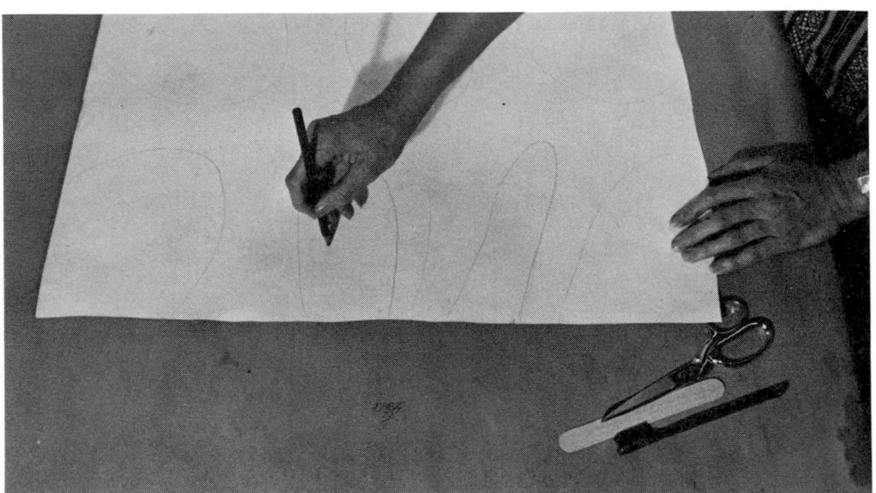

Draw the shapes which you want to protect from the spattered ink on a piece of heavy paper or cardboard.

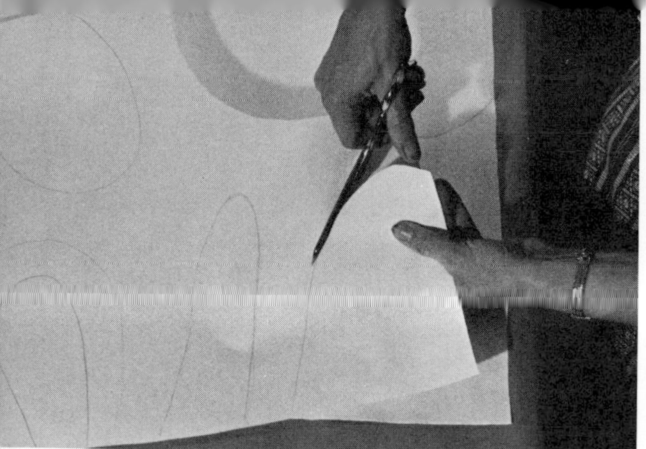

Cut these protective pieces from the sheet. Place them on the sheet to be spattered.

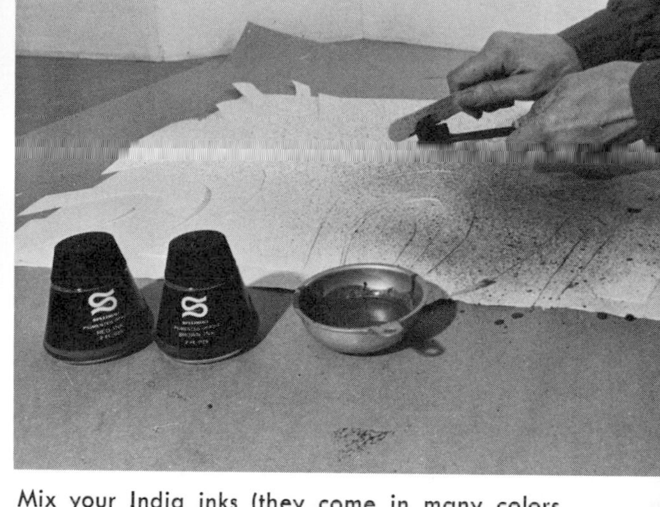

Mix your India inks (they come in many colors and can be combined to form more colors). Then dip an old toothbrush in the ink. Run a tongue depressor across the bristles so that the toothbrush fires a spray of ink across the kite face. Be careful that your clothes and surroundings are sufficiently covered to avoid stains caused by stray spray. Continue the spraying process until the unprotected areas are dotted to your satisfaction.

Now remove the protective cardboard shapes . . .

. . . to reveal the result of this technique.

PAINT AND INK

Sheets of fine kite papers can be colored and "textured" with a combination of paint and ink, too.

Wet down the sheet of paper on a wooden board. Paint with watercolors and occasional splashes of India ink. When the paper dries slightly, remove it from the board and place it over newspaper to dry. Spray the sheet with acrylic fixative (so that the color will not later run) when fully dry.

If the paper begins to dry while painting, be certain to wet it down again. The quick flicks of ink will spread over the wet paper at different rates, depending on how soaked the paper is.

Artist Jane Bearman colors and textures her papers with a combination of paint and ink. She begins by wetting the sheet on a wooden board with water applied by brush or sponge.

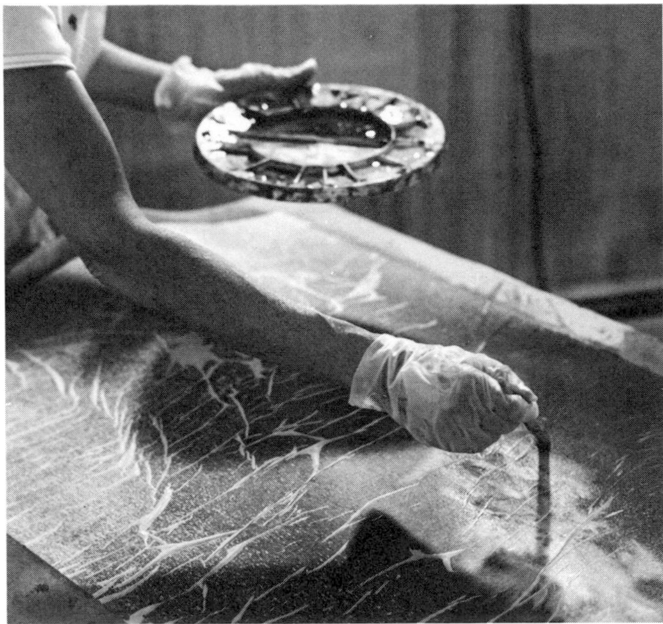

The wet sheet is then painted with watercolors. If the paper begins to dry while painting, be certain to wet it down again.

Another effect Jane Bearman uses is to flick India ink onto the paper. The ink will spread at different rates depending upon how wet the paper is.

Remove the partially dry paper from the wooden board and place it on newspaper to dry completely. When fully dry, spray the paper with a fixative. It retains its flexibility and strength.

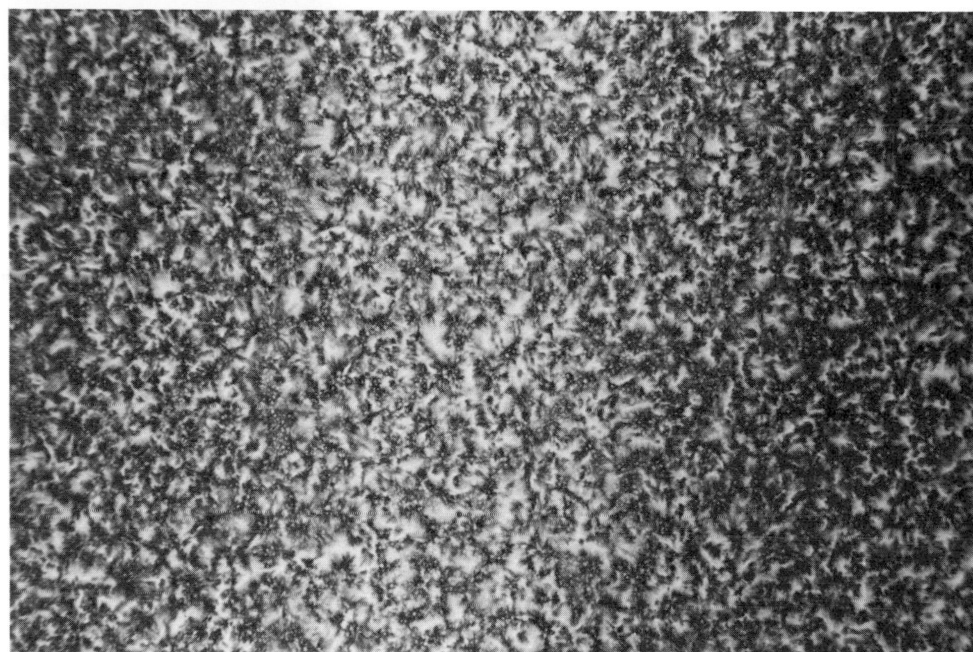

Oil color over spots of damp watercolored paper created this delightful diffused effect. The paper was made in England.

PRINTING AND STAMPING

Designs for printing can be cut from many materials: vegetables, such as potatoes, wood, Styrofoam®, urethane foam, linoleum, vinyl, cardboard, rubber from tires, erasers, RTV silicone, scrap objects like screws, spools, leaves, washers, and sponges used as stamp pads to hold paint. In fact, whatever can be incised or whatever has a ready-made pattern can be utilized. These objects can be inked and used as stamping patterns. Tempera or watered acrylic paints can be applied to the printing surface with a brush.

Designs can be repeated in several ways. Some methods for linking one unit to another are: with a random effect, where your eye judges negative and positive space relationships and the distribution of texture and color; repeat designs that line up blocks one over the other, like bricks in a wall, half dropped blocks in alternating columns; diagonal repeats such as diamond shapes and chevron effects. Butt joints allow units to meet in straight lines. Dovetail joints permit one unit to fit into another without overlapping. And overlapping joints occur where units overlap.

STAMPING WITH SPONGES

Different sized household sponges, with an end dipped in acrylic or tempera paint offer a speckled design for kite faces. Dip the end in the paint, then press the sponge onto the paper or cloth. The small air pockets in the sponges are transferred to the fabric as a block of intermingling fine lines and blotches. Sponge printing, starting from a light color and progressively getting darker in hue, can be useful in forming a nonsymmetrical random pattern as well as any of the more intricate butted patterns. Don't work with too many wet colors at one time because too many colors may run together to form "mud."

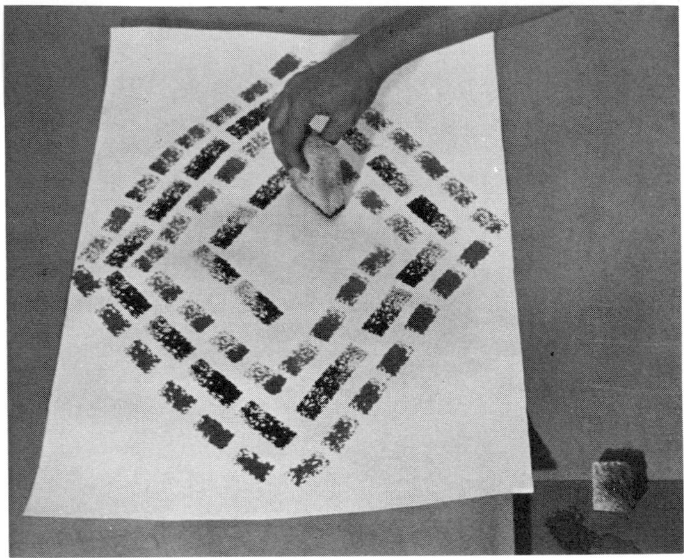

A sponge dipped in thinned acrylic or tempera paint makes an elementary printing block when stamped on paper or cloth.

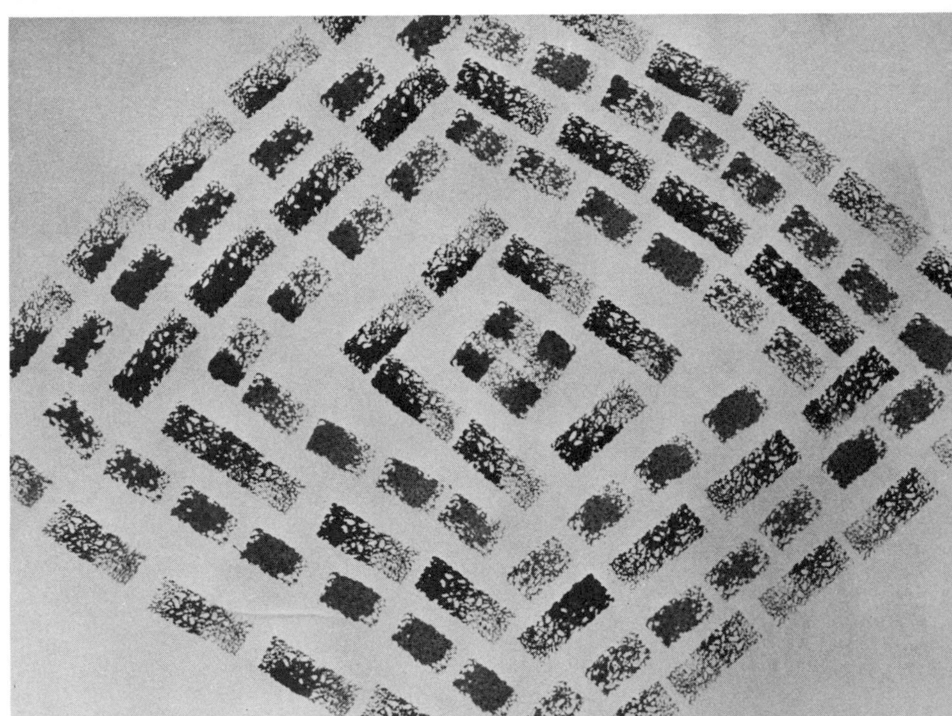

PRINTING WITH RIGID POLYSTYRENE FOAM BLOCKS

Polystyrene may be carved with almost any tool. Block carving knives and even kitchen knives will give you accurate results. Carve your design, remembering the principles of relating block print designs to one another.

Commonly known as "Styrofoam," polystyrene blocks may also be easily heat-carved with a soldering pen.

The pen is an efficient controlled heat source that "melts" away the foam plastic. Simply draw your design into the polystyrene with the hot soldering pencil, inscribing the foam. The heat leaves a carved channel in its wake. Different widths may be carved by using different widths on the soldering pencil.

Polyurethane foam blocks may also be used in block printing on cloth and paper, but do not use heat on the polyurethane—it gives off toxic odors.

After washing and ironing your cloth, or just flattening your paper, apply ink to the block. You may brush the acrylic paint directly onto the block or you may apply it with a soft rubber brayer (roller).

Press the foam block firmly onto the fabric, then turn over the fabric and block (still together) so that the cloth is now on top of the block. Burnish the surface with the back of a spoon to make certain that the paint is being evenly transferred. With thin fabrics the acrylic paint will penetrate. It is not a mistake if this happens—in fact it makes it easier to see which areas need more pressure to transfer the paint to the textile. Just be careful, especially with paper, that you do not rub the surface with the spoon too vigorously. If you do you will either tear the paper or almost surely dent and crush the soft plastic foam, losing its definition.

Repeat this process, continuing it until the entire piece of material is covered. Variations may be obtained by printing over the first color with another acrylic color, or printing on the reverse side.

Allow the acrylic paint to dry thoroughly. When it is dry, the paint will be permanent and the cloth may be washed by hand with mild soap and water.

A tip on block printing with paper: try dampening the paper before applying the inked block; the paper is more likely to "take" the paint evenly.

Pieces of polystyrene (and also polyurethane) can be carved with knives, linoleum cutting tools, chisels, almost anything to form relief designs which are inked and printed onto cloth and paper.

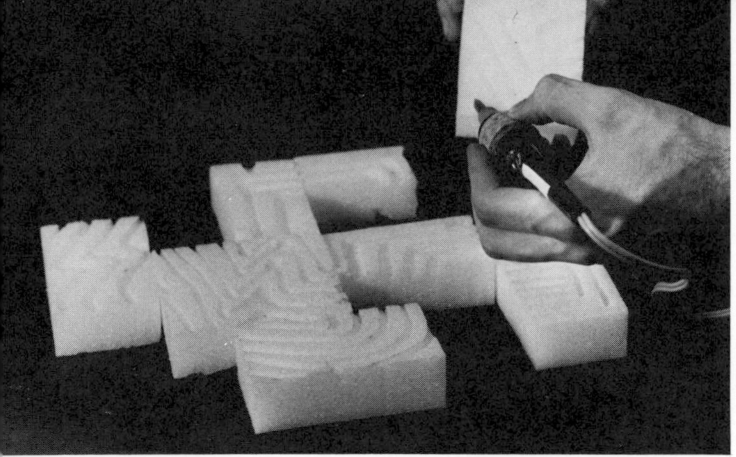

Polystyrene blocks may also be "carved" with heat. A soldering pen here melts channels in the blocks. Do not use heat with the other plastic foam—polyurethane. Exposed to heat, the polyurethane emits toxic odors.

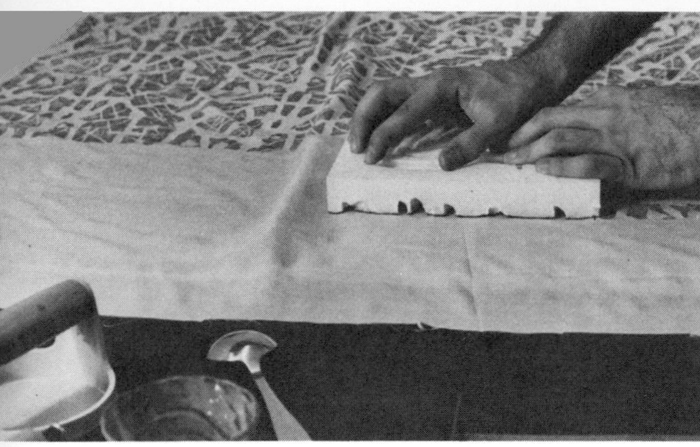

Paint the block with a brush or spread the acrylic paint with a soft rubber brayer. Press the painted block onto the cloth.

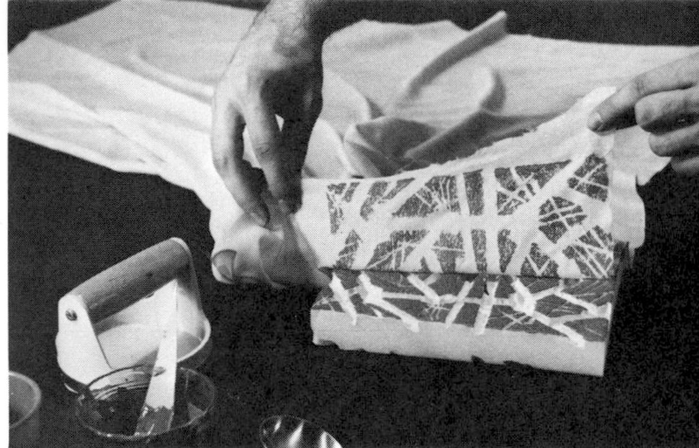

Flip the whole thing over so that the cloth lies on top of the block, and burnish the surface with a baren or the back of a spoon. Lift off the cloth, and repeat this process until the fabric is completely covered.

This appealing print will make a unique kite.

This print uses an overlapping repeat design of simple concentric circles.

Ways of repeating designs include units that butt against one another in straight lines such as the block repeat, the brick repeat with its horizontal emphasis, the half-drop repeat with a vertical emphasis, and angle repeats using diagonals. Dovetail repeats allow one unit to fit into another, and overlapping superimposes one part of a unit over another.

Block Repeat

Diagonal Repeat

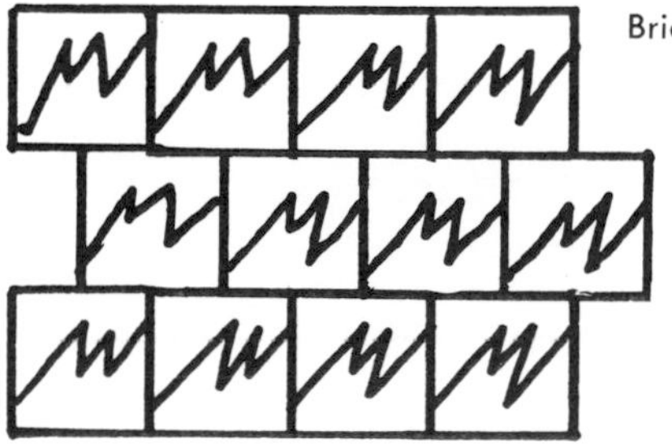

Brick Repeat

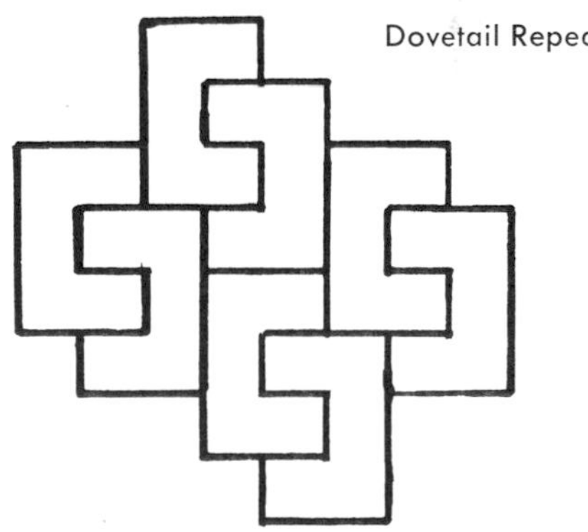

Dovetail Repeat

Half Drop Repeat

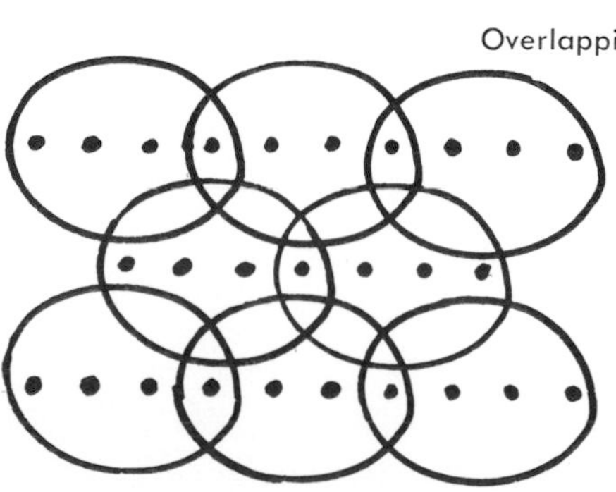

Overlapping Repeat

An assortment of decorative papers made by stamping and printing with small units.

A Japanese paper with a one-color block repeat.

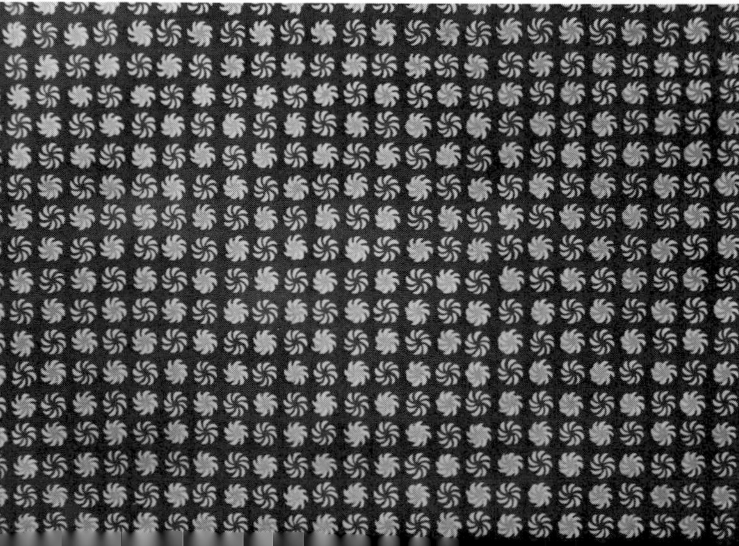

Another Japanese repeat with different color circles superimposed over alternating design units.

PRINTING WITH A PATTERNED BRAYER

An extension of simple block printing involves the use of a soft rubber brayer in rolling on a continuous pattern.

Apply rubber cement to a rubber roller. Then stick soft heavy cotton cord onto the roller to create a repeat design. Mix acrylic paint with a little water on a flat surface. Ink the brayer by running it back and forth through the paint until the cord receives an even inking.

In a smooth, evenly pressured, continuous motion, run the brayer across the cloth, paper, or Tyvek. Repeat the process until the fabric is covered—it yields a handsome rhythmic pattern.

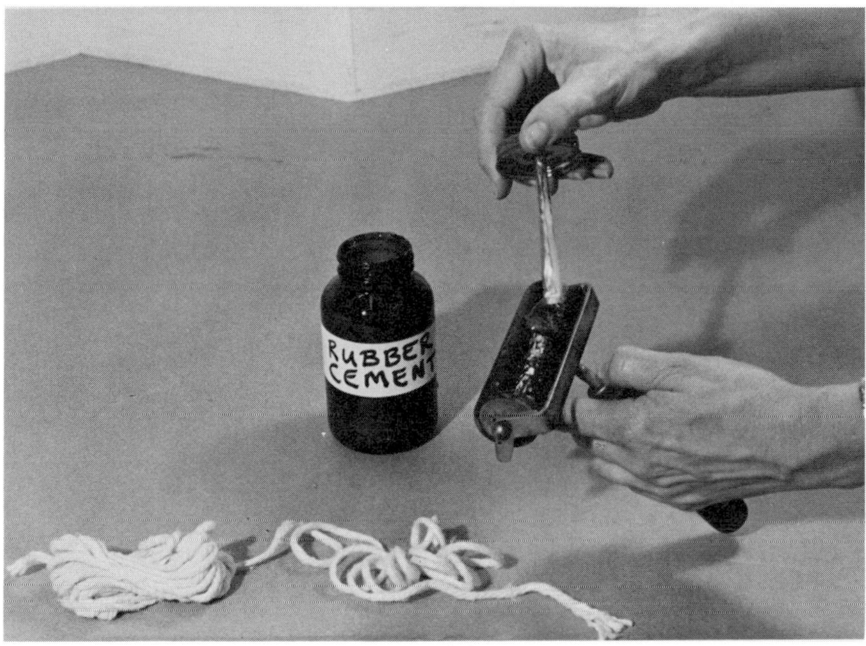

A soft rubber roller can be used for printing a continuous pattern on cloth or paper. Apply rubber cement to the brayer.

Then take soft braided string and press it onto the sticky cement on the brayer in any pattern you choose.

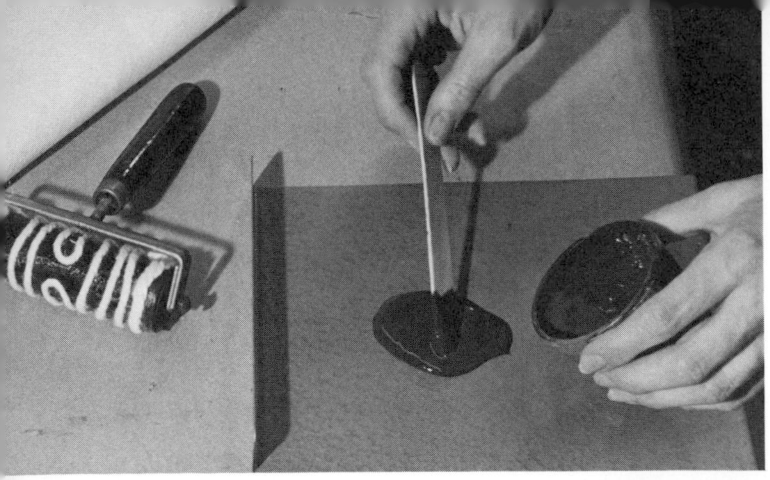

Use acrylic paint thinned with a little water.

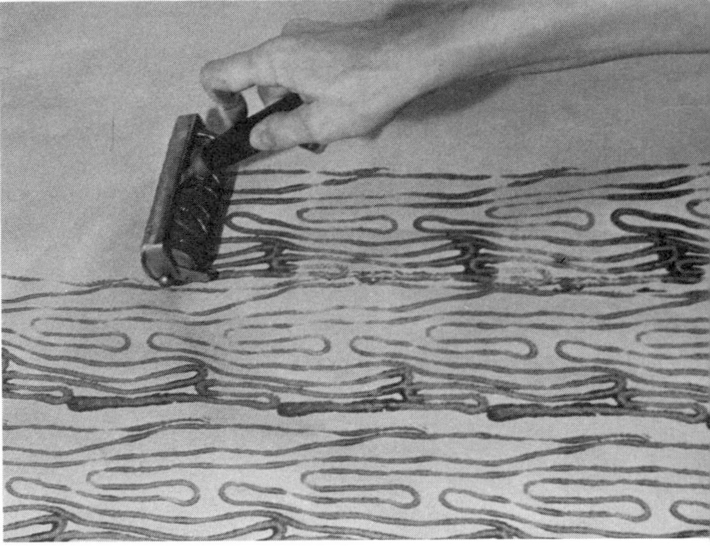

Coat the brayer evenly with the paint, then run the roller in a continuous motion across the cloth or paper. Repeat the process.

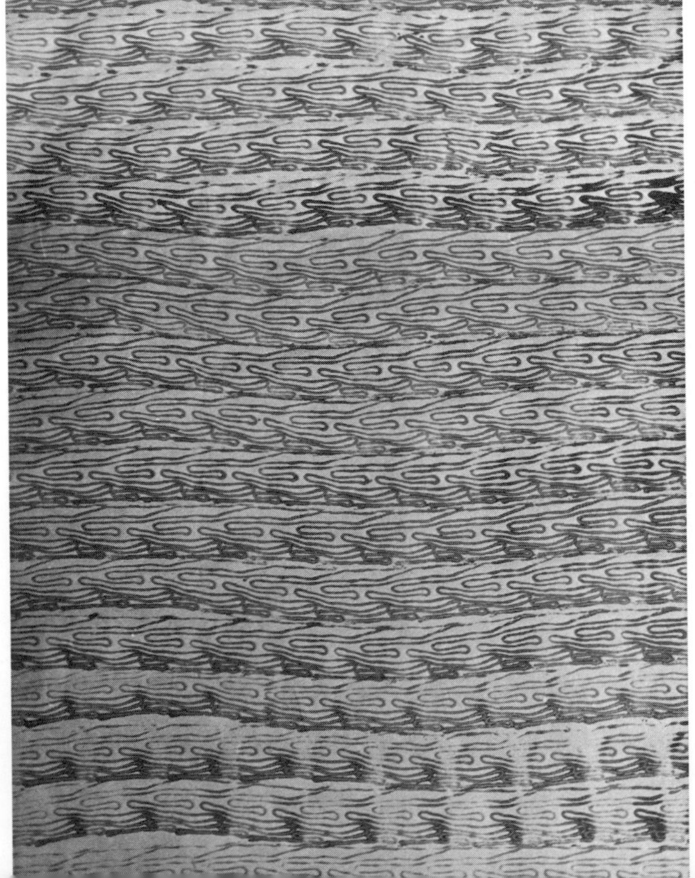

An exciting design can be produced on an enormous sheet in just minutes with this procedure. The repeating design bands would lend themselves nicely to a box kite covering.

MARBLING

The invention of marbling was credited to the Persians about A.D. 1550. Persian marbled papers were introduced into Europe in 1590. The first examples were of the "fine combed" variety. In 1750 marbled papers were used for the first time in North America in bookbinding, and can, naturally, be applied to kite design as well.

Marbling produces patterns on paper that are similar in appearance to the graining in marble. Oil color is suspended on a sizing of water and carrageen moss extract or gum of tragacanth. Patterns are drawn in the color and then paper is placed over the pattern to lift off the color. There are many variations on this concept; all meet with varying degrees of success and each pattern is different.

The size, which is a gelatinous material, can vary. Carrageen moss (or Irish seaweed), is a form of algae that is found along rocky coastlines. The size is prepared by boiling a cup of carrageen moss in two quarts of soft water for about five minutes. Then add two cups of cold water and allow the mixture to stand uncovered at room temperature for 24 hours. Put it in a blender to stir away large particles, or strain it. It will last for three or four days without a preservative and can also be frozen.

Gum of tragacanth can also be used as a size. Mix ½ cup of gum of tragacanth flakes with 2 quarts of water. Allow it to sit for 24 hours. Then blend it in blender, or strain out the lumps. The consistency should be like pourable honey.

Another size is diluted white library-type paste. Beat in water until the paste mixture pours and use that as a base on which to suspend color.

Color should be oil-based; oil paint, oil-based printer's ink, etching ink. It is best to dilute these colors with mineral spirits, which work better than turpentine. The consistency should be pourable so that you can flick the color off a straw, swab stick, brush, or nail. Any kind and color of nonglossy paper can be used.

Pour the size into a shallow tray or pan. Do not let a skin form on the size. To release surface tension, place a piece of newspaper over the size and lift it off. The consistency should permit a drop of paint to spread immediately into a large circle. If it does not, add more water to the size. Drop different colors onto the size and then allow the corners to drop gradually onto the size. These methods help to eliminate large air bubbles which would interfere with the design.

The pattern on the size will immediately transfer to the paper. Lift off the paper and rinse away the size, or blot it off with a sponge. Set the paper on newspaper to dry, pattern upward.

Before a second pattern is made, pick up the remaining ink by dropping a sheet of newspaper on the size the same way you did for transferring the original design.

If you add a few drops of ox gall to diluted oil paints you will find more life and action in the colors.

Another simple method of creating marbling effects for a kite surface is by using water in the pan instead of a size, and using colored inks instead of oil paints. Ink can be spattered on the water surface with a brush charged with color. One color touched on another makes a spot within a spot without mixing. Color is less controlled on water than on size, but some organization of color and pattern is possible. The paper is laid on the water in the same manner as in the other processes. It should be removed and allowed to dry face up on newspaper. Any surplus color on the water can be blotted off with newspaper.

Gum tragacanth flake is mixed with water and allowed to stand overnight.

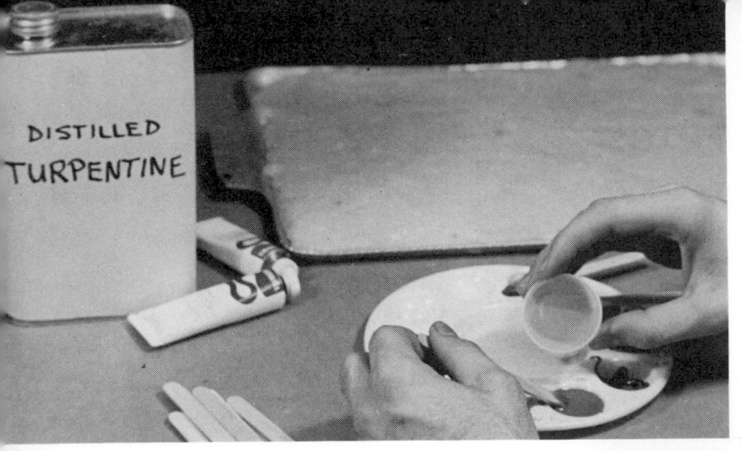

Enough water is added so that the flakes dissolve, and the mixture is blended or strained to eliminate lumps. The mixture is then poured into a shallow tray. Oil-based colors mixed with mineral spirits or turpentine are flicked off a brush or a stick onto the size. The colors should flow.

These colors are a bit too thick, as is the gum tragacanth. Both have to be thinned, but they are still usable in the meantime.

With a swab stick (or nail) move the paint into patterns.

Place the paper carefully over the ink—be certain not to trap any air bubbles in the process.

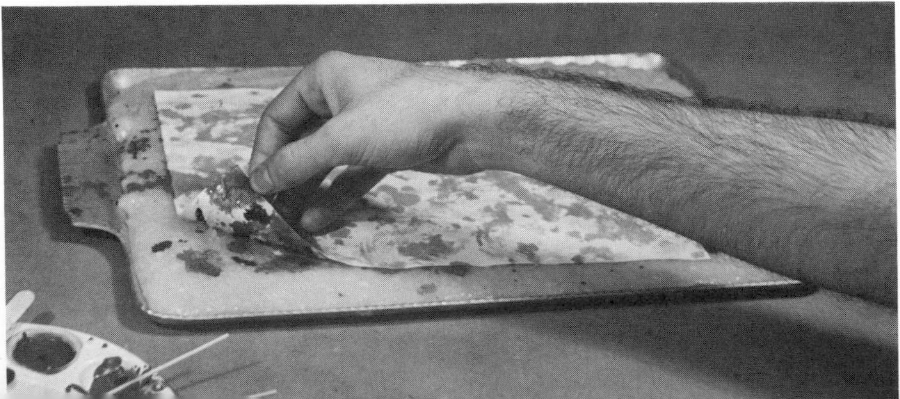

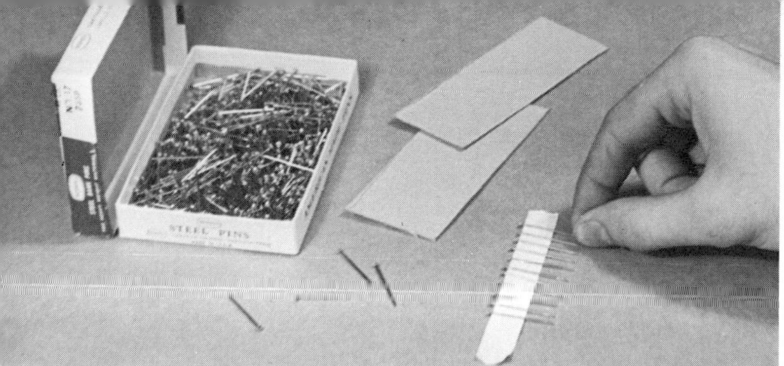

A pin comb can be made to distribute color, too. Banker's pins are attached to cardboard with adhesive tape.

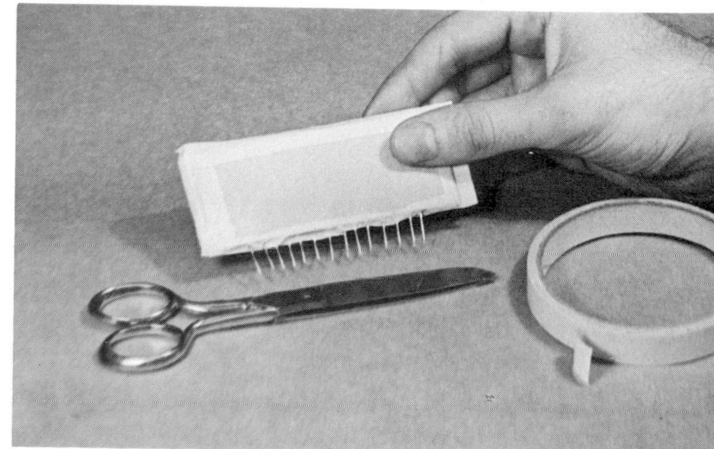

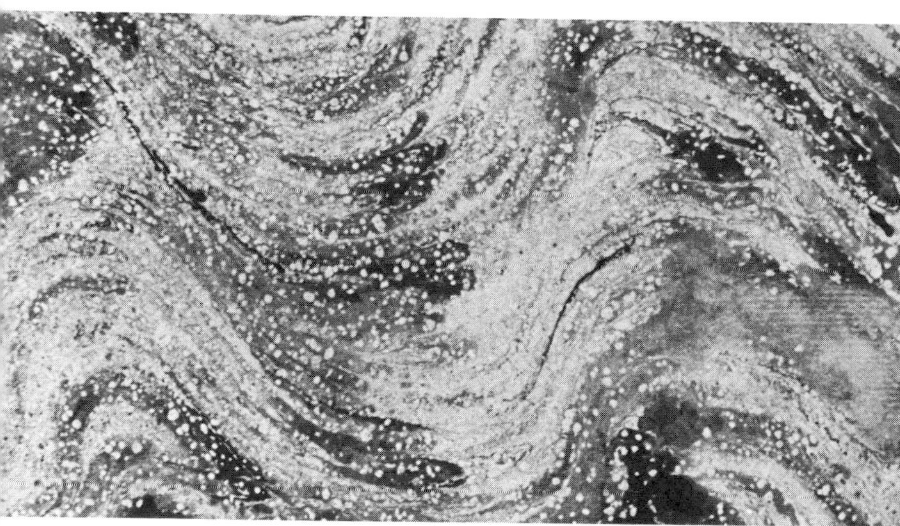

One marbling design. These can vary tremendously, depending on the mixture of paint, the suspension vehicle (size)—whether it is a carrageen moss, gum tragacanth, or water.

You may want to apply a light coating of wax to the paper.

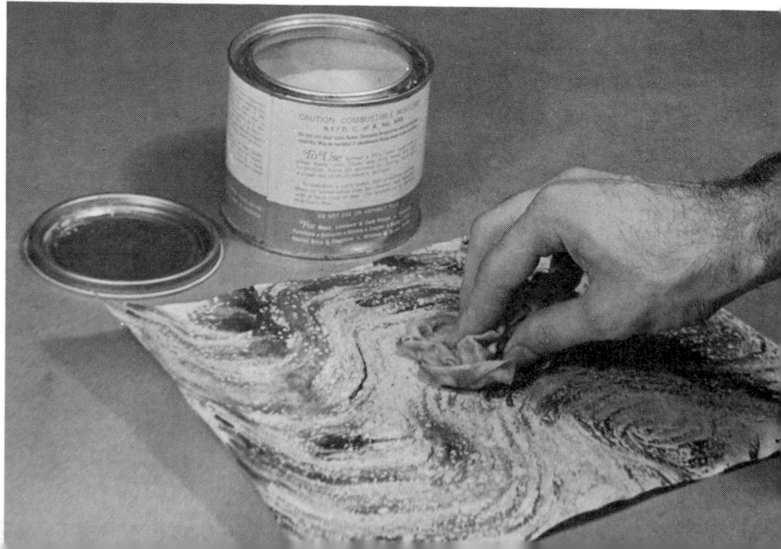

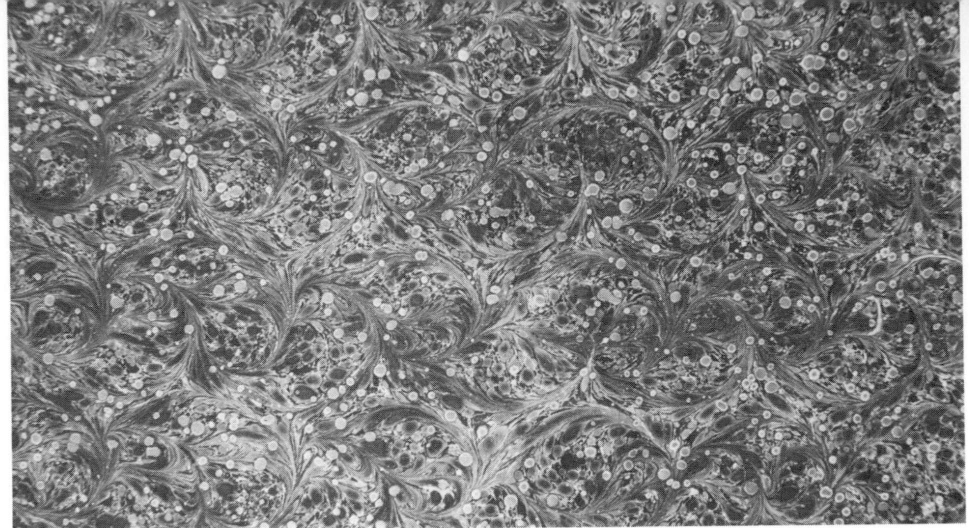

Notice that a repeat pattern does exist within a random design on this hand-marbled paper from England.

FOLD AND DYE

One of the most dramatic and successful techniques for decorating cloth and paper utilizes soft absorbent cloths and paper such as the Japanese papers of the Hoshoshi type: *gasenchi*, *echizen*, mulberry student grade, *torinokogami*, or *minogami*. Colorants may be watercolor, food dye, batik dye, or India ink. They are all water soluble and may later be fixed to the paper with a spray acrylic fixative.

There are several basic ways to fold cloth and paper for dyeing. Each begins by folding the material into accordion pleats along the material's length. This makes for a repeat design along one axis.

One variation is to fold the accordion-pleated strip to produce square or rectangular areas—effectively pleating the material along a perpendicular axis. Another folding design is to fold the paper accordion fashion into a series of equilateral (60°) or isosceles (45°, 60°, 45°) triangles. For repeat designs, folds should all be the same size. The thinner the paper or fabric the more folds possible.

Uneven and irregular folding is another variation. Instead of folding the sheet into an accordion with equal pleats, try unequal widths. Or fold the paper into a fan shape and then into triangles or random shapes. Each fold will produce a very different effect.

The next step is to dip the folded paper into dyes. The area, color, and position of the dyeing will determine the shapes and colors in the repeat design. Try dipping just corners, then edges. Dip into one color first, then a second, then even a third. Permit different degrees of color saturation by removing the material more quickly or allowing it to absorb more color—thereby dyeing a larger area. The amount of pressure you apply with your fingers (or with pliers) will help distribute the color. Designs vary according to the amount of pressure applied. After the dyeing process, very gently open the cloth or paper and place it on newspaper to dry. When dry, the cloth may be pressed with a warm iron to eliminate folds. For paper, press with an iron by putting the sheet under several sheets of newspaper.

Fold the paper or cloth into accordion pleats.

Then fold the accordion pleats into equilateral triangles which also form pleats.

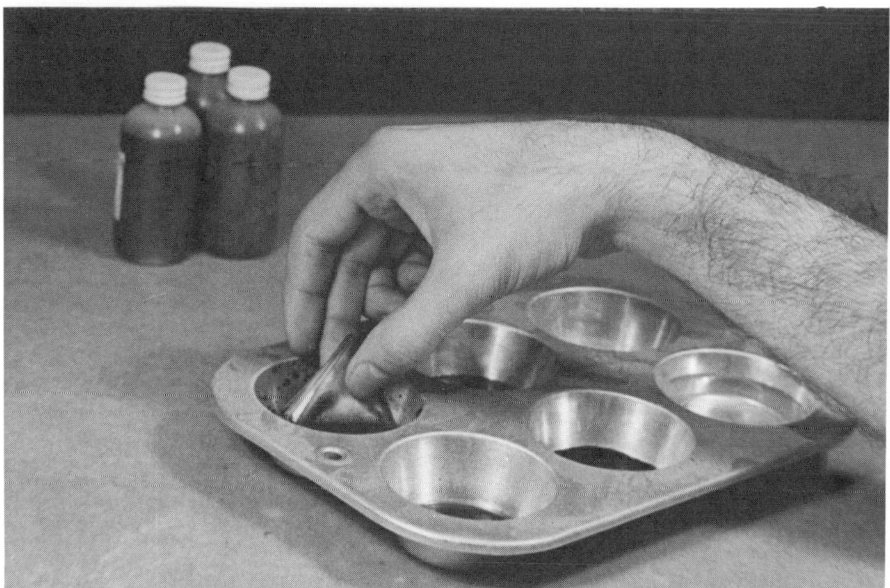

Dip the corners into different colors of water-soluble dyes. Continue the process, sometimes overlapping colors. This fold and dye process can be done on any scale needed for any size kite.

Very carefully open the wet paper and place the paper flat on newspaper to dry.

The finished sheet is pressed between newspaper with a warm iron.

A square folded dyed paper.

A straight folded accordion sheet dipped into a light color and then into a dark color dye.

TIE AND DYE

Tie and dye or tie-dyeing is a resist-dyeing process of knotting, binding, folding, or sewing paper and cloth in various ways so that when it is dyed, the dye cannot penetrate the tied areas.

Tie dye also dates back to the Orient. The Japanese make a beautiful decorative paper using spot techniques called *shibori*. In China, the craft, using spot sewing and folding, is known as *tritik*, in Malay *plangi*, and in West Nigeria *adire*, *adire ido*, or *adire alabere*. Indigo was the usual dye coloring. Indians used a tritik technique in Mexico, Central America, and South America as well.

To tie-dye, use the same cloth or paper as in "paper fold and dye." Prepare the paper by folding, knotting, binding, sewing, or a combination of these methods. Coat the string with wax or use rubber bands to effect certain bindings. These prevent dye from being absorbed under and through the string and maintain the original color of the paper.

Tying can be accomplished three basic ways. A length of fabric can be folded or gathered and tied at intervals. A square or rectangle can be folded from the center out and tied, or knots can be sewn or tied tightly in spots. Individual ties can be dipped in dye.

Use the same dyes as for folding and dying. You may dip the individual knotted areas into dye, or starting with a light color, dip into one color first and then into a second color. This creates a pattern in the dye. Knots may be held in a cluster and only the background dipped into another color. Dipping an area into water first dilutes the color and softens edges, if this is what you want in your kite face design.

Linen threads are excellent for binding, but yarn, cord, raffia, tape, and rubber bands are good too. Use a strong thread that will permit pulling and tension. To maintain an area in a stronger pattern than waxed string can provide, melt some paraffin and paint it around the tied string. Bindings should be taut and firm.

After dyeing to the proper degree of color intensity (colors usually dry lighter), carefully untie the string and unfold the cloth or paper. Dry flat on newspaper. Later press your piece with a warm iron, as described in folding and dyeing. It is also possible to allow the fabric to dry and then to untie and press it.

A sheet of paper is folded into accordion pleats. Cloth may also be used just as well (sometimes better).

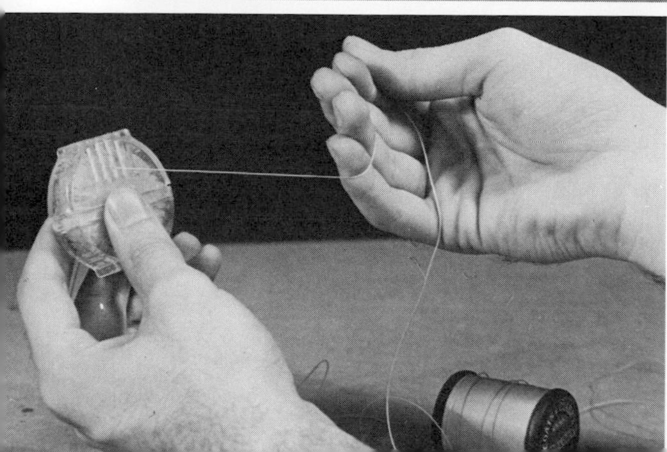

Heavy thread is waxed by running it through beeswax.

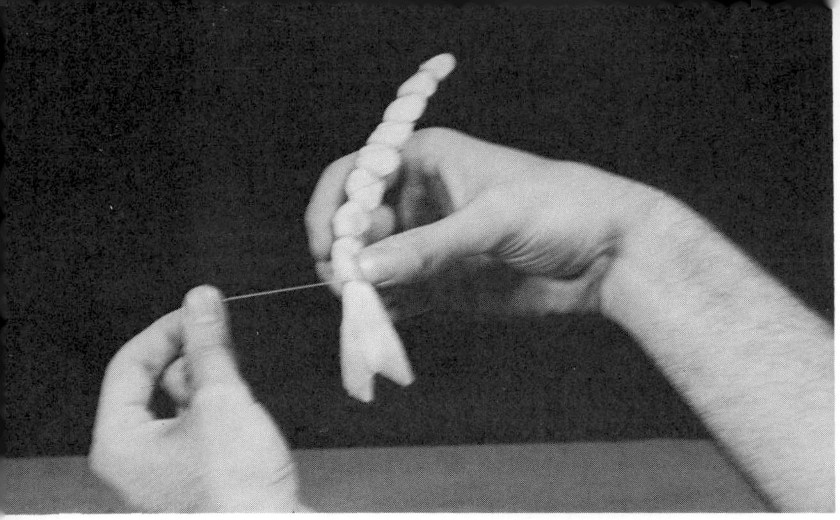

The sheet is folded in half and then tied with the waxed thread at intervals.

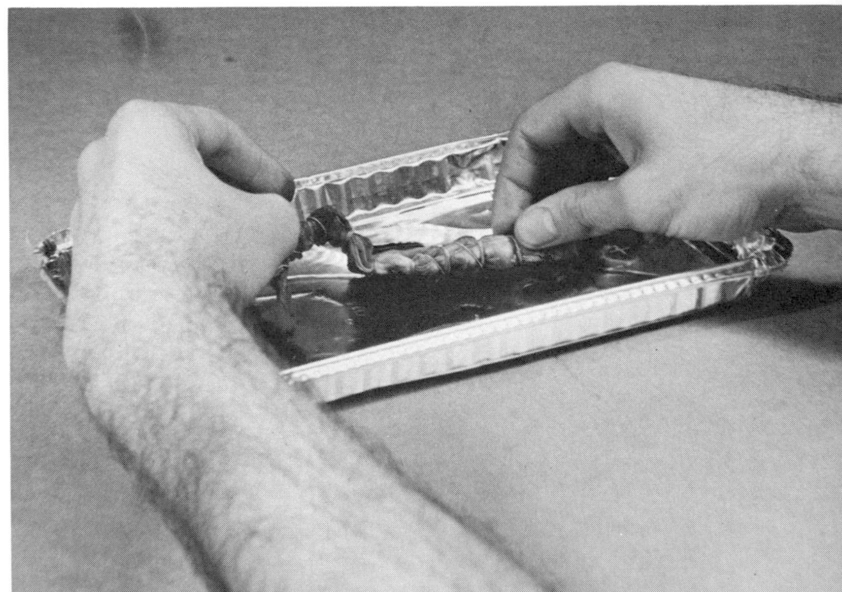

The piece is dipped into water-soluble dye of one color. Then another section is dipped into a second color.

Remove the string carefully and unfold the wet paper or cloth.

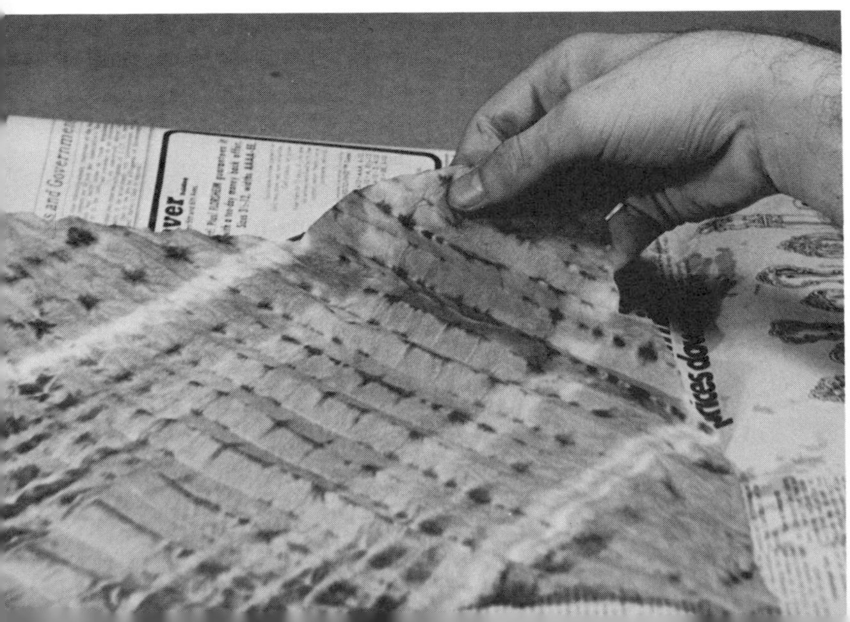

The finished tie and dye is pressed between sheets of newspaper with a warm iron to eliminate wrinkles. The cloth version may be pressed directly with the iron.

Another tie and dye method is to fold paper or cloth along its central diagonal, tie, and dip it. Also try gathering smaller sections, tying, and dipping to produce a repeat design.

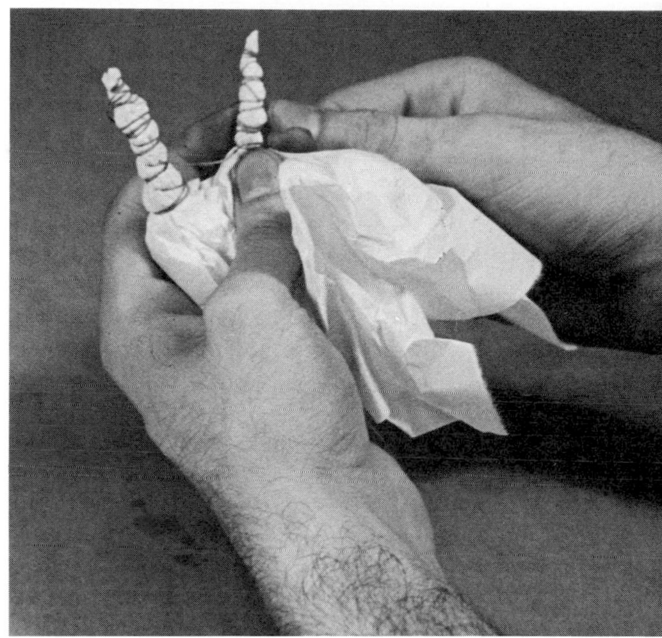

A possible kite covering with a repeat circular tie and dye design.

ORIENTAL KITES

Chapter 5

China, Japan, Indonesia, Thailand, India, countries with long traditions of making and flying kites, have appreciated the kite as more than a child's toy. It has been an art form closely linked to other elements of culture.

Folklore, history, tradition, religion, and superstition all played a part in the development of the kite as an indigenous art form. Interest in and influence of the kite was substantial until recent years.

Soaring kites seemed, for the greatest part of a two-thousand-year history, to be a link to the heavens. They were the tools and toys of emperors, and were thought to be sacred to many gods. In most oriental nations, the kite often figured in religious and ceremonial occasions. In Japan, kites brought prayers closer to the gods. In China, the kite had symbolic significance in the festival of Ascending on High. Kites have been thought to have conjured good luck and repelled evil. In Korea, on the last day of the flying season, kites are released to carry off bad fortune, and no one claims those stray kites for fear of the ill wind that carried them.

Throughout the Orient kites record folklore. Famous battles are remembered in kite faces. Traditional tales of deeds, heroes, and deities painted on kite faces link generations. The wind sock carp celebrates a boy's birth in Japan, and the kite picturing a monkey sipping wine reminds sake-sotted men to be temperate. Farmers and fishermen still call upon the kite to prophesy, and a good catch is announced before arrival with an airborne messenger.

Kites recall history, too. The red, white, and blue colors of the Nagasaki-hata suggest early Japanese contact with the Dutch. The modern Hokkaido kite depicts a pale, bearded old man of the Ainu weeping because his persecuted people face extinction.

The themes are innumerable; kite history is the history of the Far East. As the kite spread from China it brought many influences from each country it passed through. Heritages and legends became intertwined. But as much as kites were shared, indigenous forms evolved. The variety that has survived is great.

The gallery of oriental kites which follows attempts to draw together examples from many countries, but the concentration of Japanese kites is greatest—a testament to Japan's long respect for the kite as an art and craft form. Every kite here tells a story. Every kite reflects something of the culture which devised it. Nothing can better convey the fact that kites are more than mere machines than kites like these.

A GALLERY OF KITES

Outsider (*tojin*) is the name given to this type of crudely painted, oddly shaped kite. Built in Fukuoka at the southern end of Japan, it earned its name because of the strong influences from Southeast Asia in its design.

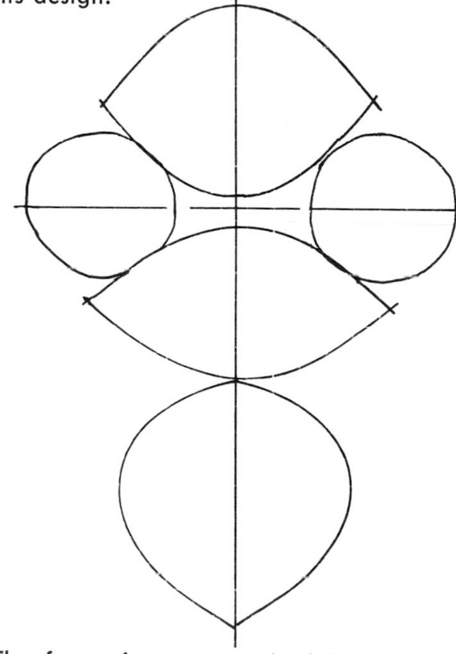

The frame is constructed of bent and lashed bamboo. The face is painted after the paper has been applied to the frame. Strips of paper glued onto the back sandwich the bamboo supports.

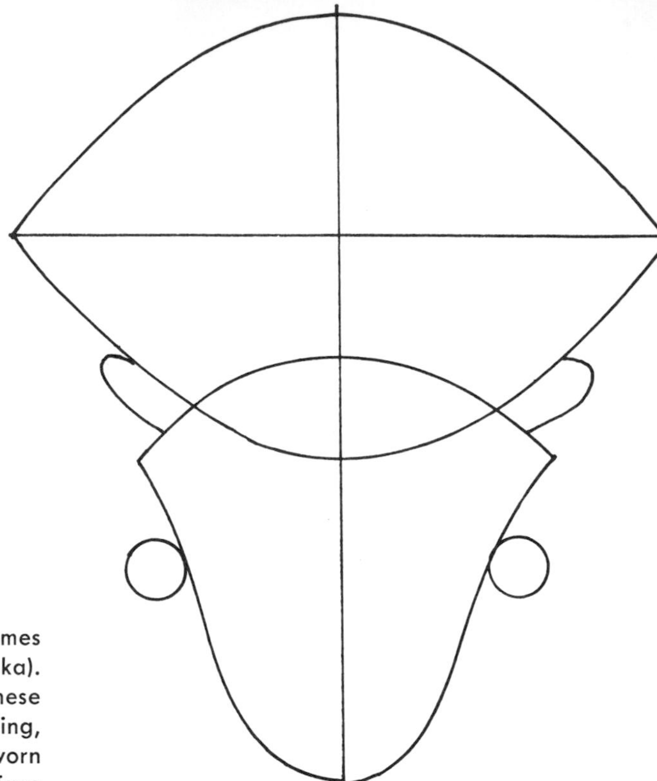

The *Oniyocho* framework.

A close relative of the *Tojin,* the *Oniyocho* comes from the Hirato-Nagasaki area (near Fukuoka). The painting has special significance in Japanese tradition. The large head, eyes, and gaping, toothy mouth symbolize the helmet once worn by the samurai warrior. If the kite has a face painted beneath the helmet, it should only be flown, traditionally, by children of the samurai.

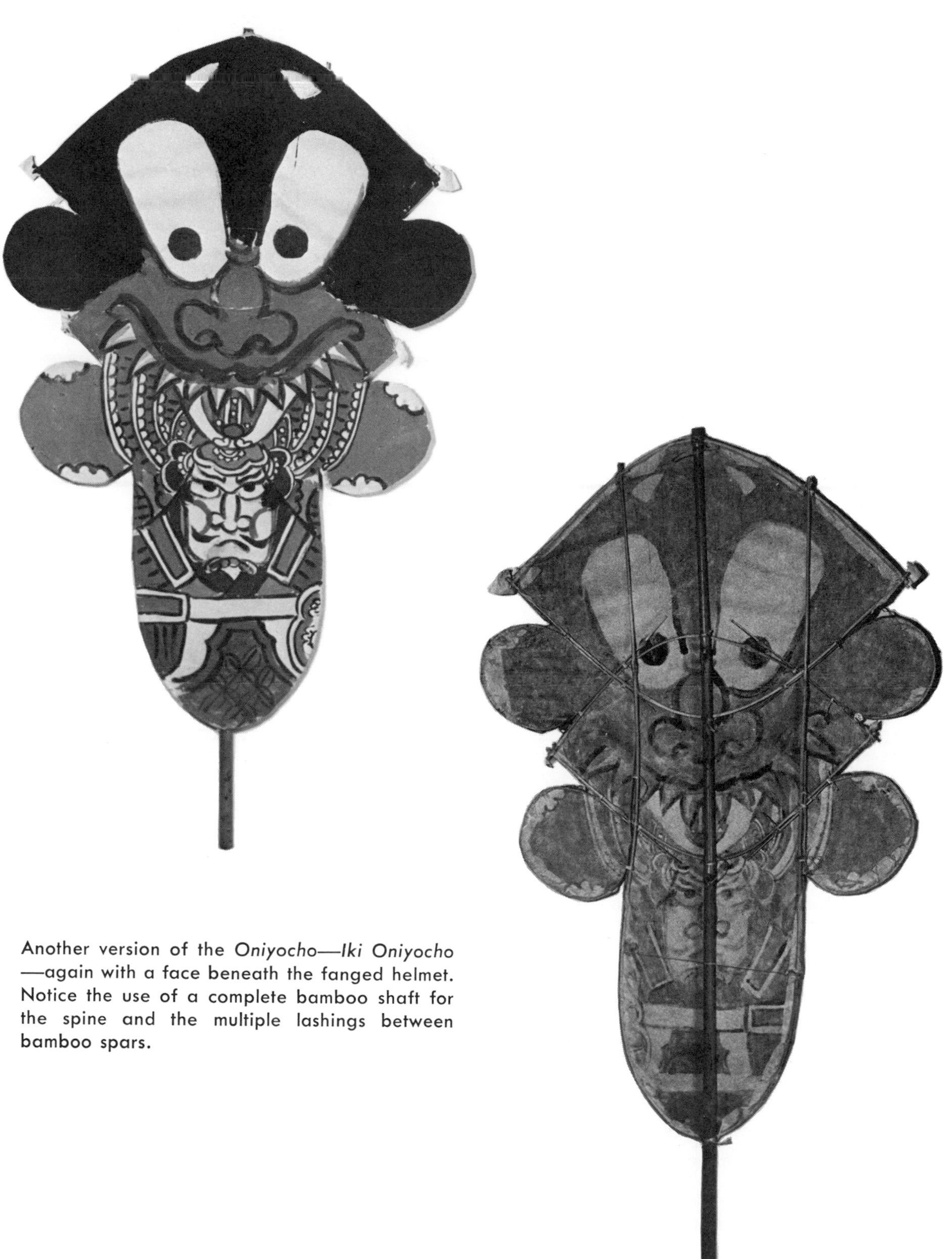

Another version of the *Oniyocho*—*Iki Oniyocho* —again with a face beneath the fanged helmet. Notice the use of a complete bamboo shaft for the spine and the multiple lashings between bamboo spars.

South of Tokyo, on the Pacific Ocean, is Shizuoka—a center for traditional kite design where the rectangular forms of the north merged with the oddly shaped frameworks from the south of Japan. The *Kashira-gire* kite, crane and tortoise, illustrates the Japanese respect for age and longevity. Folklore has it that the crane lives for 1000 years and the tortoise for 10,000. *Kashira-gire* means "cut off head"—implying that since the top is missing it is meant to be flown by the children of nonsamurai classes.

Kashira-gire is made with three thicknesses of bamboo. The curved outlines are very thin strips.

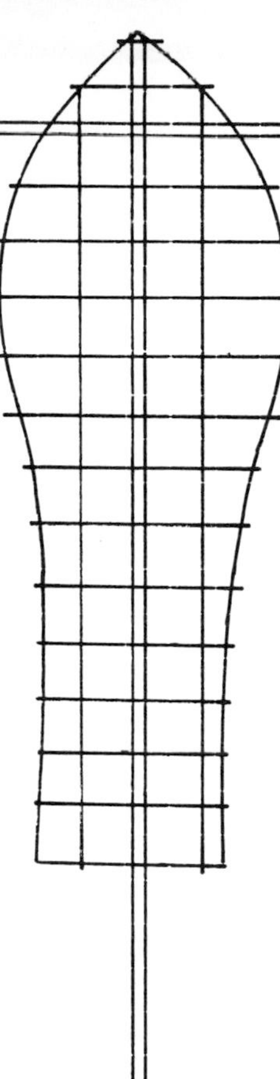

Three weights of bamboo are also used in the *Tongari* (high up) kite. This is the brother of the *Kashira-gire;* only samurai may use it.

The *Tomoe* is a kite for all seasons. The circular part, forming the leading edge of the kite, represents, symbolically, a religious shrine. The crisscrossed squares beneath it signify the temple, and beneath the temple is a Japanese fan. It too is from Shizuoka.

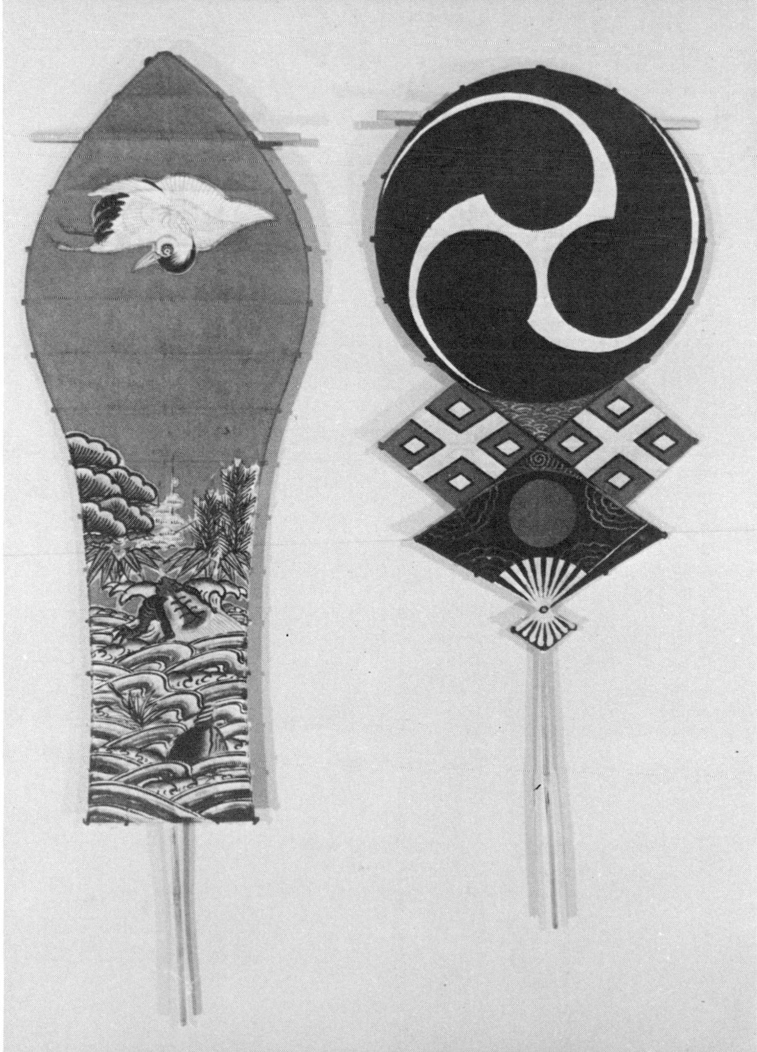

Named *Baramon* for the "inhumanly sharp bite" of the general's power, this shows the complete fighting helmet with the back of the general's head. Such kites, with only the pony tail showing beneath the sharp teeth, are flown by children of the three castes below samurai: craftsmen, merchants, and farmers. This *Baramon* stands 42″ high.

Many parts of Japan express the same traditional concepts through kites. These characters, for example, denote the long-lived tortoise (left) and crane. From the Shimane Prefecture, the nearest state to Korea, both are flown with bamboo and rattan hummers. Often flown in tandem, their name is *Izumo Iwai*.

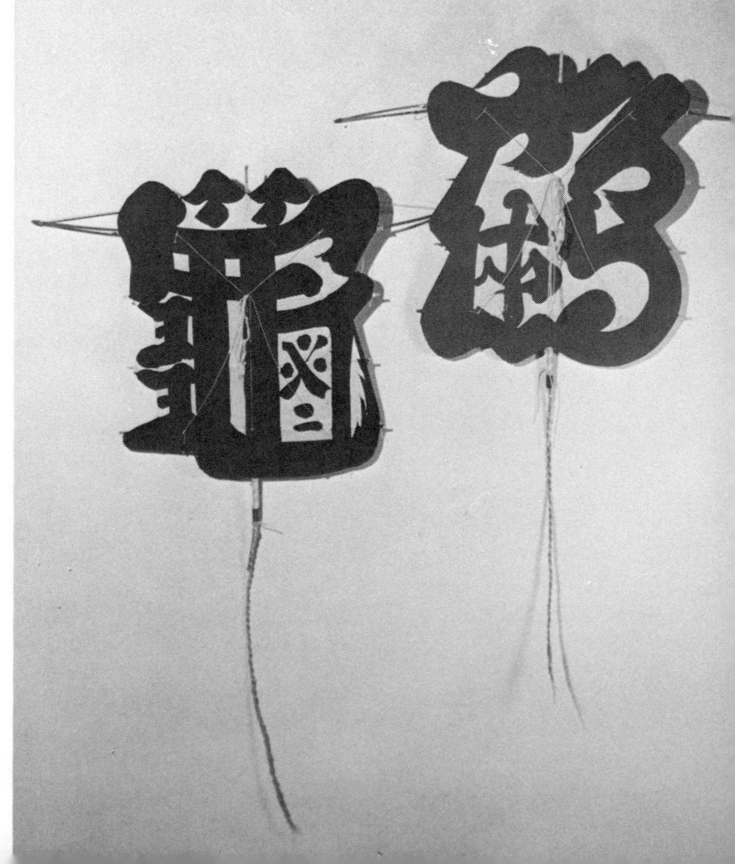

Miniatures of the giant kites launched during the Hamamatsu festivals, the *machi-jirushi* usually display a family crest. A fighter, the kite is flown with no tail. For the Hamamatsu festival, each of the sixty-six block divisions in the town makes (or has made) a set of kites with its symbol. Teams assemble on the flying field, and, with rhythmic battle cries, set about severing the lines of the opposition. Portable winches and lots of manpower are used to control these large structures.

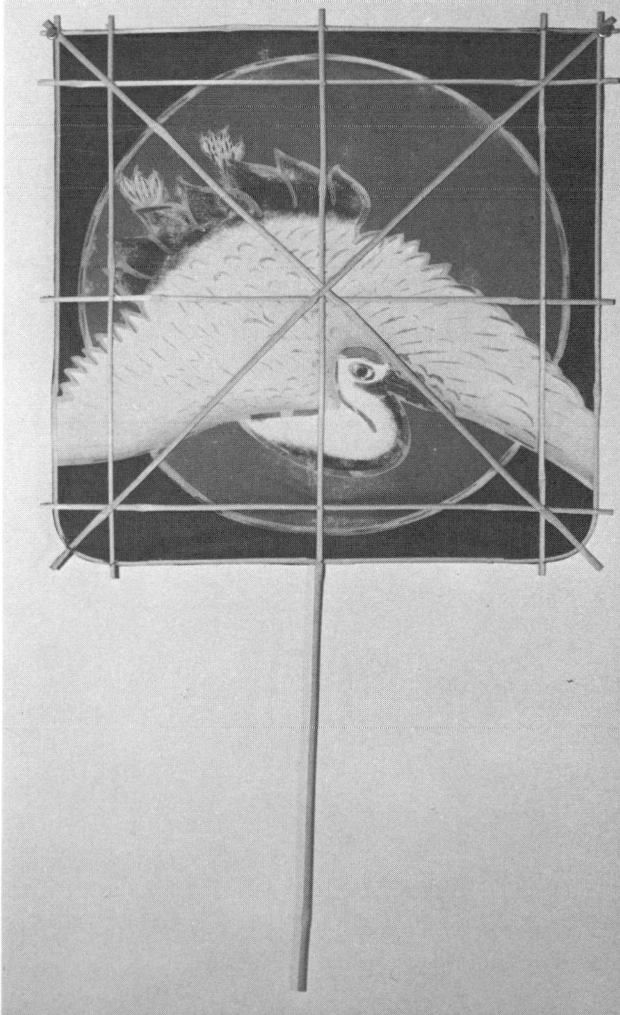

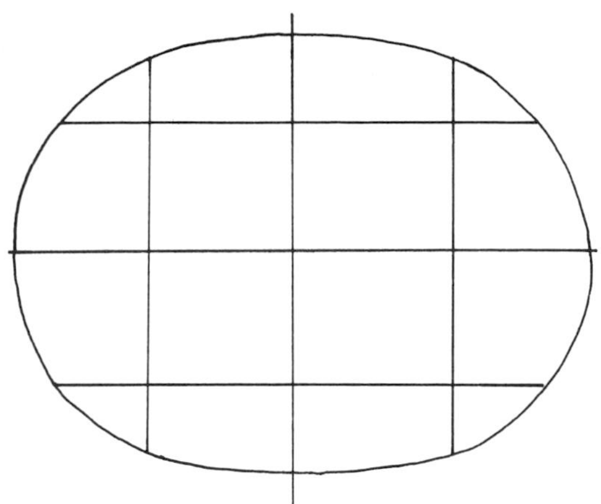

Another fighting kite, which is no longer built in the large sizes it once was, is the *wan-wan*. Once the largest kite in Japan, it is traditionally built on the island of Tokushima off the Pacific Coast. According to experts, the original kites were up to 90 feet in diameter, used nearly 3000 sheets of Japanese paper, and weighed a ton. Tails were constructed from enormous lengths of intertwined ropes. Although actually elliptical in shape, the kite is flown with a deep bow and appears to be circular when in flight. Courtesy: Tal Streeter, *The Art of the Japanese Kite*.

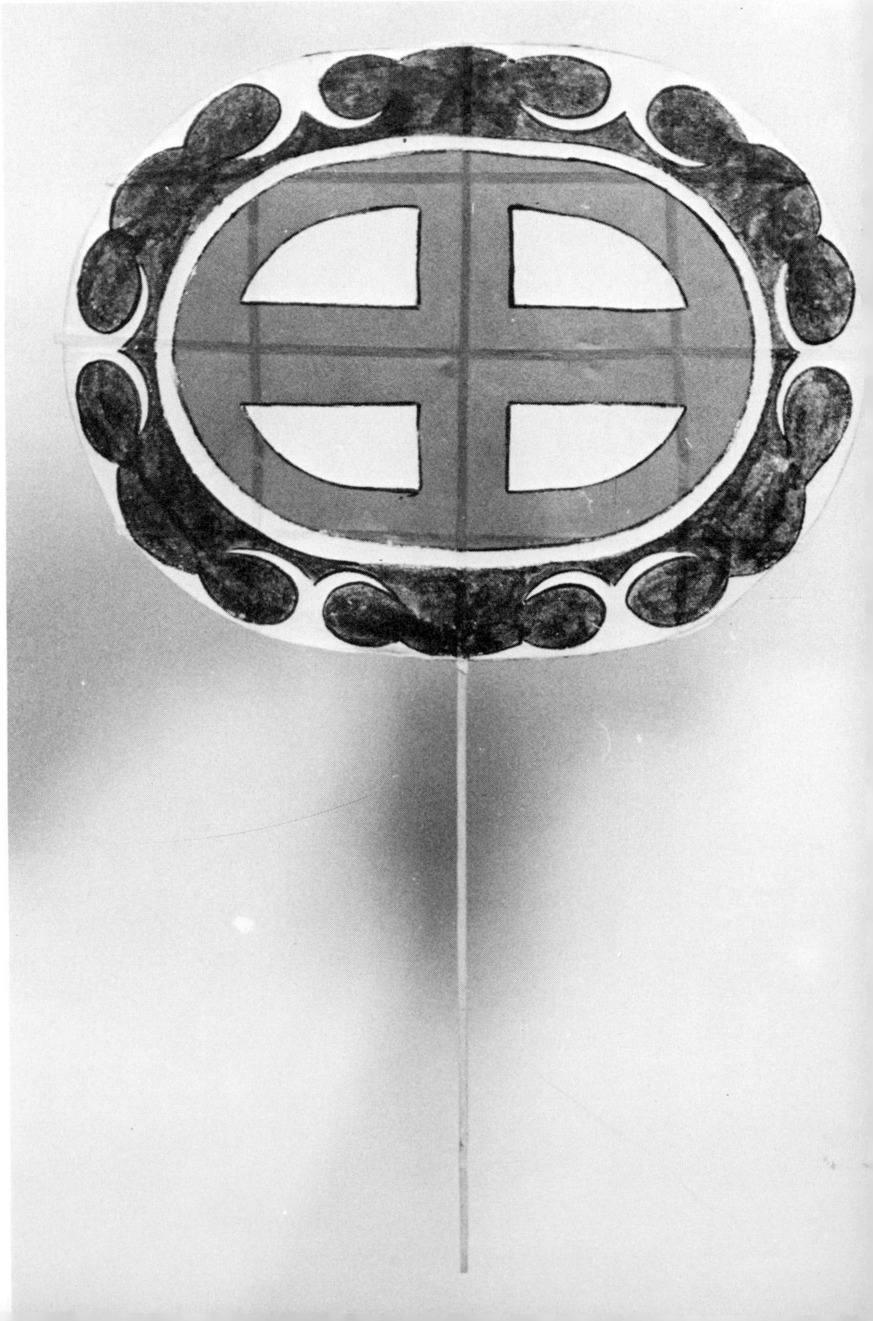

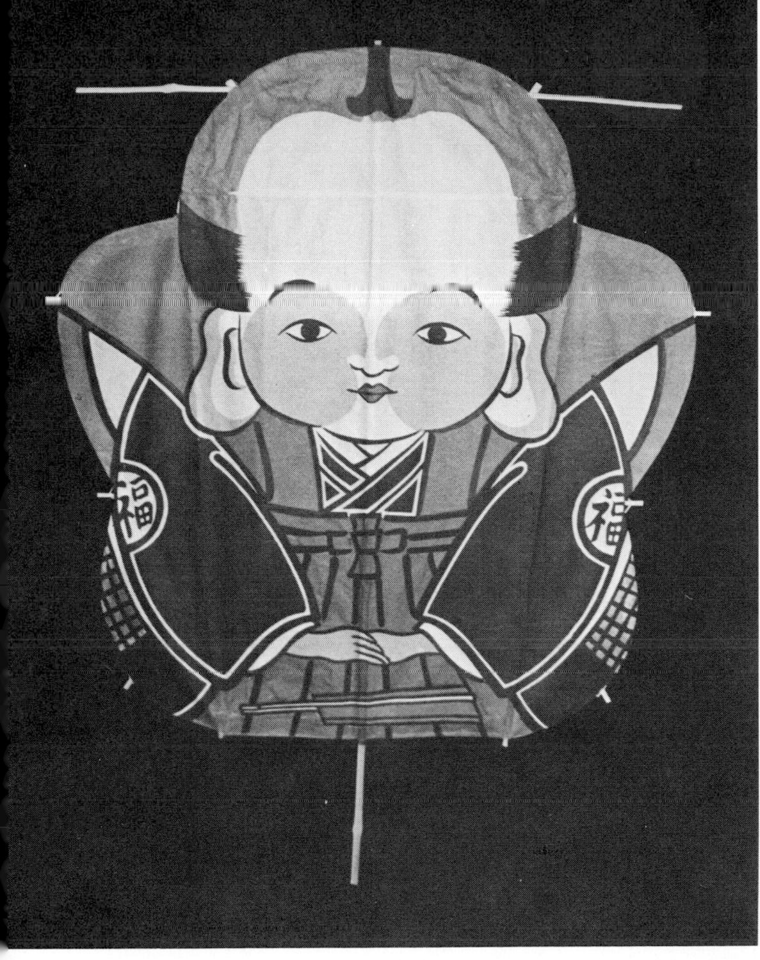

Fukusuke, with orange eyes and a long, streaming tail, traditionally comes from the south of Japan. The Japanese, like all peoples, have their superstitions and talismans—the number four is bad luck, for example, because it sounds like the word for death. Some hotels do not have fourth floors, and tea sets will never come with four cups. *Fukusuke* is the lucky dwarf. The framework is bamboo with a string guideline reinforcing the paper.

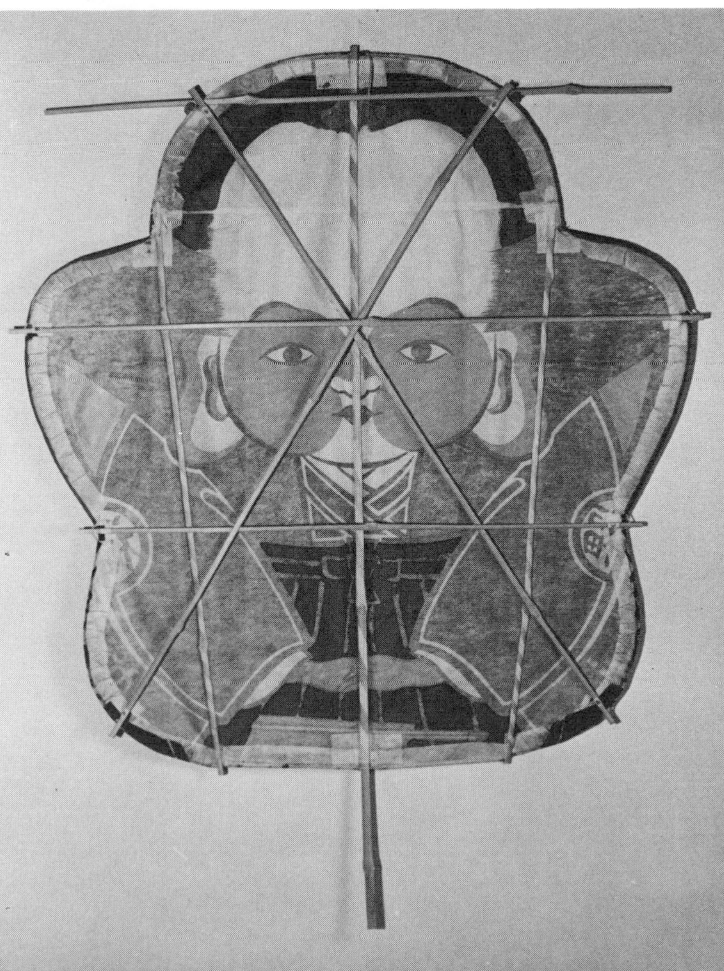

Another luck figure is *Daruma,* the Buddhist monk. Heavily cloaked in red and sitting on ocean waves, the *Daruma* is built of bamboo, string, and paper. Most often, this kite will have bright bulging eyes which are later painted by the owner when good luck has arrived.

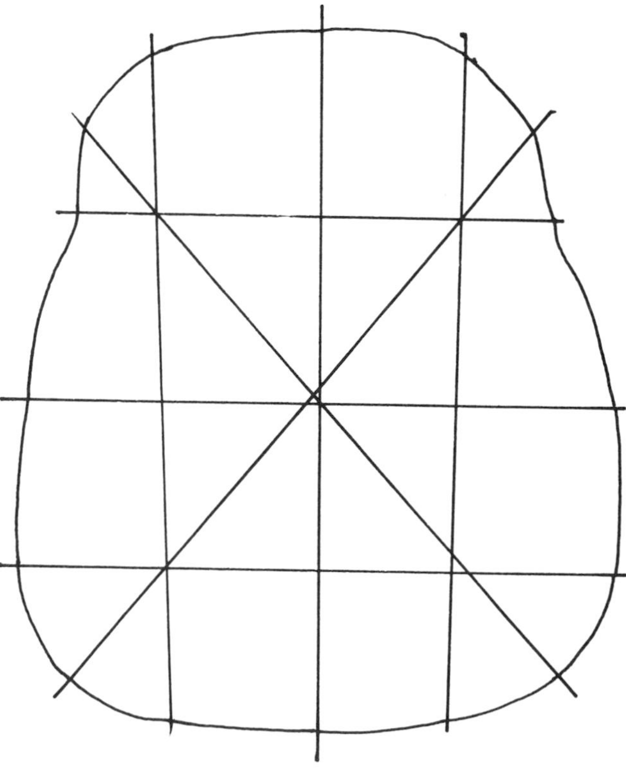

Smile. The happy *Bekkako* kite has eyes which twirl, spinning in the wind on thin bamboo sticks. The tongue is flapping red crepe paper.

A true talisman, the fanged face of the *Oniyozu* frightens evil spirits away from the newborn. Large *Oniyozu* kites cover the ceiling above new children to protect them from evil. Traditionally, the grandfather paints the demonic face, and at New Year's the entire family flies it together in the cold sea breeze. As the kite rises, it carries with it all chance of evil, and guarantees health and happiness for the child and the family.

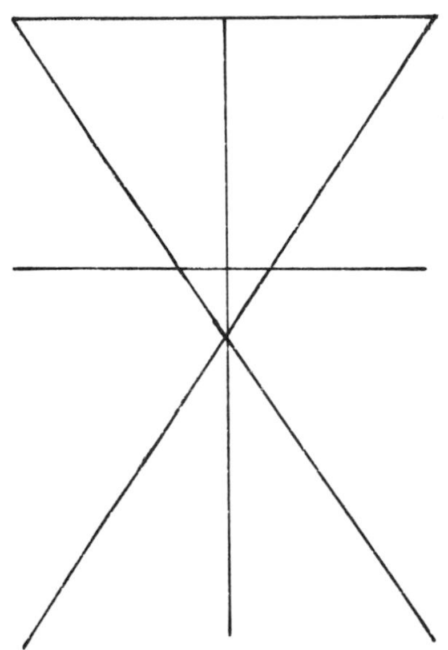

Shosuke-yakko, the samurai's servant, comes from Shizuoka. Openings in the sleeves permit air to escape around an otherwise broad lift surface. The lower legs and feet are paper tails. The rest of the body does not have string guidelines, but it is supported by a folded paper edge.

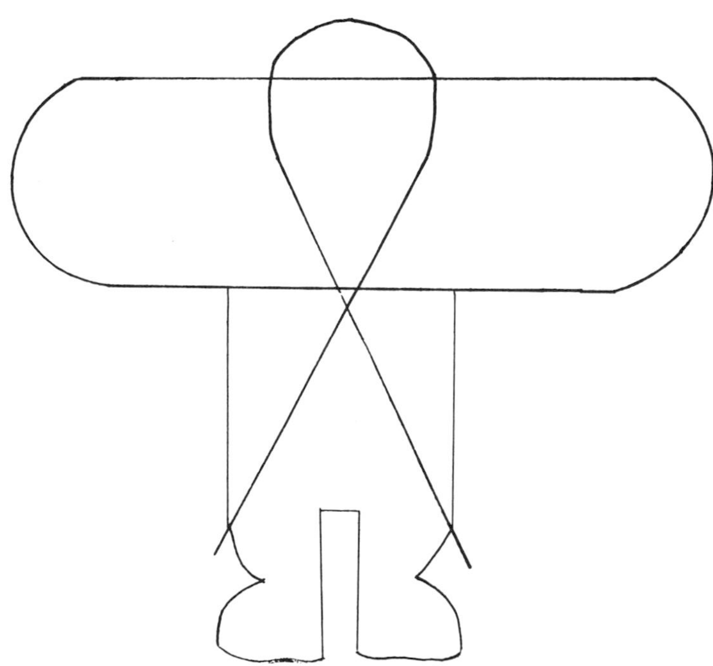

This Chinese figure kite is a distant relative of the sleeve kite. Courtesy: Smithsonian Institution.

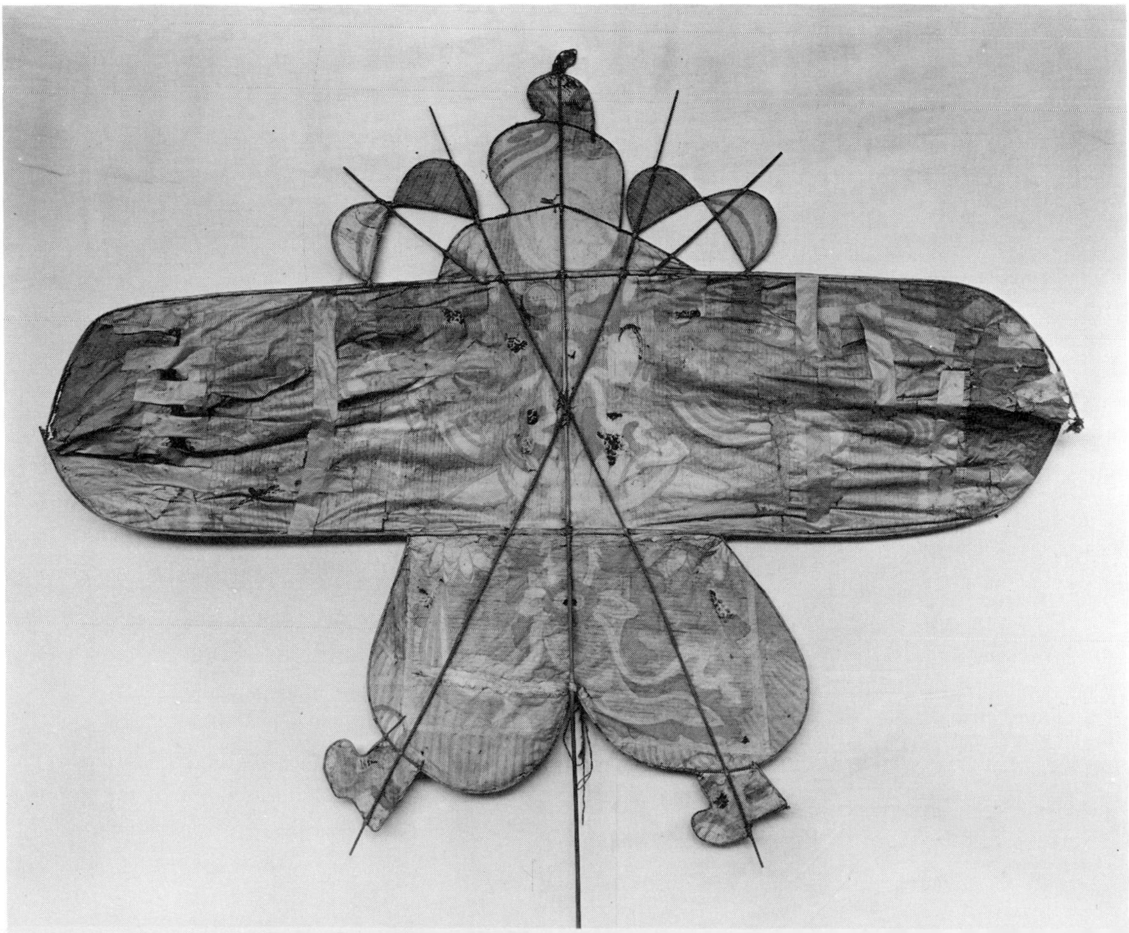

In the Chiba prefecture, fishermen make this kite to resemble the kimonos worn by men during festivals. The heroic swimmer here snatches a carp.

Before setting out on a long fishing trip these kites are flown from the ships; on return they are sent aloft again to tell the families that they have brought a good catch. Kites are readily distinguishable because each bears the family crest.

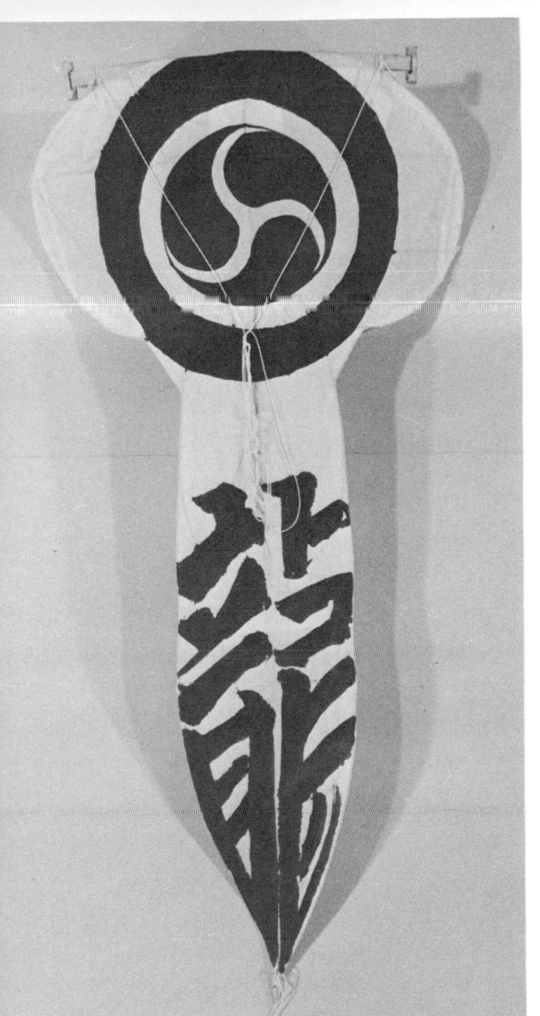

This *Tojin* kite, with a humming *unari* across its leading edge, also bears a family seal.

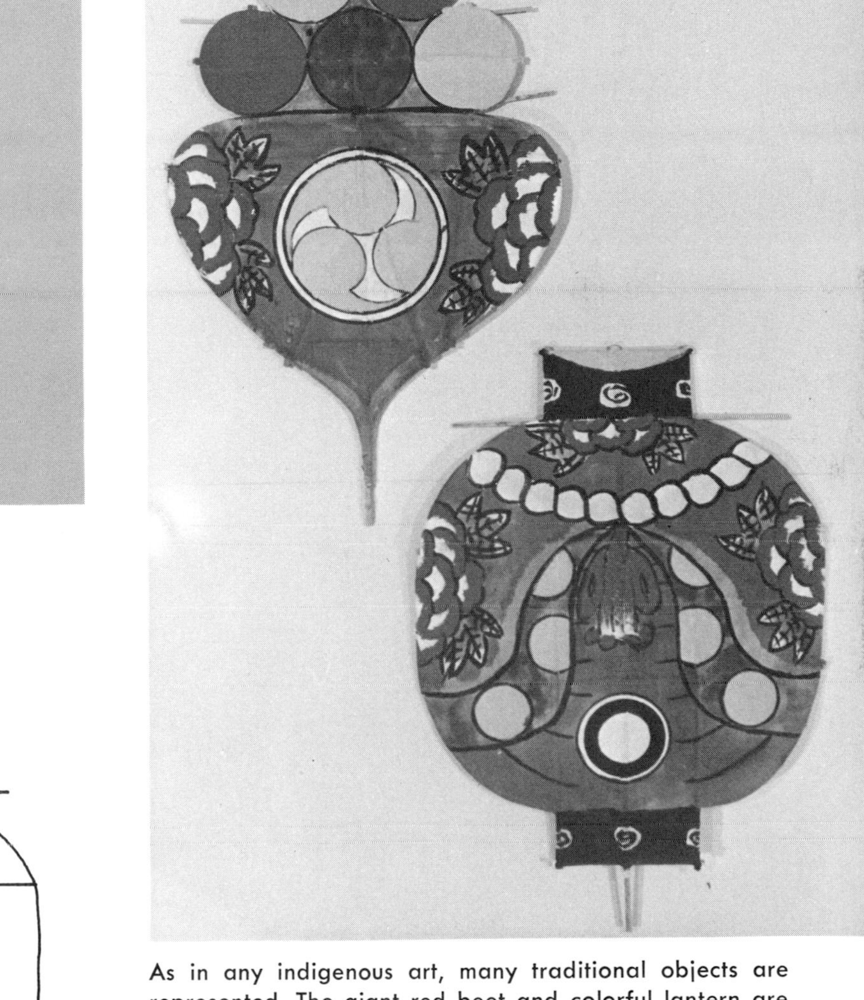

As in any indigenous art, many traditional objects are represented. The giant red beet and colorful lantern are from Takamatsu and Shokoku respectively.

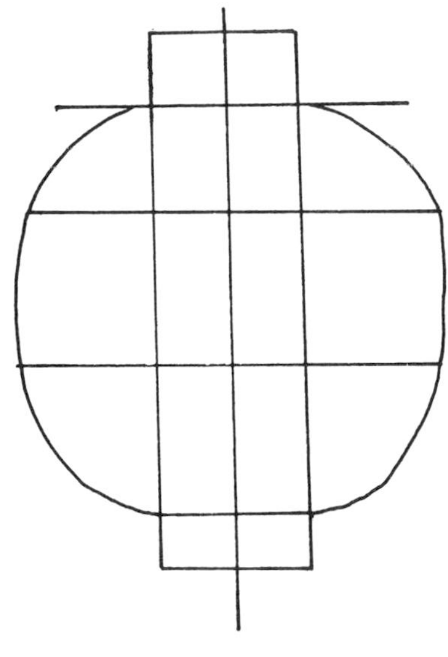

A charming version of the Chinese lantern kite. Courtesy: Smithsonian Institution.

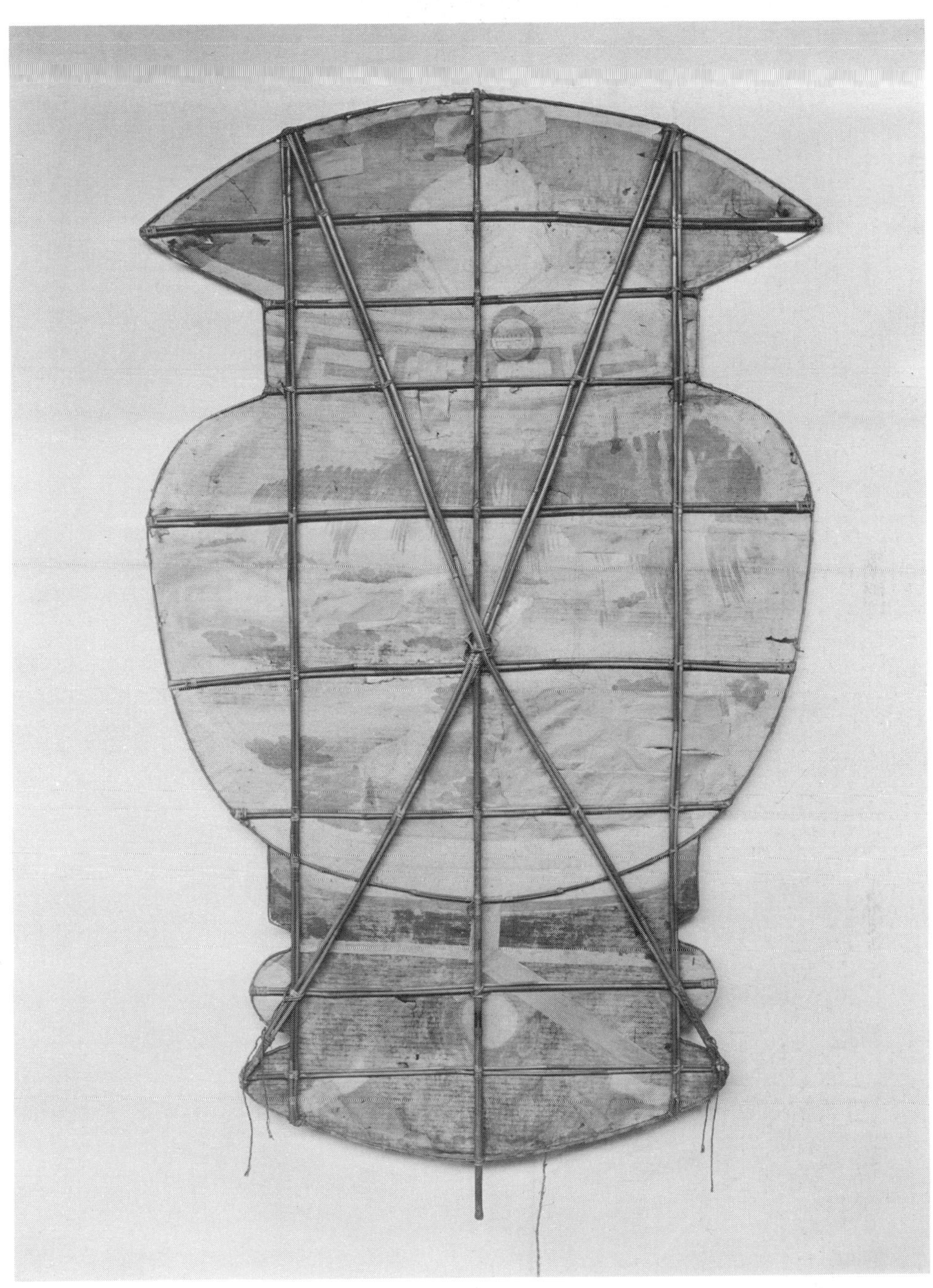

Rear view.

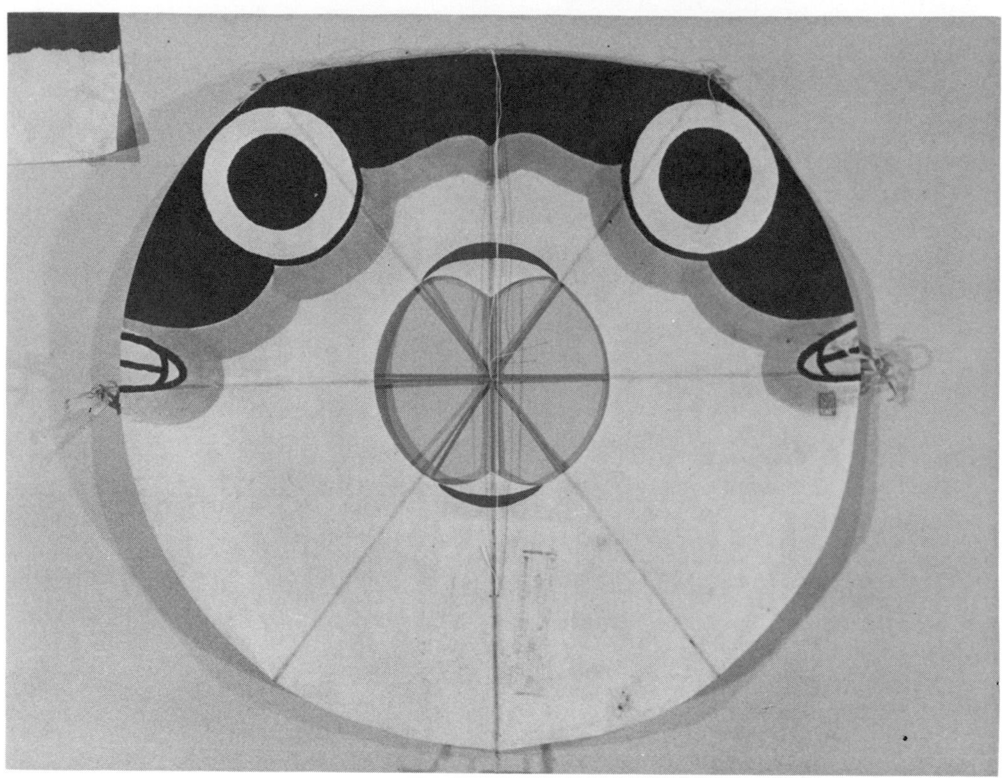

Blowfish kites have vents in their centers. The kites, from Yamaguchi in the south of Japan, are made of very thin bamboo; they are quite light.

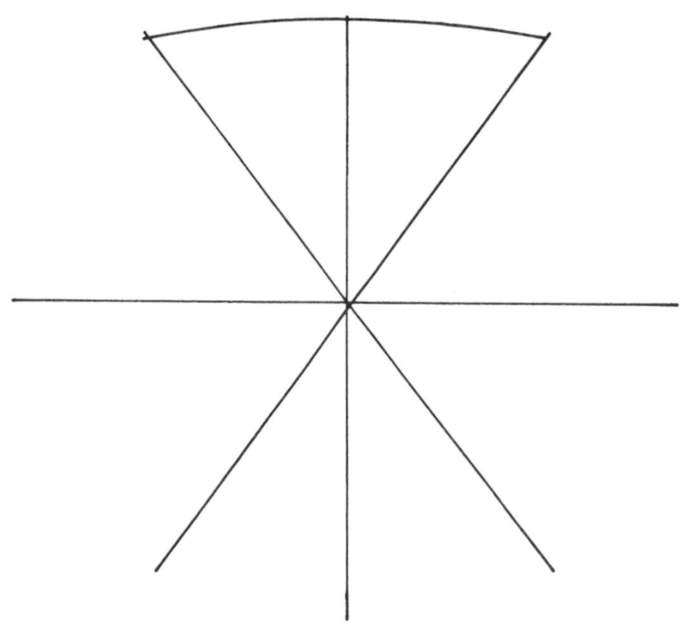

Comical cat and owl kites from Thailand and Taiwan. Courtesy: The Kite Shop.

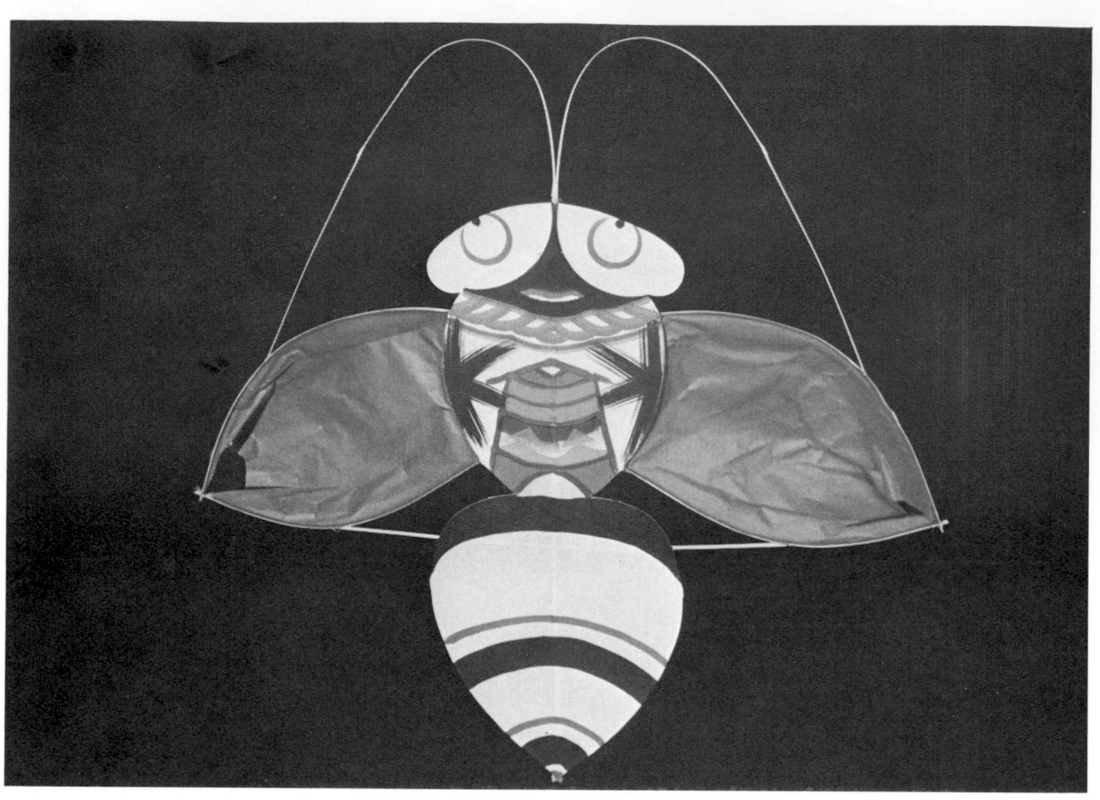

The Bee Kite has open wing tips. Its structure is clean but complex.

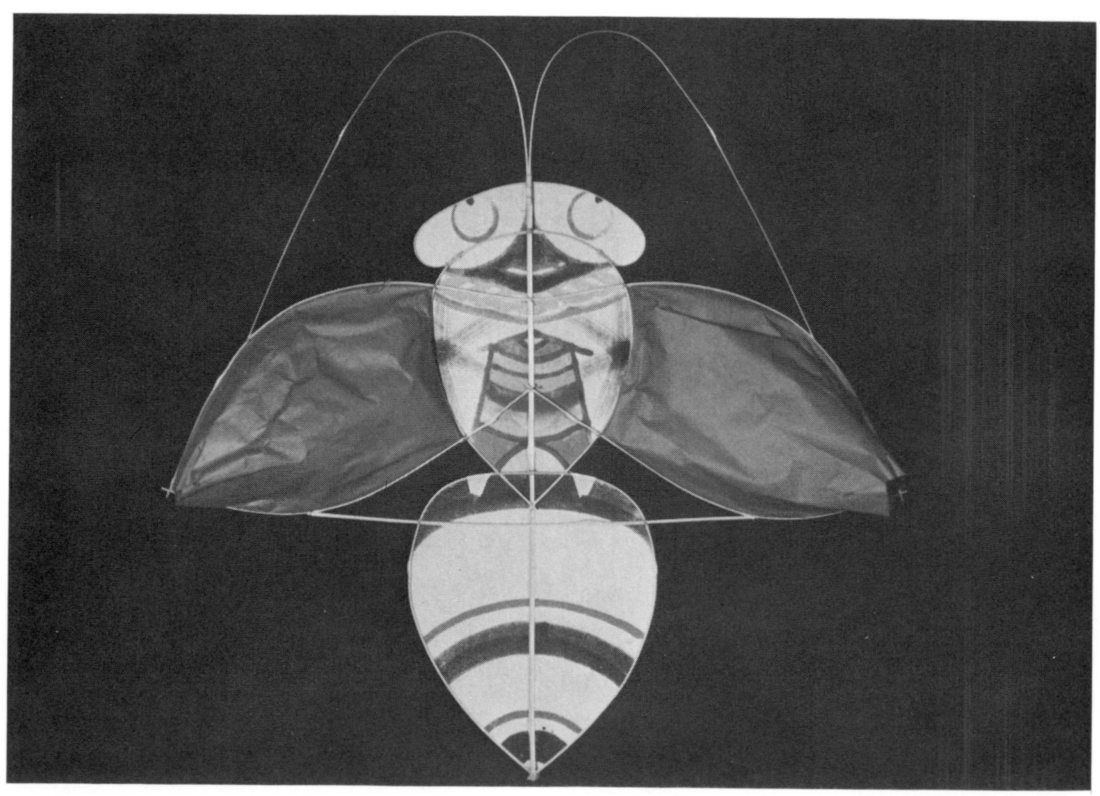

Tenjin is colored in subtle hues of purple, red, brown, and amber.

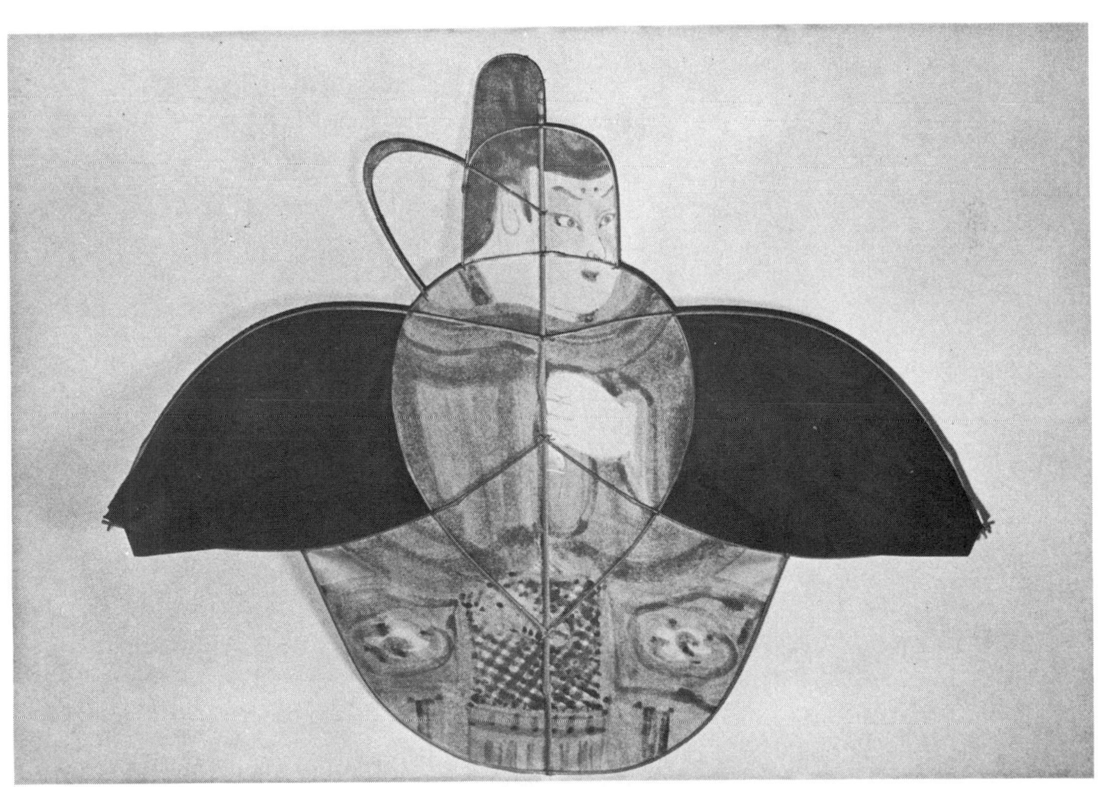

The snake kite with a simple flat body and flowing tail is indigenous to Thailand. Courtesy: Go Fly a Kite Store.

Patched tissue papers create a design on this Indian kite. Metallic papers hold spars in place.

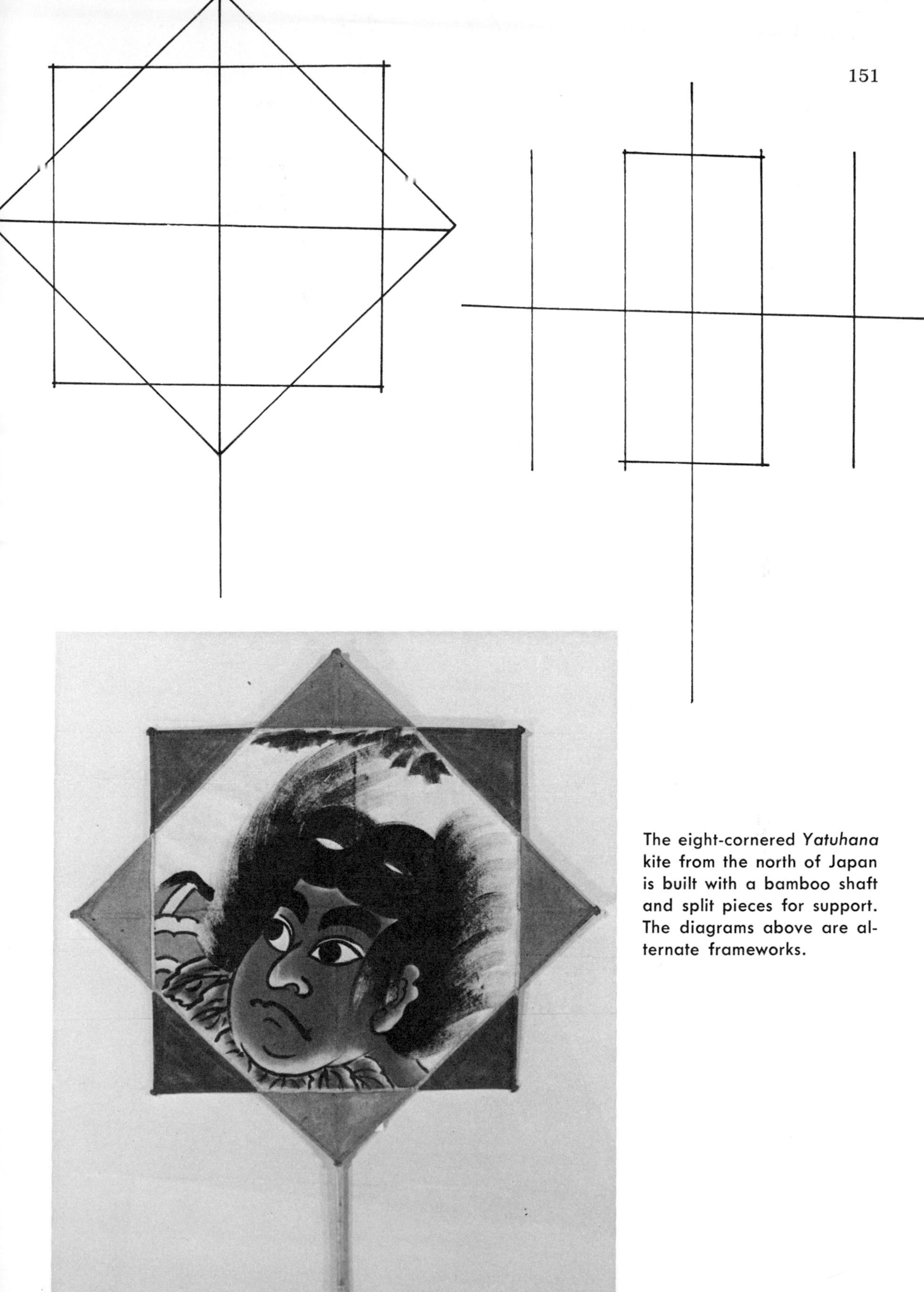

The eight-cornered *Yatuhana* kite from the north of Japan is built with a bamboo shaft and split pieces for support. The diagrams above are alternate frameworks.

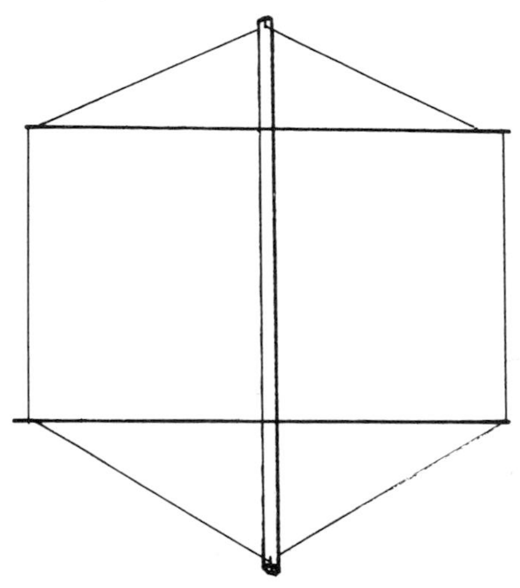

Among the most beautifully painted kites in Japan are the *Tsugaru* group. This one represents *Dakki-ohyaku,* a female thief famous in folklore who was won over by a good man and became a good woman. It is a heavy kite supported with cypress, and it is flown in strong winds.

Two Kabuki theatre characters grace these kites. Kite from Go Fly a Kite Store.

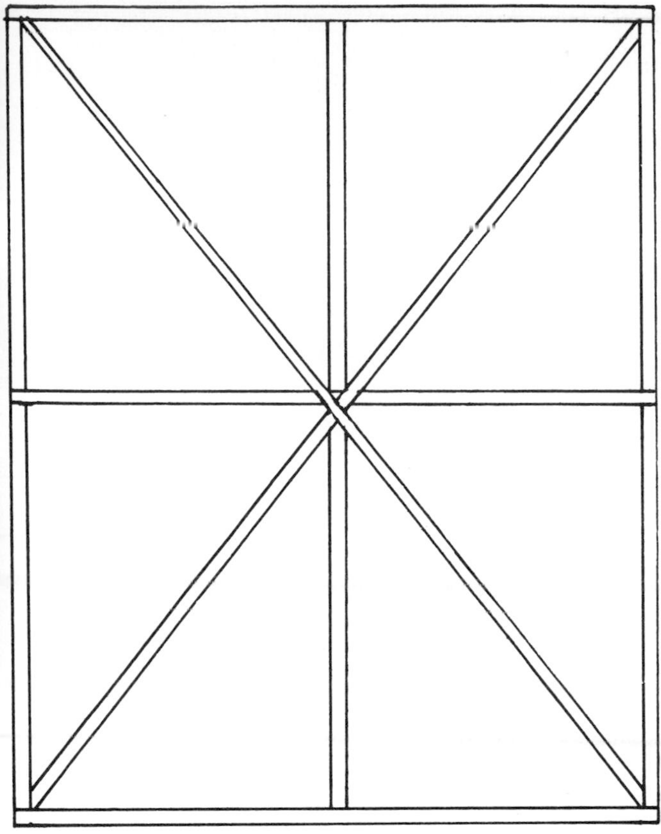

Revered by children, the legendary *Kintoki* was raised by bears in the mountains and later became an aide to the emperor. Made at the northern tip of Honshu Island. Courtesy: Tal Streeter, *The Art of the Japanese Kite*.

Kites were said to have spread to northern Japan from Tokyo along mountain roads. They transmitted legends as well. These *Musha* kites depict confrontations between priest-general and samurai. The two were said to have met, as commanders in a great battle, in hand-to-hand combat.

The eye kite, identical in structure to the *Musha*, is finely painted in black on white, with ink.

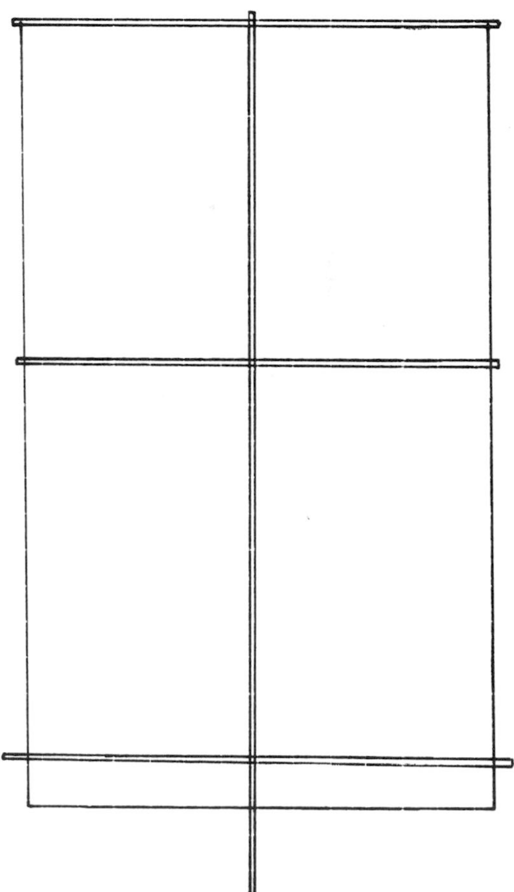

The *Beka* Kite is so named because when it flies the thin bamboo cross spars snap back and forth crying "beka, beka, beka."

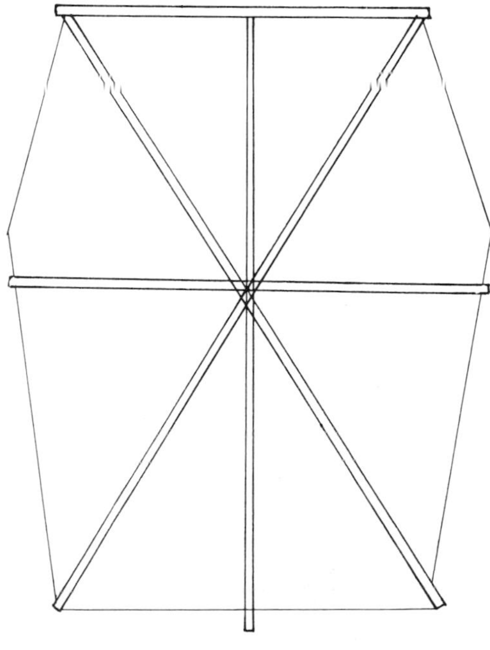

The island of Hokkaido claims only one kite design, and it is a recent development. It celebrates the inhabitants' centennial. The six-sided shape is meant to reflect the shape of the island; the painting depicts an Ainu chief lamenting the decline of his people. The Ainu, said to have been the original inhabitants of the Japanese islands, are subject to racial prejudice and their numbers are dwindling.

The classic *Nagasaki-hata* kite, related to the Indian Fighter, is still popular. The design is executed in cut and pasted paper.

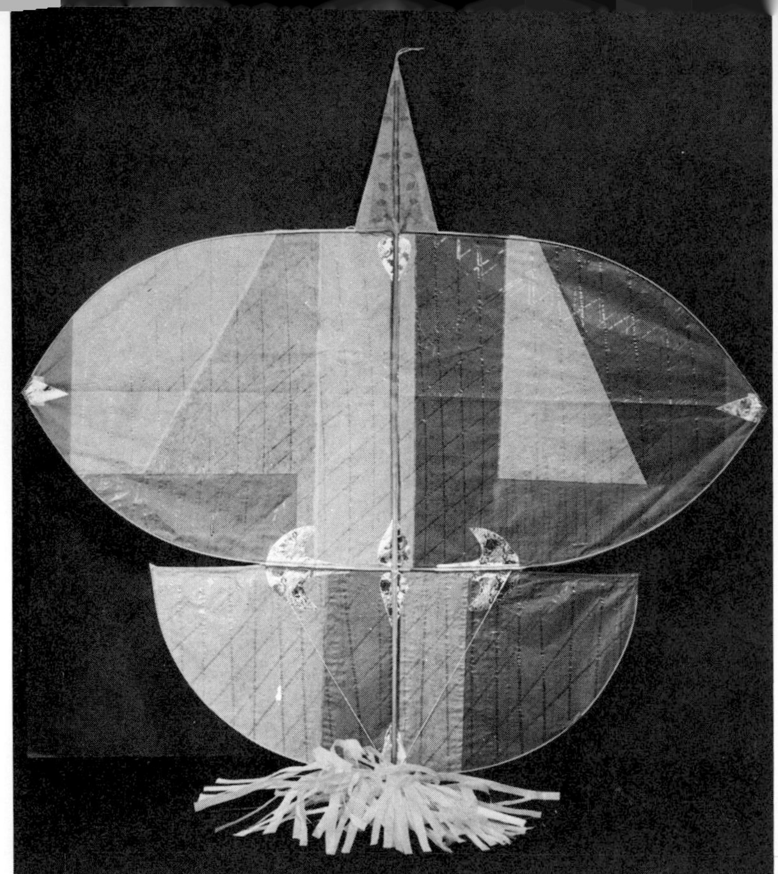

The Indian Fighter, an object of delicate balance.

Another classic fighter is the Korean design. With venting similar to that used in the *Fugu* blowfish, it is one of the few Korean designs which survive. It is gently bowed across the leading edge.

China, of course, has the longest history of kites. Their structure has, as in Japan, reached a high degree of sophistication. This is a flat kite with flowing wings and spinning eyes.

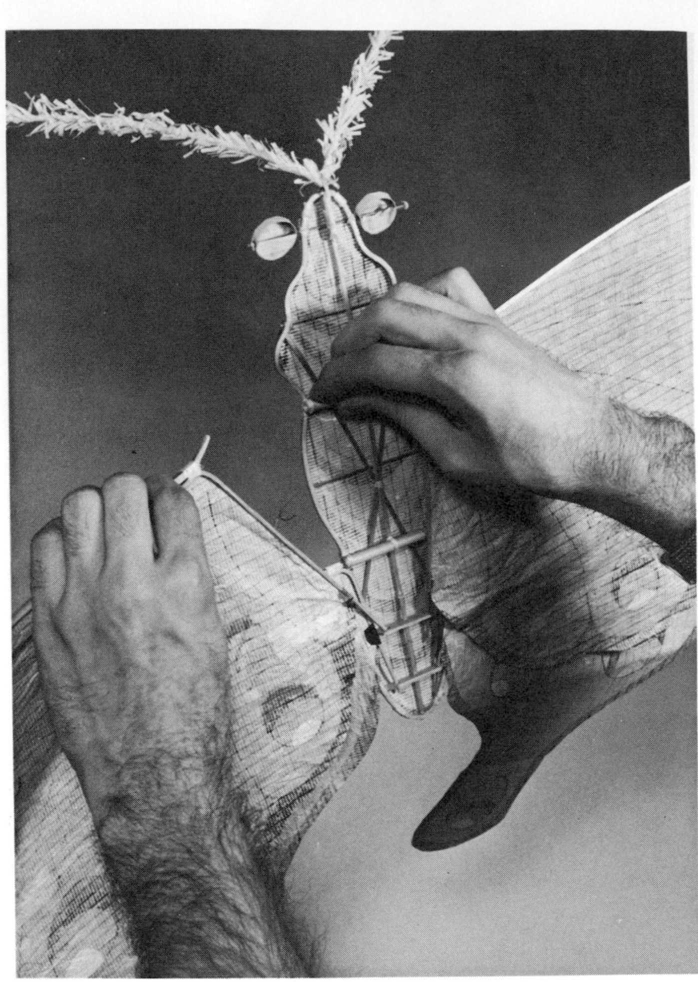

A more elaborate Chinese butterfly has detachable wings. Kite from Go Fly a Kite Store.

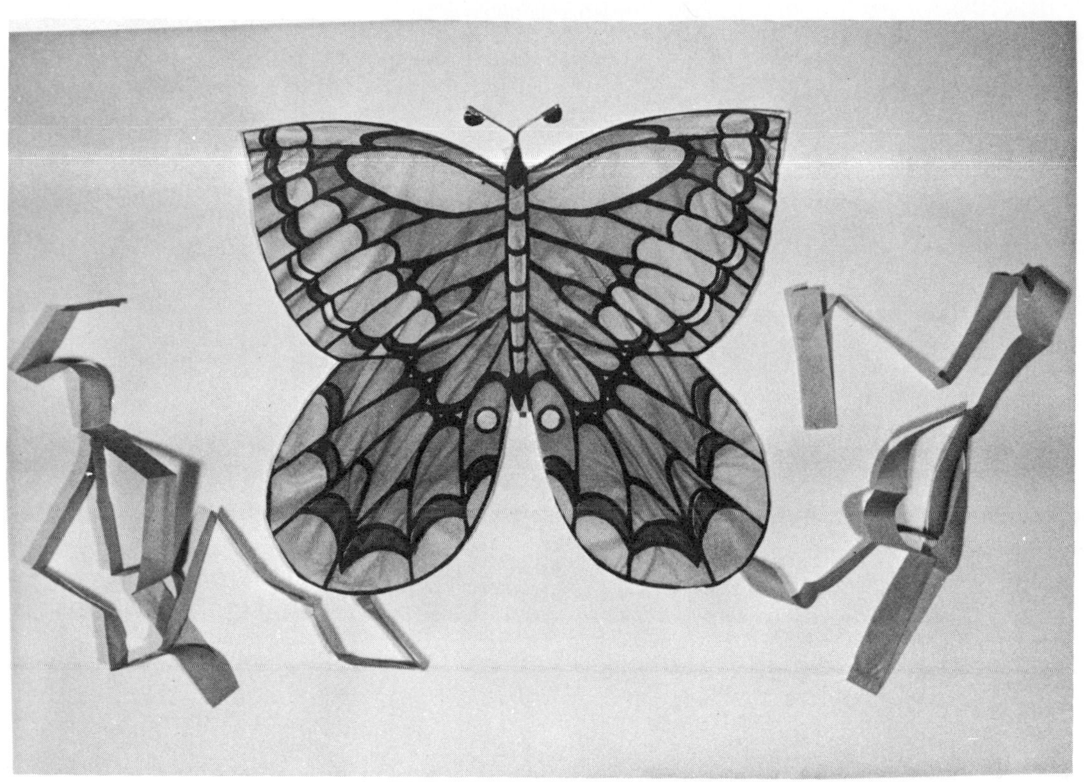

The Taiwan butterfly kite is constructed in the Indian tradition.

In addition to an intricate bamboo body in three segments, this Chinese kite has detachable wings which are swept back slightly. Such a great face!

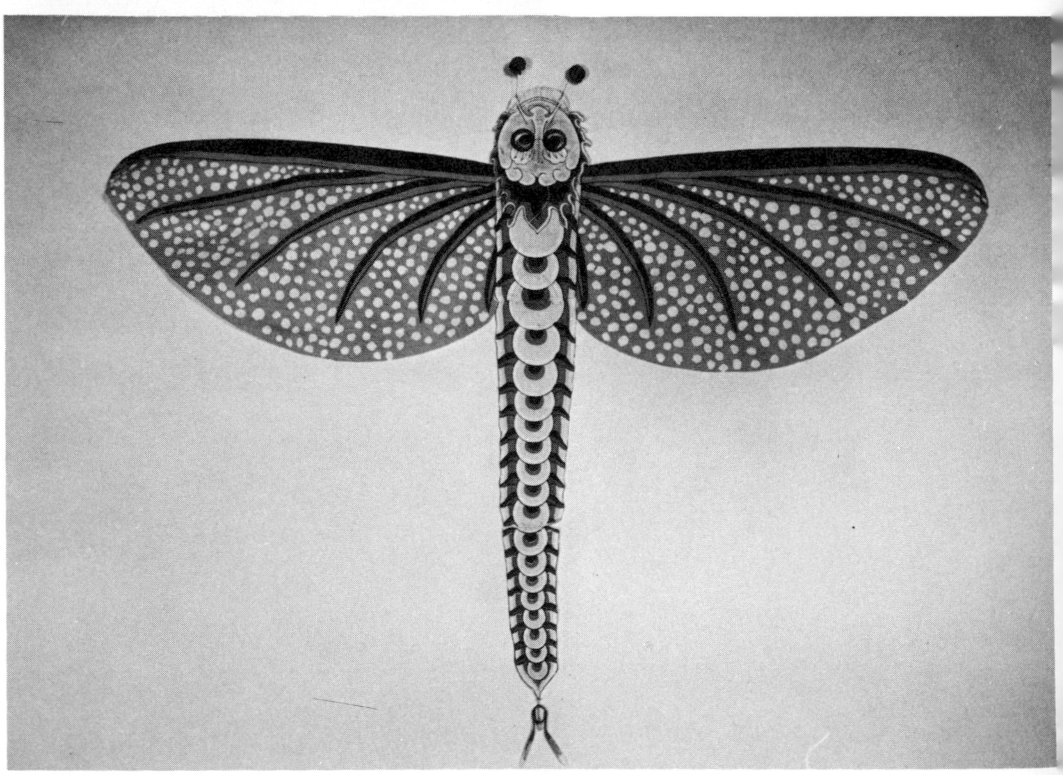

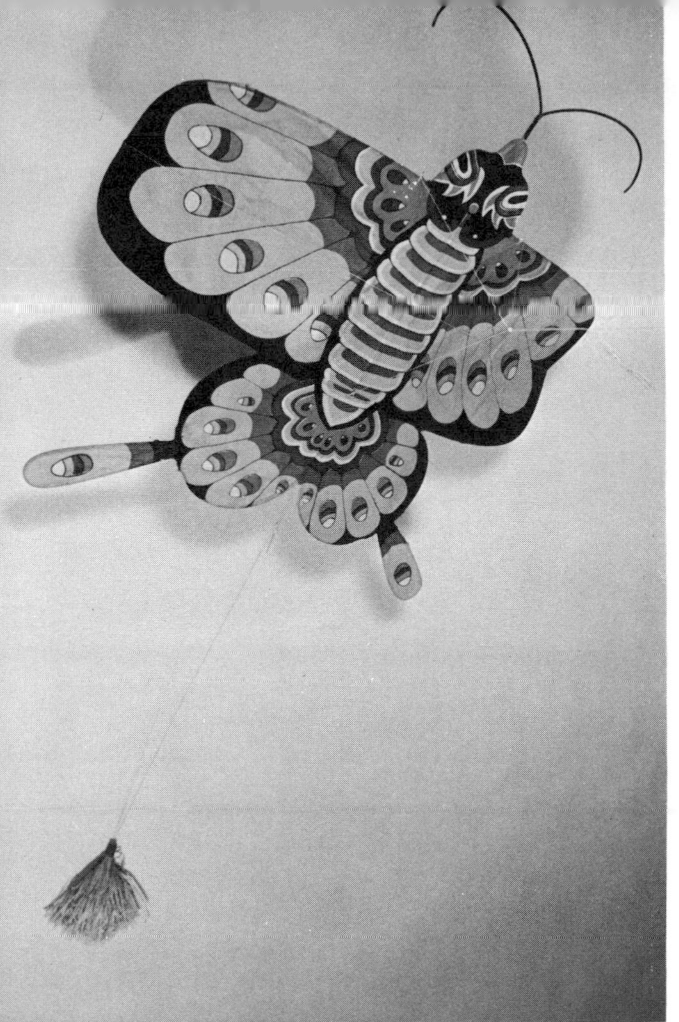

All wings on this contemporary Chinese kite are constructed with a dihedral angle.

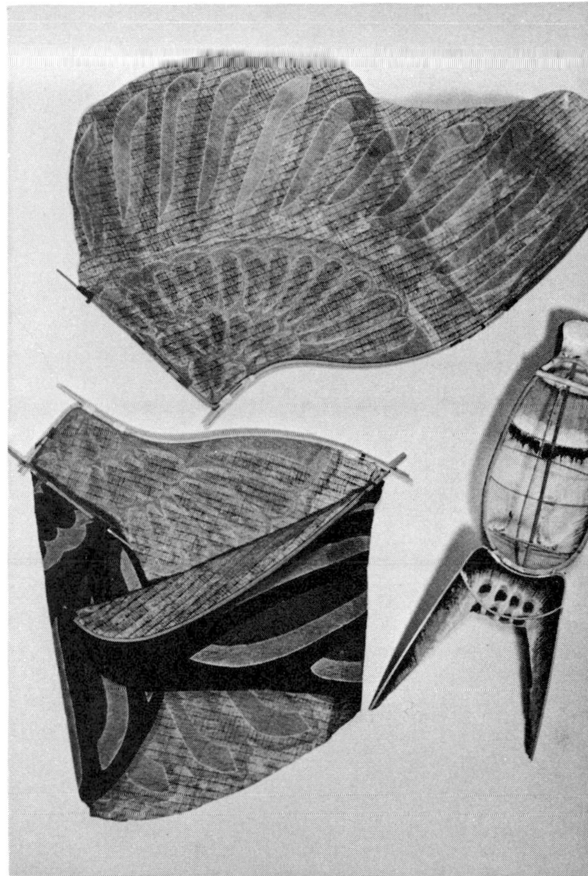

Another Chinese design employs three-dimensional bodies with hinged tails and folding wings. This bird, for example . . .

. . . not only has a plump body and a free-swinging set of tail feathers, but a pair of wings which fold to make packaging and transportation easy.

A nineteenth-century bird kite, predecessor of the modern Chinese design. Courtesy: Smithsonian Institution.

A devilish bat in a similar framework style of construction. The tail detaches as well.

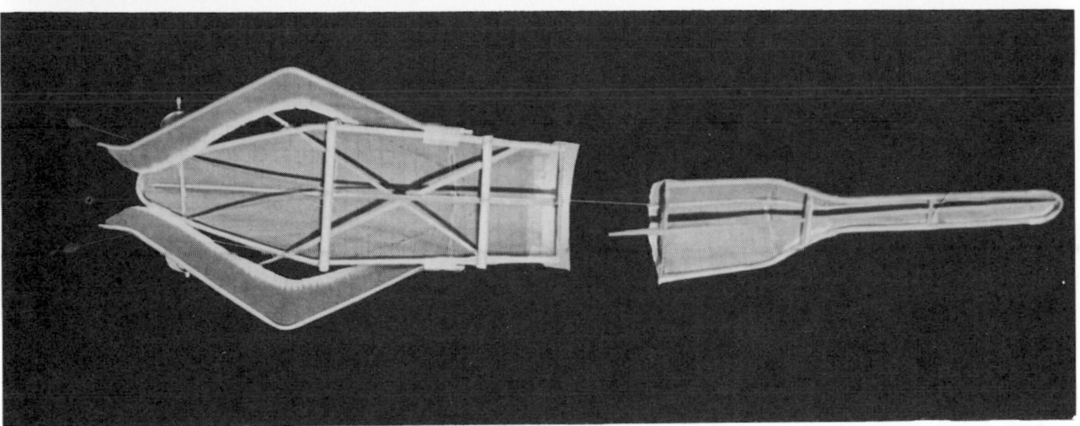

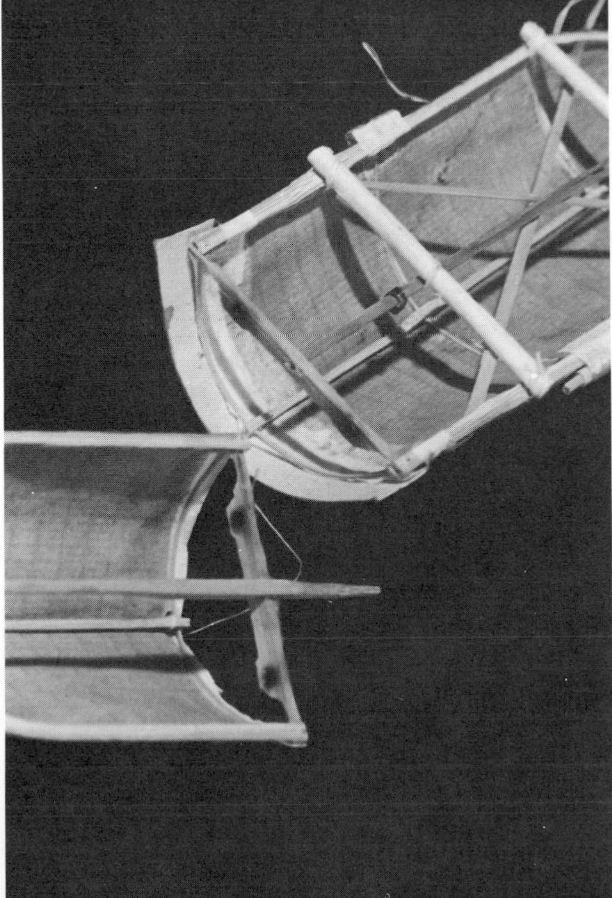

The flying insect boasts green, shocking pink, and orange coloring as well as detachable wings and legs.

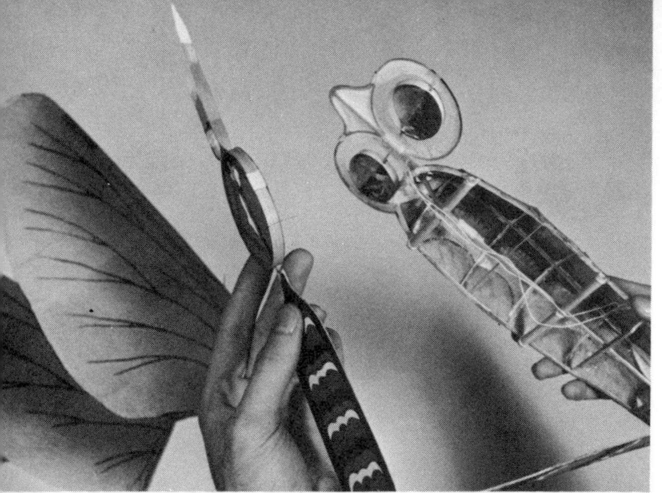

The beautiful Chinese dragonfly kite. In flight, eyes and tail spin in the wind.

Modern Chinese designs, from indigenous techniques and traditions, offer marvelous inspiration to kite craftsmen.

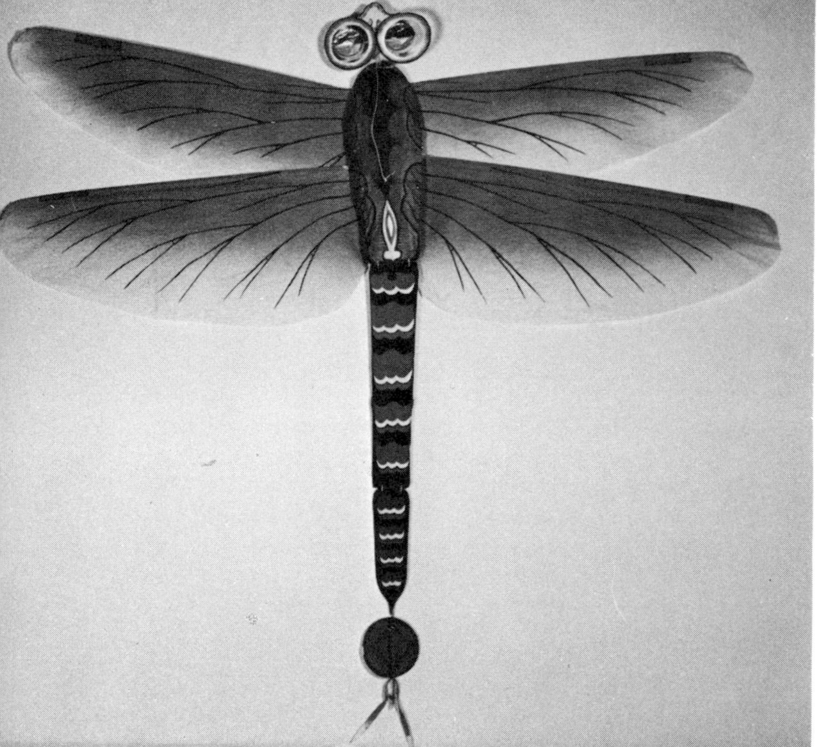

A modern Cambodian kite. The long bow across the top is a hummer, and the kite is flown with two very long, thin paper tails. Courtesy: Huot Kimleang.

CELLULAR KITES

Chapter 6

The modern history of the kite has recorded the search for stability and lifting power. For Australian Lawrence Hargrave this led to the revolutionary invention of the cellular kite. Hargrave's search for a kite that would lift a man was not a new goal; in fact, the Chinese succeeded at that centuries ago. Nor was the principle that the power of two superposed planes is greater than that of a single larger plane his own discovery. The combination of goal and structure did, however, lead him to a unique solution.

Some work suggested that horizontal planes stacked vertically might develop substantial lift in the face of wind, and it was later reasoned that spaces between those surfaces could make such machines even more efficient. Hargrave added the essential element; vertical planes connecting the horizontals. The result was Hargrave's box kite, and the start of cellular kite construction.

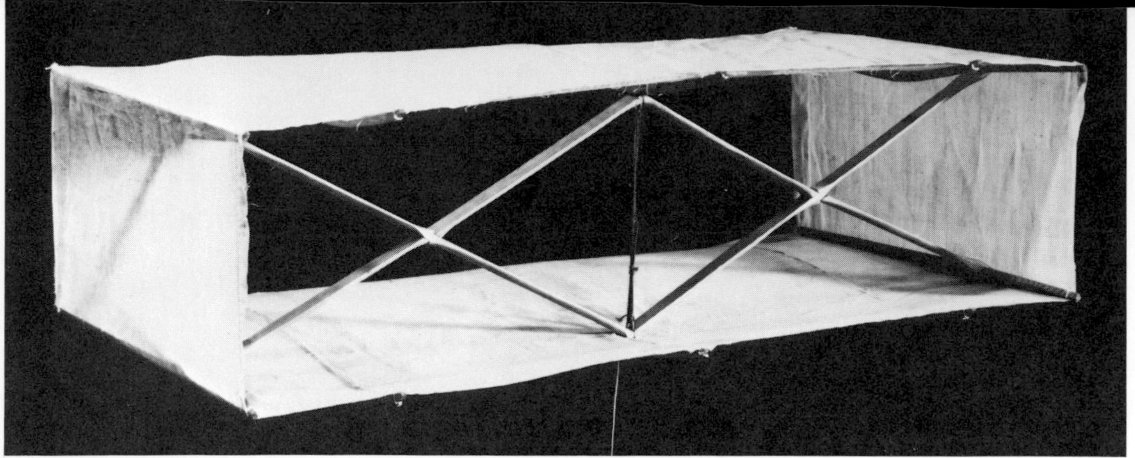

Hargrave's reflex curve kite was one of many he designed to test the effect of cambered lift surfaces on kite flight. Braces for the leading plane (inside the kite cell) and braces for the top surface are all curved so that the wind forces both planes to assume curved rather than flat postures. Hargrave's experiments along this line can readily be compared to the work of early airplane designers who tested many designs for celled wings of different camber before discovering the best combinations of curve, reinforcement, and power source. Lent to the Science Museum, London, by Mrs. Lacey.

The Skyscraper® box kite designed by the Airplane Kite Company is constructed of ⅛″ wooden dowels and Tyvek. Because the kite is extremely light, the comparatively small lifting surfaces are more than ample. The construction technique, clearly visible here, shows how easily a light kite can be built. Four spines are braced in each cell by two crosspieces. The Tyvek coverings were taped together and then were taped to the frame. Courtesy: Airplane Kite Company.

Six Skyscraper kites of wooden dowel and Tyvek were tied together to create this compound multicellular kite. The addition of single cells is the easiest way to create a large structure such as this one, but it is not the most efficient kite. Since the inside walls and spines are all doubled, the kite is carrying excessive weight—it still flies, though, and for ease of assembly and transportation the method is great.

BOX KITES

The basic box kite (see Chapter 3) has a rigid frame and a covering of paper or cloth. It is a totally rigid structure. Not only is the frame entirely solid, but internal supports, too, are solidly lashed and glued in. One variety, whose construction is described in Chapter 3, shows the use of four separate panels which may then be assembled by tying at four points and adding structural supports of cord. The truly collapsible box usually has four rigid spines and internal supports that are hinged so that these dowels can be pressed together and the whole apparatus slipped into a tube.

Construction of the rigid kite is elementary. After the frame has been lashed and glued together, covering material is glued or sewn on. For a nonrigid kite, begin with two strips of covering material. The fabric or paper should be long enough to cover all four sides of the intended box, and it should be as wide as you want each cell to be. In the standard design, the covering strip for each cell will be four times as long as it is wide. With each unit complete, the problem is how to keep the kite rigid. One viable solution calls for the use of flexibly joined wood Xs. Tack together two pieces of wood at their centers with a small wire brad so that they can swivel at that point. Each piece of wood should be as long as the diagonal of the cell. Make four of these cross units, and notch the end of each stick so that the spines will fit in snugly. The structure can be reinforced and firmed with cord and adhesive tape. Check the alignment to make certain that everything is square—then bridle and fly.

Box kites can be easily lashed together to create huge structures. At least one modern sculptor and Japanese kitemaster, Tsutomu Hiroi, has experimented with multicelled box kites. Even as individual kites, box kites have been made very large. The U.S. Weather Bureau used wood-framed cloth-covered kites for years to hoist instruments and cameras. Countless daredevils ascended on trains of box kites. And, importantly, many airplane designers took inspiration from this and the cambered box kites that Hargrave also designed.

Weather bureau kites of the design used early in this century provided meteorologists with a ready vehicle to send instruments aloft during the years before the airplane became a practical tool. Although they were replaced as soon as air travel became feasible, the design has remained popular because of its strength and stability. Most often built with ¼″ dowels reinforced by metal and covered by weatherproof cloth, these kites harken back to an era when kites ruled the skies.

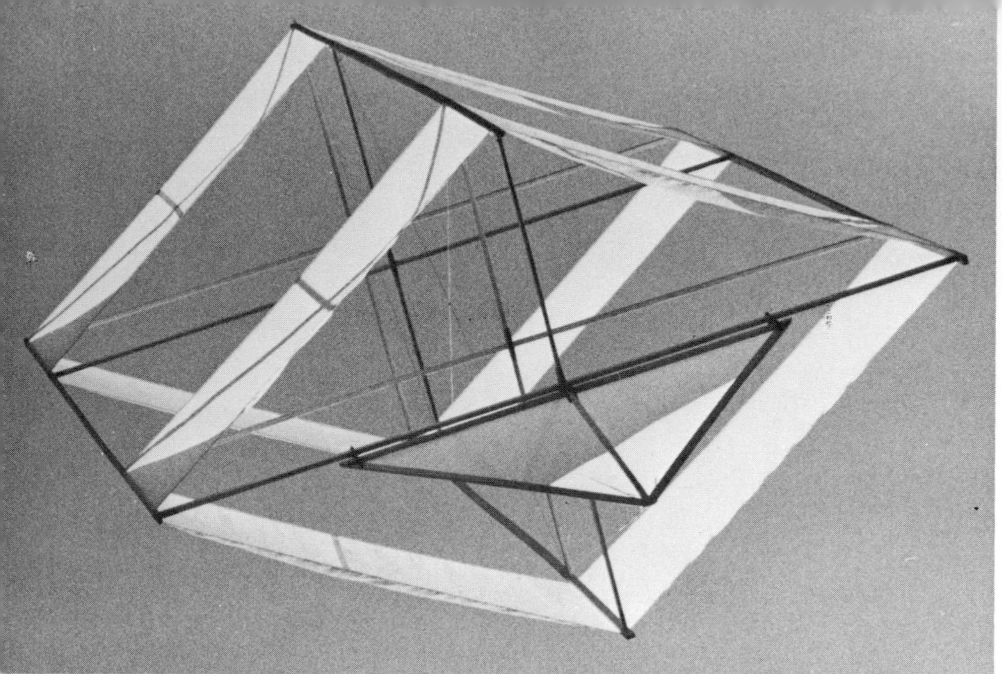

This diamond-celled box kite, viewed from behind and beneath just after launching, illustrates the use of a dihedral angle to achieve stability. The triangular rudder provides added directional steadiness and control.

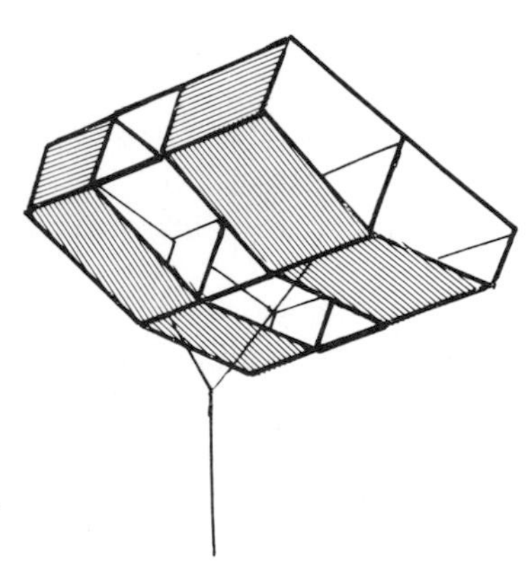

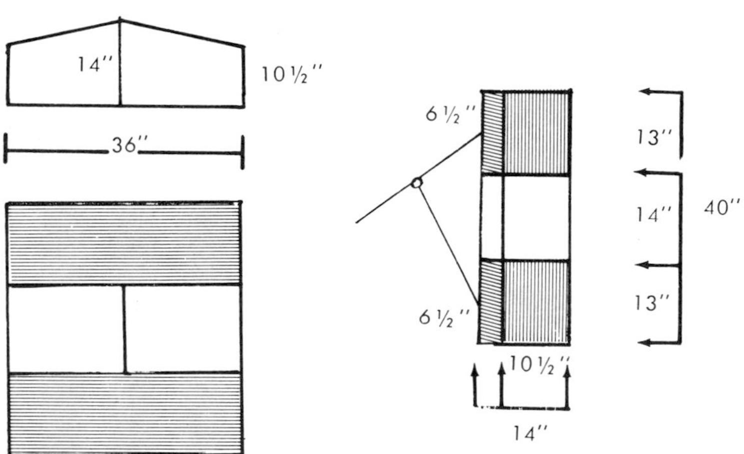

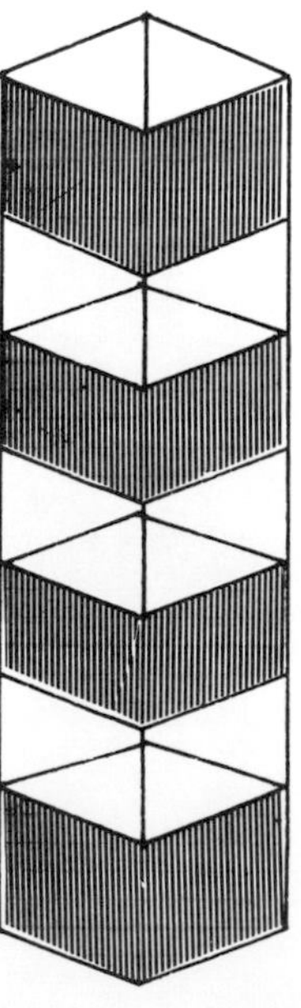

A modification of the Hargrave box kite makes use of the dihedral. By making the frame wider at the center of the cell and thereby causing the front plane to face the wind in two angled sections, you can experiment with this design tool. Different angles will, of course, result in different flight characteristics. The kite is bridled at two points: on the keel at the midpoint of each cell.

Cells can be combined in almost any configuration as long as the structure is strong. Four or forty squares can be assembled together. Where many cells are used, experiment with different methods of bridling. The larger the kite the more shroud lines will be needed to provide direction and support. An advantage of multilegged bridles over simpler versions—especially for larger kites—is that they distribute stress more evenly.

BOX KITE VARIATIONS

In addition to the rectangular celled box kite for which Hargrave is most famous, there are a number of equally skyworthy variations. A modified Hargrave, which makes use of a dihedral angle in the forward plane, has some added stability.

An important species is the stub-winged box kite. It is a standard box with wings extending diagonally from two corners. The wings provide a great deal of additional lift surface and add only a negligible amount of weight.

Besides kites in the box configuration, a number of kites have evolved which are combinations of many and often diverse cellular and lift surface elements. The navy barrage kite designed by Harry Sauls is one example. During World War II, the barrage kite was flown from ships to frustrate the attacks of dive bombers by providing interference, obscuring the ships, and making accurate aim difficult.

Hargrave himself flew a variety of kite shapes in the 1890s: circular-celled, ovate-celled, and triangular-celled kites were all sent aloft, proving the soundness of cellular structure for efficient tethered flight.

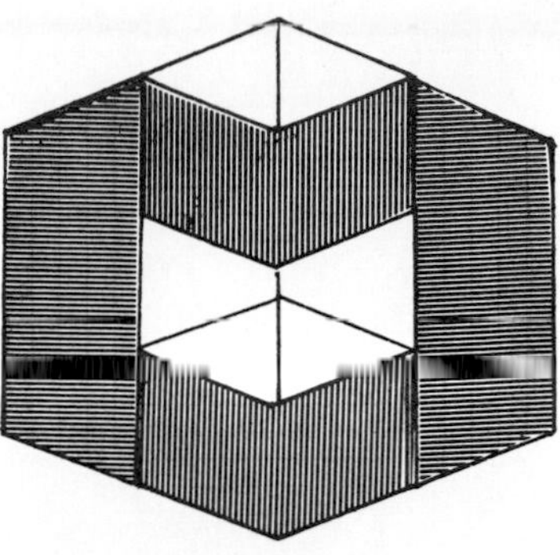

Besides using cells as elements of compound kites, wings should be combined too. In this example wings extend on the diagonal of the cell from two corners.

This variation of wing design employs two stub wings extended diagonally from the back corners of this flat-flown elongated cell box kite.

Other versions employ wings on each corner.

The naval barrage kite, designed by Harry Sauls, became a useful tool in providing interference for ships during World War II. The kite is launched here by several midshipmen at Annapolis.

This plan describes a barrage kite somewhat smaller than the original version which requires several men to launch and fly. Since the original version was meant to fly from ships at sea, weight was not a primary consideration—large size was. For land-bound fliers a smaller replica should suffice.

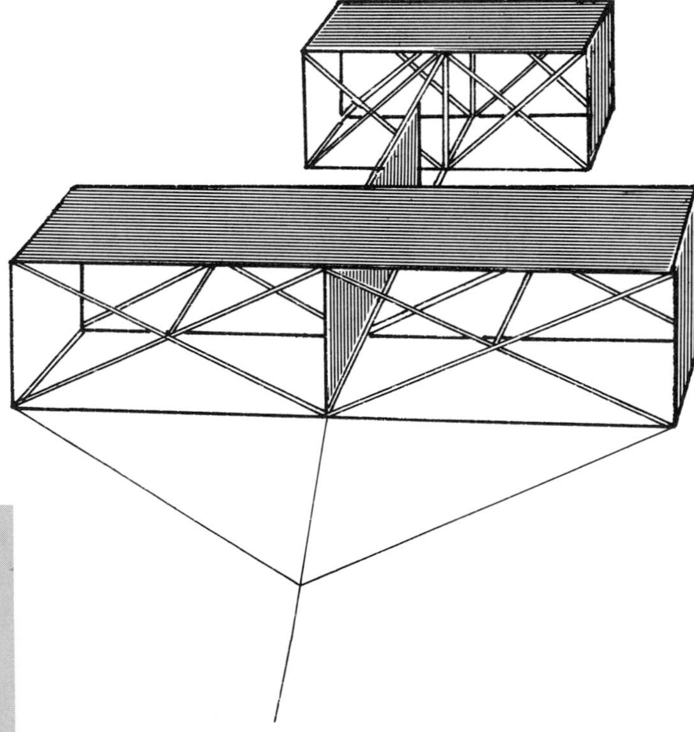

The kite, with a central panel as a type of keel, as it was flown at the Smithsonian Kite Day in Washington, D.C.

THE CONYNE KITE

Of the experiments with cells of shapes other than rectangular, only the triangular cell has survived as a viable structural unit in larger and compound kites. This kite is essentially a box kite with cells of triangles in place of squares. Compared to a box kite flown face to the wind, this kite has much less surface area, but the angled sides contribute greatly to stability. Most often, the triangular box kite is combined with other structures to create a multicelled compound kite.

The most popular form of the triangular celled compound kite is the Conyne kite or French Military kite, invented by Silas Conyne in 1902. The Conyne kite is a triangular box kite with a spar across the back to support a pair of wings. Since the stability offered by the dihedral is maintained and additional lift is supplied by the flanking wings, the Conyne is an exceptionally well-designed high flier. The French, who recognized its value, used it so much that it is now better known by its alias.

Built usually of 3/16" or 1/4" dowels, the Conyne, like the box kite, can be constructed either rigidly or nonrigidly. The most important factor for successful flight of this kite is to keep the cells open. In a rigid structure this can be achieved by inserting internal braces (or even using detachable braces for a nonrigid version). To be sure, the tendency to stay open is inherent in this design anyway, since the force of the wind against the wings pulls the back of the cell away from the keel which is attached to the flying line. Because the Conyne pulls very strongly, use a fairly heavy braided or nylon line—at least 25-pound test. Bridle the kite from the top and bottom of the keel or from the centerpoints of each cell. In a heavy wind also adjust the two-leg bridle so that the kite is angled closer to the horizontal.

Included here are some examples of variations in wing design which have been successfully developed so far. Like all cellular kites, the Conyne can be made very large and in many combinations, and the dihedral angle will always help to keep it stable and well oriented.

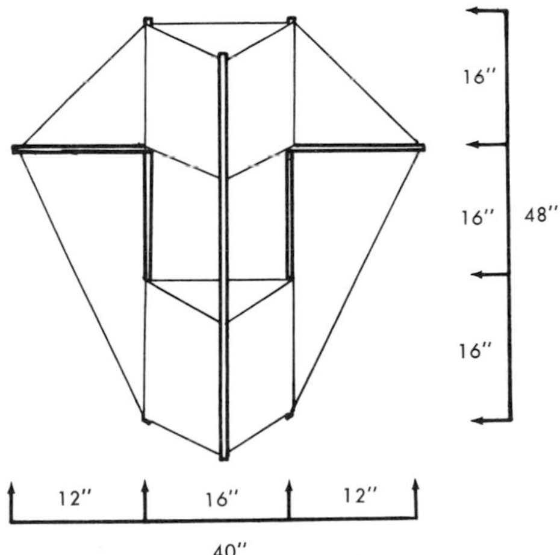

The Conyne kite, a triangular box kite with two wings added, is one of the most stable and powerful kites yet invented. Many daredevils, who sought public attention and rode to acclaim by boarding skybound kites, chose this kite as their vehicle.

Cells and wing planes can be combined in innumerable ways. Like the box kite, single triangular cells can be erected on top of one another. Two-celled kites can be bound laterally as well.

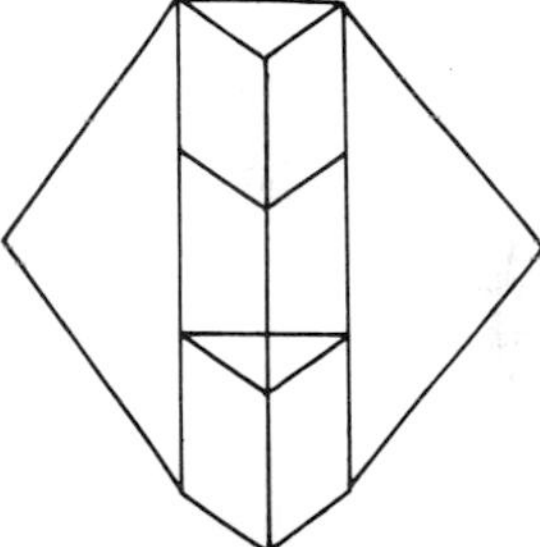

Cellular kites lend themselves to variation and the Conyne kite is no exception. Wing changes will affect flight greatly. These two suggestions are only a beginning. Many other designs have been proved successful and efficient kites—as many more remain untried. The top sketch here shows increased surface area and a slight change in shape. The bottom design carries more than a suggestion of the delta wing.

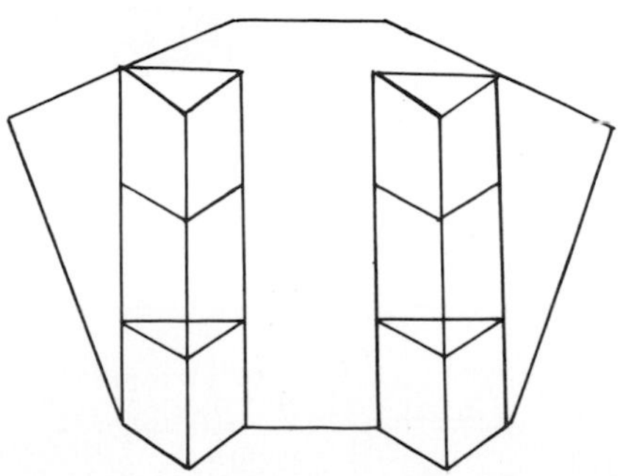

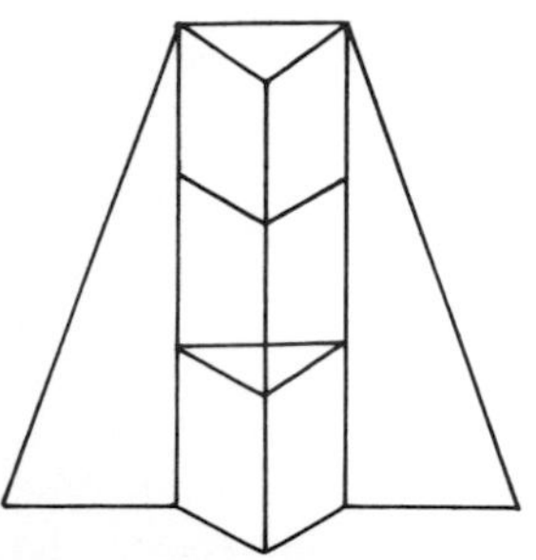

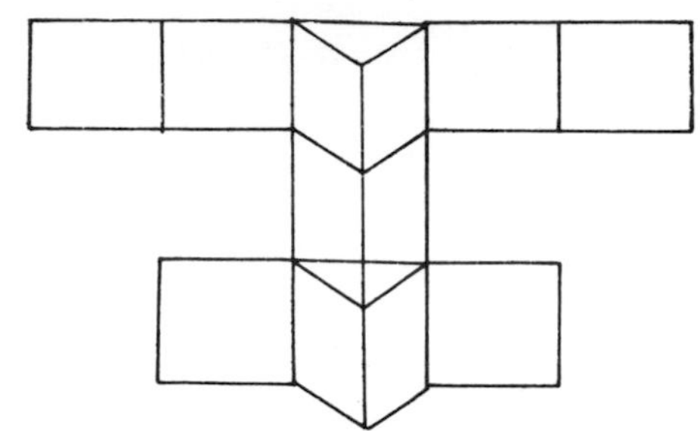

Rigid wing extensions provide even a greater lift surface by making more wind do more work.

Striegel's French military kite (or Conyne kite) is constructed of tough Tyvek and wooden dowels. The cell is kept open by opposing forces of wind against its wings and line pulling the keel earthward.

Alan-Whitney Company's Space Bird kite is a variation of the Conyne theme. The wings, instead of squared in shape, are more like real wings. The border of contrasting material under each wing flutters in the wind; the kite flies extremely well. Nylon cloth, used here, stands up well.

The Flying Man, a kite by Jean-Michel Folon, shows design possibilities. The techniques illustrated in Chapter 4 should provide other inspirations for decorating kite coverings.

TETRAHEDRAL KITES

In the early twentieth century, Alexander Graham Bell, inventor of the telephone, also experimented with kites. Bell was intrigued by the problem of manned powered flight, and he saw kites as a means toward that end. He took up where Hargrave, whose work he regarded as the "high-water mark of progress in the nineteenth century," left off. Bell felt that he needed a structure which was much more rigid, but he still sought a design that would lift a great load without being too heavy itself. The kite building unit he decided upon was the regular tetrahedron —a four-sided pyramid composed of triangles, and now considered by some scientists to be the basic structural "building block" of all matter.

Bell's tetrahedron was a regular pyramid, and each unit had four equilateral triangle sides. He covered two sides to create dihedral lift surfaces, but allowed the rest of the framework to remain open. Because of the acute angle of the lift surfaces, Bell found that a great deal of wind was required to lift this small ship, but he soon discovered that the regular nature of the tetrahedron allowed for almost infinite combinations of the elements. Since single spars could be shared by several units, the ratio of lift area to weight increased, making his kites more efficient.

Bell proceeded to construct enormous kites, the largest of which was his famed *Cygnet*. This huge cellular structure was built with the intention that it either be powered or that it be towed. Made up of over four thousand cells, it needed very heavy winds to launch it. It did fly (behind a steamer), and it even carried a man nearly two hundred feet up.

Part of the fascination of tetrahedral kites, in spite of the fact that they often require strong winds to fly, is that they are large, complex, and beautiful in flight. There is a point of diminishing return in every endeavor, however, and if your tetrahedral becomes too large it may either fly you or not fly at all.

Construction techniques for tetrahedral

kites are varied. Several companies offer kits that contain connectors, rods, and coverings, but tetrahedrals are easy to build from scratch as well. Small tetrahedral kites can be built with drinking straws. First construct individual units of six straws each, and cover two sides with tissue paper; then glue and/or lash several such units together. Especially in a larger structure, dowels should be lashed together—or you can screw small wire "eyes" into the dowels' ends and attach the units with wire. This allows a great deal of flexibility in arranging the cells, but, as your kite becomes more elaborate and weighty, it also becomes more difficult to fly.

When finally attaching the individual tetrahedral units, make certain that all the lift surfaces are facing the same direction. Bridle the kite at the top and bottom of the leading edge, and choose a breezy day for launching.

Cellular kites offer kite craftsmen—beginners and experts—such infinite variety that it is easy to become entranced (as Bell was) with the subleties and diversities of design.

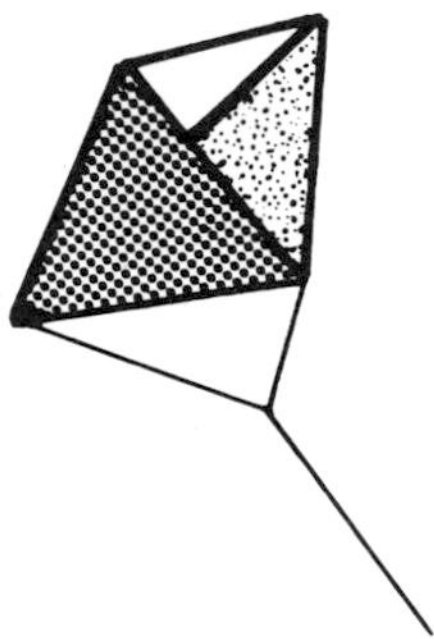

Bell chose the regular tetrahedron as his major building unit. The structure of this element, four equilateral triangles, provides great strength.

Bell experimented with many varieties of tetrahedrons before settling on the regular shape. The right-angle tetrahedron and obtuse-angled tetrahedron offer different characteristics, most notably an increase in the amount of surface area. But, since they are not regular, the possibilities of building very large structures of identical single units are forced and limited.

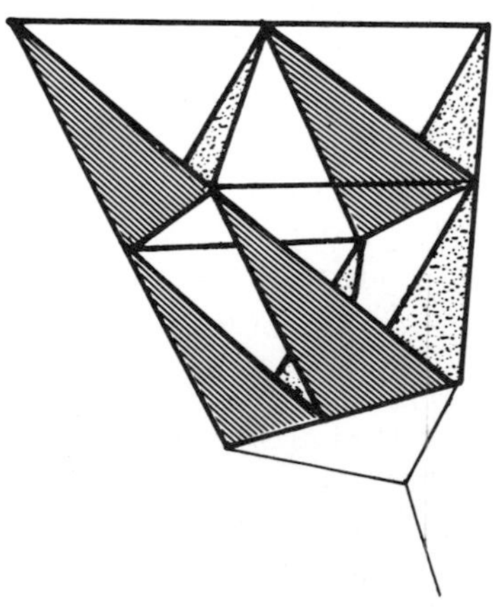

The regular tetrahedron, on the other hand, can be combined infinitely. Very large tetrahedral structures usually require heavy winds to lift them, and while Bell's 4,000-celled *Cygnet* did fly (behind a moving steamship), most kite craftsmen prefer to accept the limitations of land and work to overcome gravity within this constraint. The four-celled tetrahedron pictured here is a good starting point since it is of a manageable size. For smaller tetrahedral structures heavy frameworks are unnecessary. Ten- and sixteen-celled kites can be constructed with 5″ paper drinking straws. Larger kites can make use of thin dowels or plastic rods; the largest tetrahedral kites employ heavy wood, aluminum, or fiber glass supports.

One method of attaching supporting rods in tetrahedral kites is to screw metal eyes into the ends of the dowels. The units can then be laced together with wire. This kite was covered with white sailcloth. A single piece of diamond-shaped covering material is usually used to cover the two sides of a tetrahedral unit which act as the lift surface.

This ten-celled kite was over 8′ high.

Thin polyethylene film was stretched over fine wooden dowels in this sixteen-celled structure.

The value of plastics to the kitemaker becomes apparent when we see how light, strong, and flightworthy a kite this size can be.

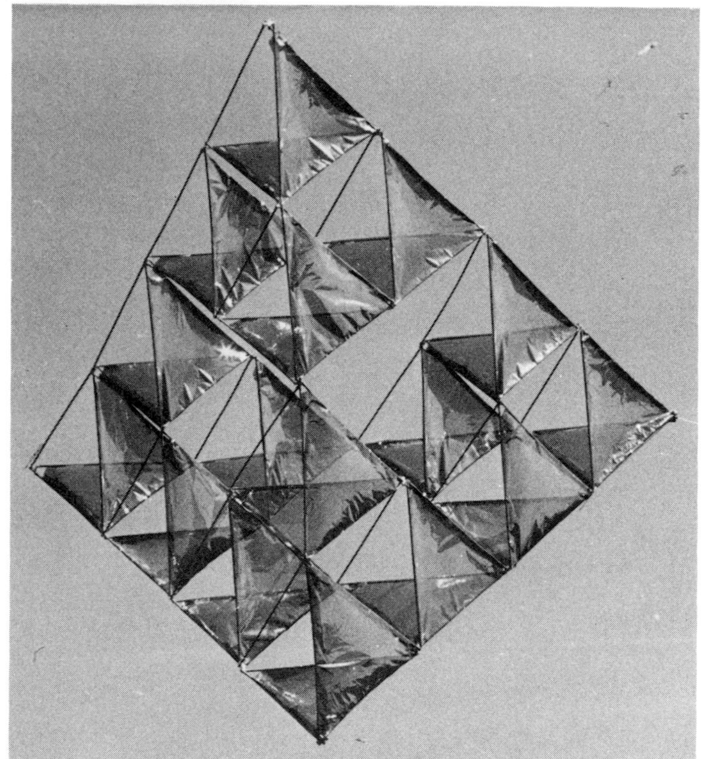

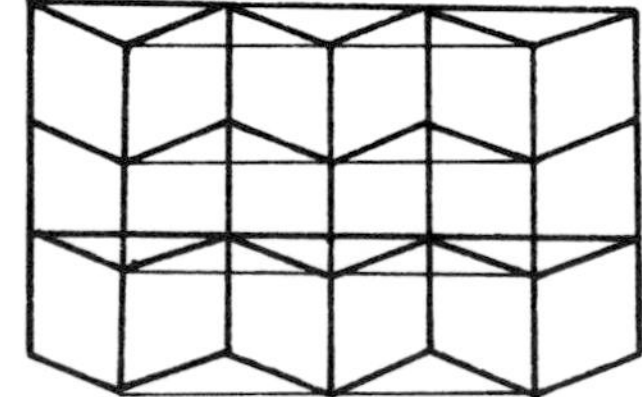

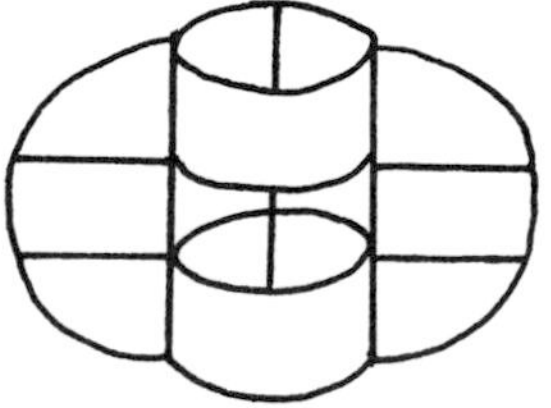

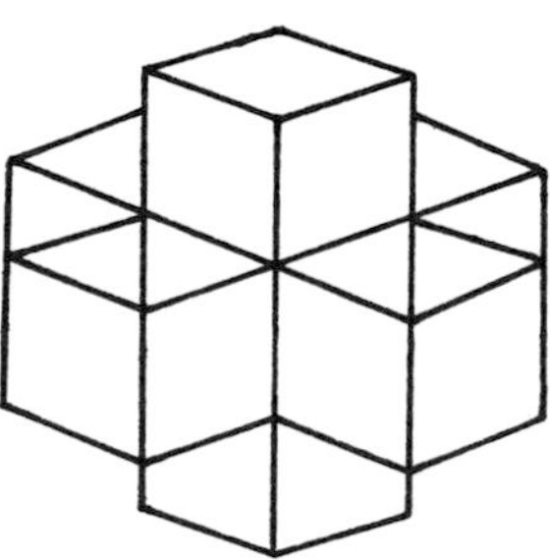

Some cell combinations vie for variety.

KITES OF THE LAST THIRTY YEARS

Chapter 7

In the past thirty years there has been a great renewal of interest in building and flying tethered aircraft in the West. Several marked advancements in kite design have resulted. The Jalbert parafoil, Rogallo parawing, Scott Sled, saillike Marconi-rigged kite, and the keel (delta wing) kites all testify to the renaissance of kite art. These advances and refinements have led modern kitemen to reevaluate parameters of kite design.

The evolution of kite form, from the first tethered palm leaf to the monstrous turn-of-the-century tetrahedral, progressed slowly with many small refinements resulting in growing sophistication. The spectacular developments of recent years are unprecedented in kite history. Hargrave's box kite was perhaps the first such innovation; the Jalbert, Rogallo, and Scott designs advanced kite construction even further.

Traditional designs persist—who can resist the joys of Indian Fighters or of a soaring Chinese bird kite—but kite design has been affected by the pace of our society. As in many other art and craft forms which have been catapulted to popularity in the leisure time '70s, progressive kitemakers seek to "explode" this craft form, experimenting at nearly every turn. Some attempts at innovation fail because they disregard the fundamentals of aerodynamics. But each attempt at creative kite design contributes positively to the medium's growth. Successful designs necessarily exhibit a keen observation of form and function enhanced by inspirations from the environment. Jalbert resolved his parafoil design in direct response to a need to lift heavy loads. His inspiration was the application of the airfoil to kite design. Similarly, the Marconi-rigged sail kite and the keel kites (the delta wing is the most popular variety of keel kite) evolved from observations of the basics of sail function. Marconi-rigged designs exhibit just how much the two wind machines (sailboat and kite) are alike. At times it seems we "sail" rather than fly some kites. The same forces of lift which cause the kite to rise also work on the ship's sails. As a result, we have in this century adopted much of the specialized jargon of sailing for kiting (spar, keel, fore and aft, mainsail), pointing out again how one air science develops another through its language, and more importantly, through its concepts. And while kite purists argue for kiting's own lingua franca (i.e., strut, camber, leading and trailing edge, stabilizer, lateral and ventral), whatever vocabulary you choose, the inspirations and relationship between sail and kite design are apparent nevertheless, particularly in the Marconi-rigged and keel kites. All are based on the sailor's and kiteman's science of how to channel the flow of air to do the work of flying.

THE KEEL KITE

One of the oldest three-dimensional kite designs, the keel kite, has been used in many forms over the centuries because of its stability.

A keel serves as a fin does—it is a sail (or kite surface) attached at right angles to the mainsail (or lifting surface). A rigid keel which has been fitted to either side of a kite channels the wind. It distributes the forces of the wind onto both halves of the lift surface, stabilizing the kite and acting as a rudder to direct the kite into the wind. The steadying power of a keel is great and can easily be

The keel is an important element in this Thai owl kite. It uses a single leg bridle from the apex of the rounded keel.

experimented with on a variety of flat kite forms.

The most elementary keel design is one fixed to the back of a flat kite. Cut a bamboo or wooden stick so that it is about one-third or one-quarter of the length of the flat kite's spine. Drill a hole at each end. On the typical flat kite, tie this stick to the point where the spine and spar intersect, making the keel stick stand out at right angles to the lift surface. Use string running from all corners of the kite to keep the keel perpendicular, passing the framing strings through the drilled hole. Cover one of the string-outlined panels with cloth, paper, or plastic material to complete the makeshift keel.

Since a keel is so easy to construct in this fashion (and is easily changed and adjusted) we recommend experimentation with several shapes and positions. If you find a certain keel size or placement particularly significant for a particular design, you may decide to affix a more permanent keel using sewn cloth and tape, as shown in the delta wing design. But the keel must be a significant contributor to steadiness of the kite in flight, or else it is excess baggage. Be careful not to make it too big (and weighty).

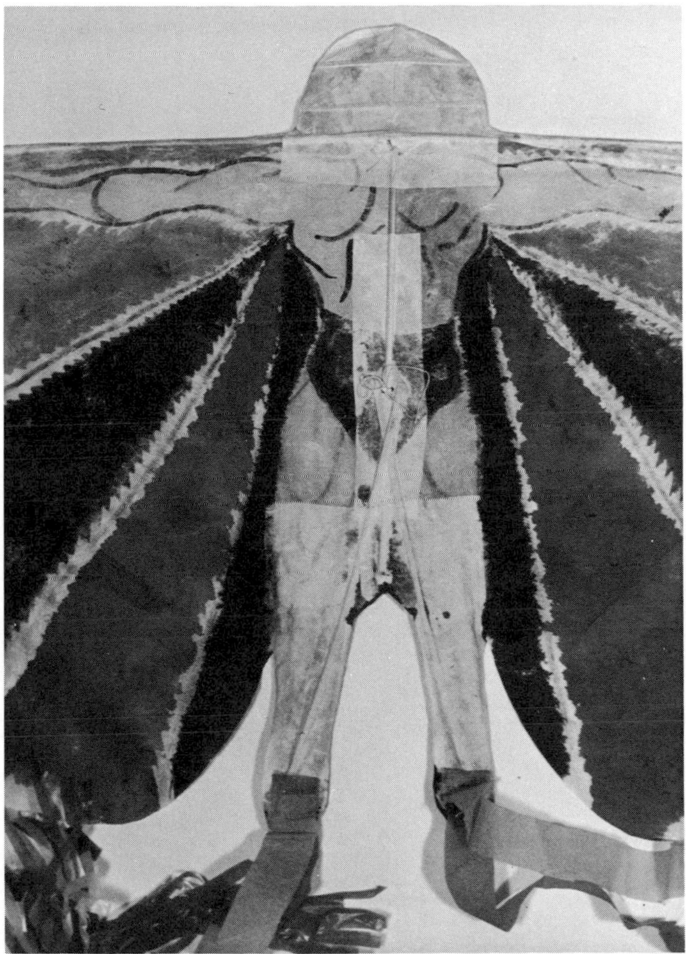

A view of the back of the Thai man kite shows how dowels are held in place in a sandwich of paper. The paper not only binds the spars but adds extra reinforcement for the paper face as well.

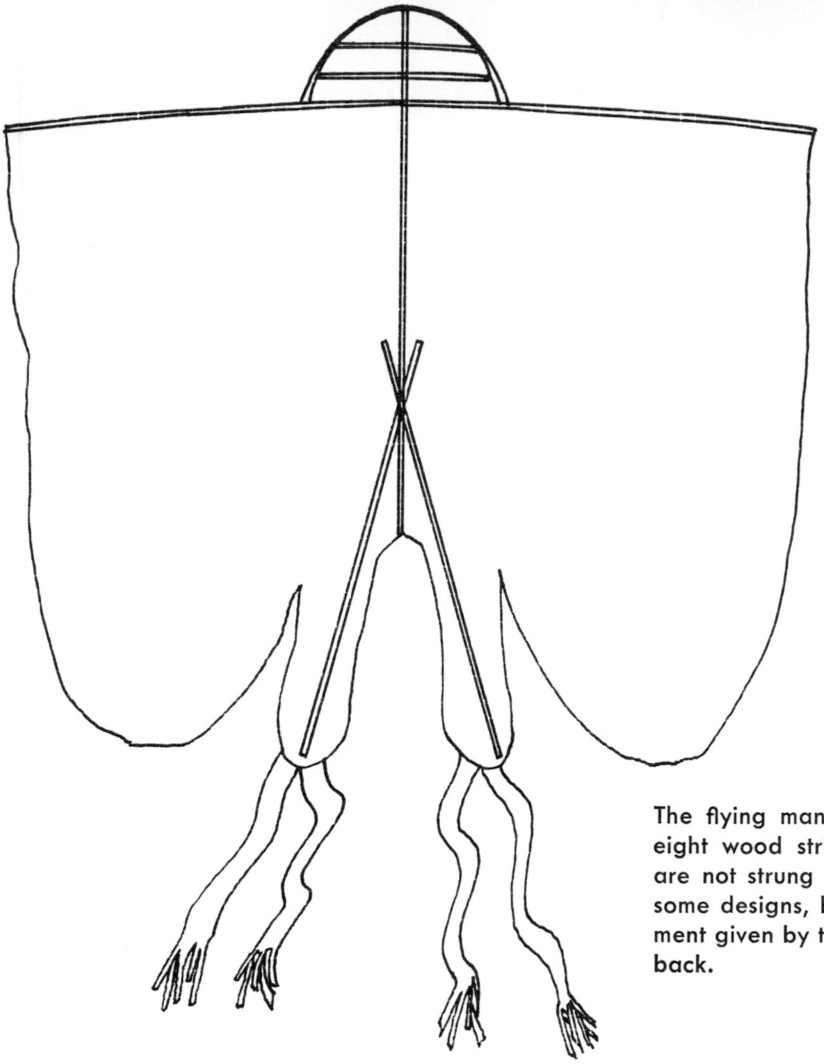

The flying man's framework consists of eight wood strips. The legs and wings are not strung with outlining cord as in some designs, because of the reinforcement given by the extra papering on the back.

The flat face of this traditive Thai kite is bisected by a keel. The crepe paper tails are shredded at the ends. The keel offers the additional lateral stability required by kites with broad wingspans.

Another keel kite design. This kite, spotted during a kite fly in New York's Central Park, has a pair of sails and many "flags" on its back side for decoration. The keel on the underside is the one that really does the work. Because of the lightness of materials and efficiency of the keel design, this kite can afford the extra weight on its back side.

DELTA WING KITE

Today's most popular version of the keel kite, the delta wing, is a modern adaptation of the traditional keel concept. Commercially quite successful, this kite design, related to the Valkyrie kite designed by Nantucket kiteman Al Hartig, is a steady, high-flying kite.

As the kite manufacturers have demonstrated, the delta wing kite can be made out of sheet plastic, but this version is more difficult to control. The delta wing is best made of cloth. As long as the proportions are maintained, the delta wing can be made almost any size. Using heavier weights of cloth, line, wood, or bamboo (and even aluminum rods), the delta wing has been successfully flown in towering sizes reminiscent of the Japanese Hamamatsu festivals.

Variations on the basic design have generally been only minor changes like flattening the nose to make the kite more trapezoidal than triangular. The kite requires (if properly measured and balanced) only a single bridle line extending from the keel.

Dan Lirot recommends the use of 1/4″ diameter wood dowel rods for the spine and the wingspars; a crosswing spar of 5/16″ wooden dowel; 1/16″ diameter steel wire to be used for the 6″ long hook on the cross brace; and #25 line for flying the kite. You may choose to use a heavier line according to flying conditions, but for a high flier the delta wing has surprisingly light pull (because of a low flight angle).

Begin by cutting the cloth larger than the final dimensions of the kite. To guarantee that both halves of the mainsail (on either side of the keel) will be identical in shape and size, fold the cloth and then cut it doubled. Also cut the keel cloth to size. Sew hems on all the edges of the keel cloth.

With the mainsail cloth doubled along the proposed central keel line, draw a line 3/4″ in from the kite center running from leading to trailing edge. Sew a straight seam along this line to form a sleeve for the spine dowel. Sew the keel to the kite on this center line, placing it 7″ down from the kite nose.

To create sleeves on both wings for the side spars, open the kite flat on the table with the keel side face down. Draw lines 1 1/2″ in from each wing edge. Fold, then sew a seam on each side so the spars can be slipped in and secured. Use tape to form sleeves in the plastic version of the delta wing.

Slide the two 36″ spars and 33″ spine into their respective sleeves. Tape the lower ends of the three sleeves so that the dowels will not slip out. Each spar and the spine should sit firmly against the trailing edge of the kite. Either staple or sew shut the cloth sleeves at the upper end to lock the dowels in place.

Measure 19 1/2″ from the nose of the kite along each wing. At that point attach cloth tape to serve as reinforcement for eyelets. (This is the point where the cross-spar will be attached to the back side of the kite.) Sink eyelets through tape and cloth as shown. Make two eyelet holes in each wing if you plan to just tie the spar in place. But if you plan to make small wire hooks for the cross-spar, only one eyelet in each wing is needed.

To make the hook, saw a ⅛″ deep notch in each end of the 5⁄16″ thick dowel. Shape two wire hooks as illustrated. They are held in place at each end of the dowel by the sawed notch and by lashing with string or thinner wire.

Insert the hooked cross-spar into the eyelets on the wings by slight bowing. If not using the hook, simply lash the stick in place with thin wire or line through the pairs of grommets.

Use tape to reinforce the protruding tip of the keel and then punch an eyelet at this bridling point. (You should also insert one or two more grommets above and below the one at the immediate apex, in case of a need to adjust flying angles.)

The kite, completed, will not be entirely rigid in flight. Known to float gracefully and to shift ground in rising gusts, a properly weighted and balanced delta wing is a lively flier. This size flies particularly well in 10+ mph winds.

The kite should weigh about five ounces; it relies heavily on precision of wing dimensions.

If the kite is too heavy for the day's wind, it can be expected to dive. It will also nose-dive if the wings are not of equal size.

To correct minor imbalances in the lifting surface, add and subtract small strips of tape or staples from the wing tips. If the kite moves to the right, either add tape to the left, or else slide the right wing's dowel upward in its sleeve by about one inch, restapling it in place.

To fly the delta wing kite you should not have to run. With about thirty-pound test line attached from the keel, the delta wing can be easily hand-tossed into the wind.

In flight the delta wing's wings will fill out, removing any minor slack in the cloth or plastic. The cross-spar will rise a few inches above the spine. The product is a combination airfoil and billowing sail.

Dan Lirot markets plans for his 30′ wingspan "dilta" wing kite (Kyte Specialties Co.). It carries the figure of a giant dill pickle here in observance of National Pickle Week. The delta wing is of such stable dimensions that it lends itself to construction in nearly any size—if you've got the wind to lift it. Courtesy: Kite Tales.

The delta wing kite is the most popular version of the keel kite. The chevron shape makes it a delight for the creative kite face decorator, too. This delta wing was built by Hod Taylor. Courtesy: Hod Taylor.

The delta wing is an isosceles triangle with a keel bisecting the lifting surface, beginning at the trailing edge and ending a few inches from the leading tip. Two options for attaching the cross-spar are shown in the details flanking the main diagrams. Taping is recommended in the plastic version, while sewing the sleeves and hems is advisable when using cloth. Courtesy: Dan Lirot.

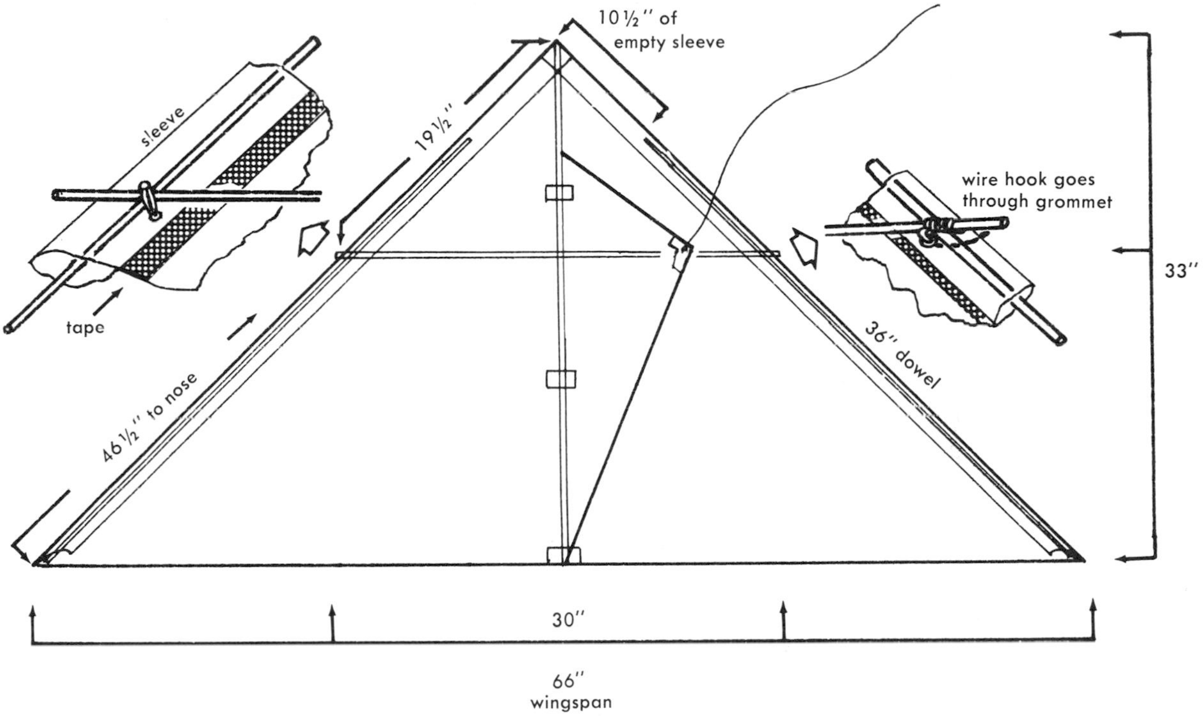

10½″ of empty sleeve
sleeve
19½″
tape
46½″ to nose
wire hook goes through grommet
36″ dowel
33″
30″
66″ wingspan

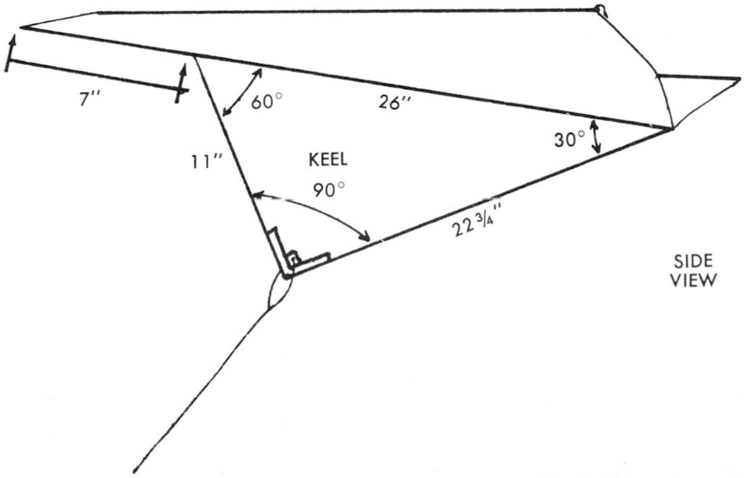

7″
60°
26″
30°
11″
KEEL
90°
22¾″
SIDE VIEW

THE MARCONI-RIGGED SAIL KITE

The so-called Marconi-rigged sail kite goes a step beyond the simple keel kite in applying sail concepts to kite design. Early seamen used the simplest form of sail—one broad surface for the wind to blow against. Later, keels were added to provide maneuverability against the direction of the wind. The aerodynamic efficiency of the single sail was later improved again with the advent of a second forward sail or jib. The jib itself is quite an efficient airfoil, but also creates a "slot" effect of directing wind behind the mainsail and thereby producing greater lift through improved airflow.

In the 1940s a series of kites using the jib principle, based on the Marconi-rigged yacht, and pioneered by W. M. Angas, became popular. The jibs on the kite can be adjusted separately allowing for precise balancing. In a strong wind, as when sailing, the kiteman can set tighter jibs. In light wind, the loosened jib will luff, fill out with wind, and give the kite remarkable lift.

The framework of the Marconi is minimal: two wooden dowels of 54″ and 72″ (spine and spar, respectively) intersect at their midpoints. A third dowel, one foot long, stands perpendicular to the spar and spine at this intersection, serving as part of the keel. The spine is bowed back 3″. The spar should be bowed back 6″.

Fit the cloth keel (cut to the size diagrammed) to the back of the kite along the top half of the spine using the 12″ dowel as the "mast" of the keel. This keel mast is steadied by the two bowstrings of spine and spar intersecting through sawed notches in the stick's end. The cloth keel will stand between the two jibs, directing the wind behind the mainsail.

Cut and sew hems into the triangular mainsail and two triangular jibs to dimensions shown. Thread all three sides of the mainsail with cord. The three corded corners are tied to their appropriate dowel ends with the mainsail passing not in front but *behind* the dowels. A cord is tied from the intersection of spar and spine to the bottom of the spine behind the mainsail to keep the sail in shape under wind pressure.

The mainsail covers the bottom half of the kite; the jibs form the adjustable leading edges. The small V cut out of the top of the mainsail is to facilitate tying of the mainsail to the intersection of spine and spar, giving it the proper shape. Jibs are also threaded and tied to the appropriate spar and spine ends, but *not* to the intersection of the two—the jibs are drawn *in front* of the spar and tied through a hole which must be drilled through the spine about six inches below the intersection. Tie the jibs at this special hole in the spine, using a bowknot to facilitate the adjustment of jib slack.

Bridle the Marconi from both ends of the spar, the top of the spine, and 13½″ from the bottom of the spine.

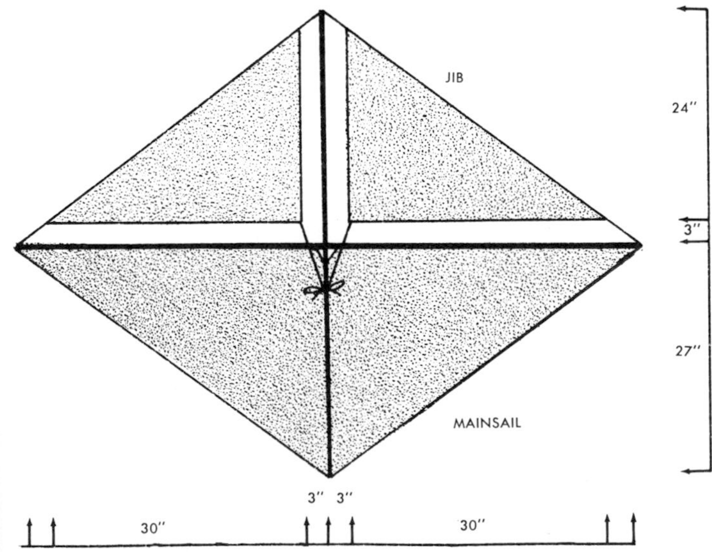

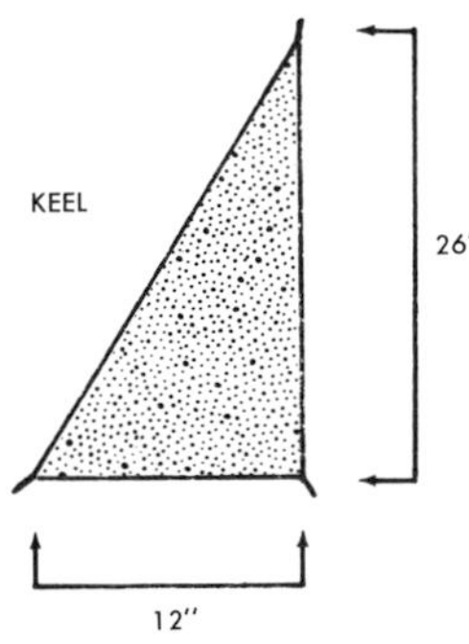

The Marconi-rigged sail kite employs two jibs and a keel to guide air to the mainsail. The keel is fixed to the back of the kite between two jibs which form the leading edge.

KEEL

12″

JIBS

CROSS SECTION

The spine is bowed back 3″, and the spar is bowed back 6″. The keel is erected from the cross section of the two sticks, and its dowel "mast" is held in place by the bowstrings (dotted line).

One variety of the Marconi-rigged sail kite.

Art Kurle built this four-masted schooner of Styrofoam® brand plastic foam, spruce, and Mylar, employing the same functional sail elements of jib (at front), mainsails (four), and keel (or rudder).

Notice the detail in the spruce framework and suspension lines.

The thin Styrofoam keel was covered with Mylar and painted in two colors.

The four-masted schooner soared well above the trees for a clear view of Washington, D.C., and the Smithsonian Institution behind it. Each successive jib or sail feeds air to the next sail.

Virginia-based sculptor Charles Henry said he had to first master some important sail concepts before developing this highly sophisticated and aesthetically pleasing white sail kite.

The framework is of fiber glass rods lashed and glued with strips of fiber glass cloth dipped in polyester resin. The sailcloth is Zephyrlite.

An efficient medium to higher wind flier, this kite was also built with a detachable bowed rudder/tail.

THE PARAWING

"Let the kite conform to the wind, not the wind to the kite," says Dr. Francis Rogallo who in 1943 introduced a kite that could assume different shapes and positions depending upon wind conditions—a kite with no rigid spars or spines, almost as light as air. The parawing kite offered kitemakers a needed transfusion in both kite construction and the philosophy of kite design.

Rogallo, who has had a major role in the National Aeronautics and Space Administration (NASA) space program, created in 1948 what he deemed his first completely successful flexible kite; he received a patent for the Flexi-kite® in 1951. But innovation in this flexible wing design was not to end there—others have found myriad applications for this kite in transportation, kiting, sports, and more.

The parawing kite is a lifting surface with "a parachute-like tension structure in which the wing surface is shaped and maintained by the balance of forces between the airload on the surfaces and the tension in the suspension lines," Rogallo explains. Not only is the kite putting wind to work in creating lift, but the kite also calls on the wind to give this airfoil its essential shape against the resistance of carefully placed bridle lines.

Being entirely flexible, the parawing is essentially indestructible. Having nothing about it which can snap or lose shape, and being so remarkably light, the kite can rise on some of the lightest drafts or in the heaviest winds without fear of breakage. Fascinating in its purity of design and in its appreciation of how to "use" the wind, the parawing defined a new direction in kite design and construction.

The key to the parawing design lies in the bridling. The bridle (shroud) lines maintain a vertical fold in the center of the kite which serves as a central keel—if this slight keel were lost, the kite would become flaccid. This fold, preserved by the force of the wind against the taut lines, serves then as a spine would, only without the use of any rigid supports.

The way in which the *wings* of the parawing are bridled resembles the use of "laterals" in some other contemporary kites—an application of the keel concept as a funneler of wind onto the main lift surfaces.

First used as a toy, the parawing has remained high in kitefliers' esteem and has found its way into the glider/parachute field as well. Ryan and North American, two U.S. aircraft corporations, have considered the Rogallo design for manned craft. Ryan used the Rogallo design in an experimental "Fleep" (flying jeep) which lifts loads up to one thousand pounds short distances over uneven, difficult terrain. In larger applications such as this, the parawing is modified with some rigid supports (more like the delta wing) and is given more elaborate bridling. Sometimes the necessary rigid members are just inflated tubes of flexible plastic, which retain the essentially flexible qualities of minimal weight and minimal structural limitations. The U.S. Army has investigated the design's potential for air delivery of cargo and equipment, too. And NASA, working with North American, developed the Gemini paraglider from the parawing.

A sport now favored by an increasing number of people—hang gliding—also relies on the parawing as a stable glider.

Thomas H. Purcell, Jr., who designed a small Flightsail glider from the Rogallo form, shares honors with Ryan's Flexi-wing plane as producer of one of the first man-carrying flexible wings. He has been researching the parawing for over a decade. Designs include a flying boat with portable flexi-wing. He hopes to soon complete a powered flexible-wing boat, too. Others inspired by the flexible concept have dreams of a flying sports car. Who could have predicted these possibilities would emerge from a simple kite—the first was made of a potato chip bag!

The true parawing is 15 to 20 inches square, and the recommended material is Mylar. With a cool iron, the Mylar can be creased diagonally to form the center keel. Mylar is strong, and bridle lines will not tear it easily. You may choose to reinforce the Mylar with tape and grommets or, if using cloth, reinforce with hems and grommets.

If working with cloth, begin by hemming a 16″ square with a ½″ hem on each side to form a 15″ square kite. Attach shroud lines as indicated. The parawing will seek a flying angle of about fifteen degrees. It hand launches easily and flies on 10- to 15-pound test line. It is not a high-altitude kite.

To increase the dimensions of the parawing you may have to experiment with rigid spines and extra shroud lines, and also add a tail. The tail is essential to most parawing designs, particularly in high winds. The parawing has little drag and comparatively little lift; it is therefore very sensitive to size and length of the tail. To find the best length and shape requires experimentation. Begin with a tail 30″ long, 1″ wide, attached on a 10″ line from the trailing edge of the kite fold.

Whatever your choice in adapting, altering, and manipulating the design, you will find best results if you bear in mind the essential philosophy of the parawing design: "Let the kite conform to the wind and not the wind to the kite."

Dr. Francis Rogallo's parawing, one of *the* kite design breakthroughs of the twentieth century, was tested along the shores of Chesapeake Bay. Courtesy: Kite Tales.

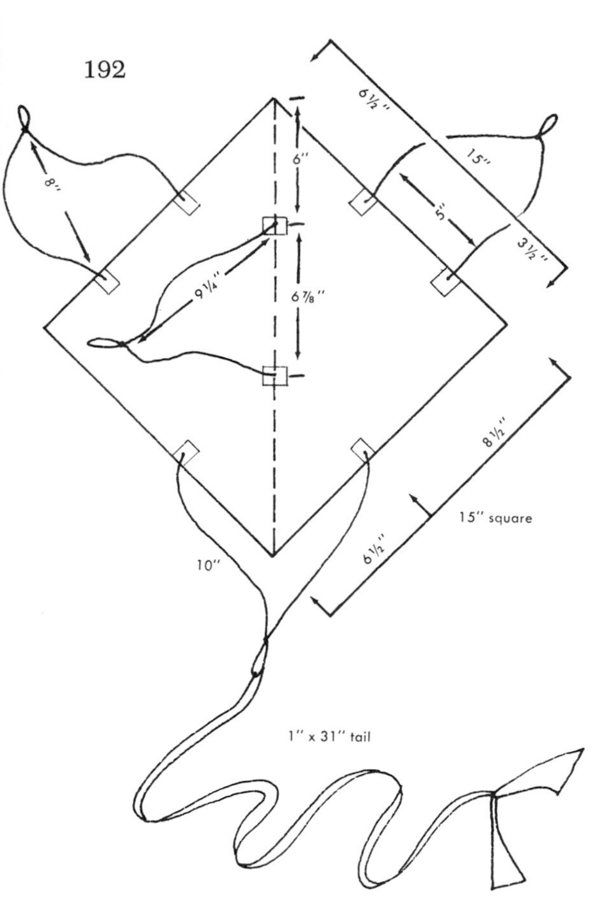

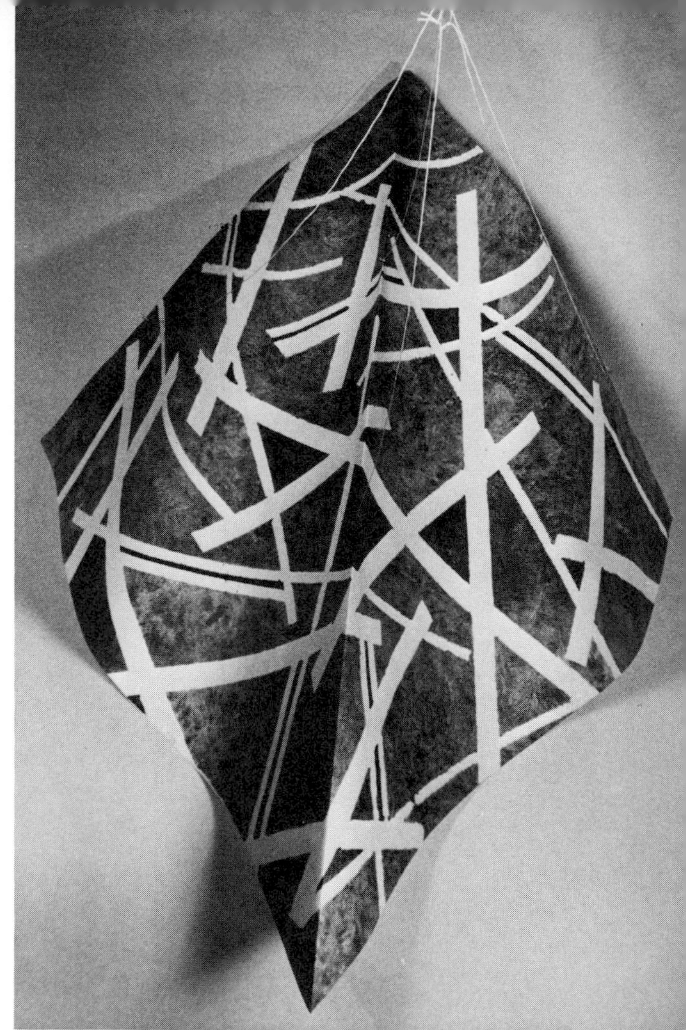

A modified parawing kite is 15′ square with a fold along the diagonal. Bridling is of primary importance.

A rectangular version of Rogallo's flexible kite.

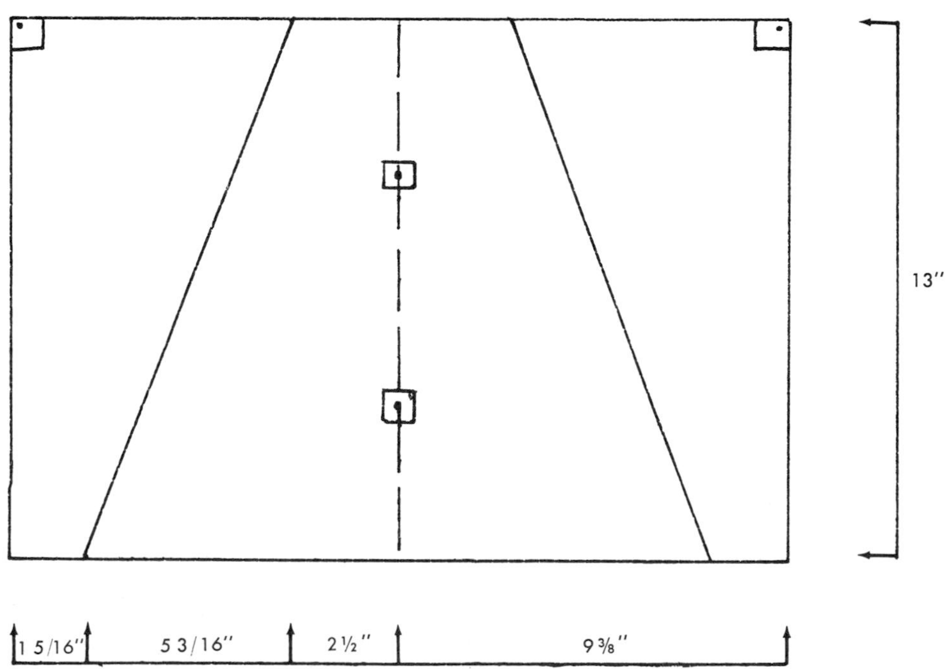

Man-lifters like the paraglider are modifications of the parawing. Because of the increased size of these "kites," it is necessary to include some rigid supports. The original Rogallo design, however, is free of any nonflexible components. Courtesy: Kite Tales.

MODIFIED PARACHUTE KITE

Following Rogallo's lead in using wind to give shape to kites, many others have adapted air devices to kiting.

Ted Maciag of El Paso, Texas, for example, is one kiteman who makes parachutes into flexible fliers. Huge kites using 2.25-ounce ripstop nylon with 21 suspension lines and no rigid braces are flown in flatlands using nylon "kite string" of 5,000-pound test.

"My original rig was constructed as a parachute," Maciag explains, "It had been jumped about a dozen times when I retrimmed it so it would fly as a kite. Those first flights were wild. It pulled an iron pole sunk three feet into the ground loose and dragged the pole and 500 pounds of concrete across the ground for a quarter of a mile before we could stop it." Maciag testifies to the power of bridled wind. He uses a drogue with the parachute design and has plans for adding extra control lines to the wing tips to see if he can make the parachute maneuver as the smaller Rogallo design kite does. But, for now, Maciag's particular parachute kite requires three people to launch it—one on the line, two on the canopy—and once it starts up nothing can stop it. "One of the launchers held onto the line and was lifted fifteen feet off the ground before he dropped off," Maciag observes—returning us to the era of the man-lifting tethered aircraft when the layman found out that not all kites were backyard toys. "Save this one for us old kids," Maciag advises.

Several serious kitemen, including Dave Williams of Kentucky, modify regulation size parachutes so they perform as kites. Spectacular fliers, yes, but powerful and dangerous too. Williams tied off six of the shroud lines and attached them to a 15-lb. weight to act as a stabilizer for this kite he modified in 1968. Courtesy: Kite Tales.

Ted Maciag's modified USAF parachute kite requires two men to hold the "wings" and one man to man the line for launch. Courtesy: E. Maciag.

Up, up, and away. Maciag says, "Better save this for us old kids." Courtesy: E. Maciag.

THE SCOTT SLED

Frank Scott's kite design follows the path of Rogallo's breakthrough. The Scott Sled is similar to the parawing in its escape from rigid lateral support and its reliance upon the wind for its shape. It does, however, use either two or three thin dowels across the main lifting surface. The Scott Sled, while relying on some of the principles already revealed by Rogallo, also employs the vent as a flying tool. The three-foot Scott Sled with a triangular vent in the lower half of the lift surface defies major changes in design—it is so reliable a flier. Some versions of the sled have been made with differently shaped vents, and even without vents. But if a Scott Sled is flown in a high wind without the vent, it is liable to begin to rudely loop and slip to a lower altitude. The sled flies best in light steady winds and rises nicely, responding to thermals. It can fly sometimes at as high an angle as 50 to 60 degrees.

A light .0015 weight of polyethylene found in department and hardware stores is a recommended covering material for the sled. It is easily cut with a sharp knife or razor blade and, if taped at all bridling points and along the exposed edges, will prove quite durable in light and medium winds. Cloth, Tyvek, and Zephyrlite are all good choices for the Scott Sled, too.

The spines should be ⅛″ birch dowels for the standard size sled. The entire kite may be made from one piece of fabric, but you may also choose to use three pieces of material in making the rectangular lift surface and the two triangular ventrals.

As in other canopy kites, much of the Scott Sled's success depends upon the bridling. Here, where there are only two bridle legs (coming from the tips of the two ventrals) the important factor is making the bridle lines sufficiently long. The sled's single drawback is that when the wind drops or it is hit by a crosswind, the kite will fold up. Unless it catches another wind gust, it will sink to the ground like a falling leaf. If the bridle lines are too short, the sled will have an even more difficult time recovering in the event of a fresh wind gust. If the sled is too short, the ventrals will flatten together. If too long, however, the bridle lines will permit the ventrals to flare and result in the loss of directional stability. When the bridling is correct, even if the sled occasionally folds up, it will usually recover.

For the standard size sled, 15-pound test line is sufficient. It is recommended that the line be braided, not monofilament.

As you might suspect, from the collapsibility of the Scott Sled, it is, when you begin, an idiosyncratic kite to fly. But the sled shortly becomes a fast favorite. A tip on flying: Don't be frustrated by launching, because once you have got the sled past the low altitudes it will climb steadily. Just beware never to give it unrestricted slack. Feed as much line as it will draw without beginning to luff (flap). If you feed too much line, the immediate tendency is for the sled to fold up and sink. The usual flying angle is around 35 to 45 degrees. Launching is most easily accomplished in the single-man hand-feed way.

A Scott Sled normally doesn't require a tail, but in high winds you may choose to use one to stabilize the kite. As mentioned earlier, the standard design seems to defy major changes—but you should feel free to experiment with different styles, shapes, vents, and tails. A great challenge is to try stretching, shortening, doubling, or otherwise altering the kite's standard. The sled raises a creative challenge to kite craftsmen.

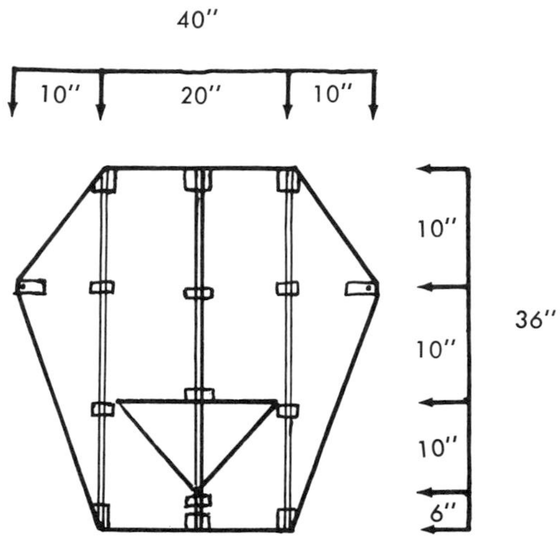

Another kite which is now commercially quite successful because it is simple and effective is the Scott Sled. The standard Scott Sled has a triangular vent in the lower half of the lift surface and has just three balsawood spines taped in place as rigid supports. Tape is also placed at points of stress and bridling.

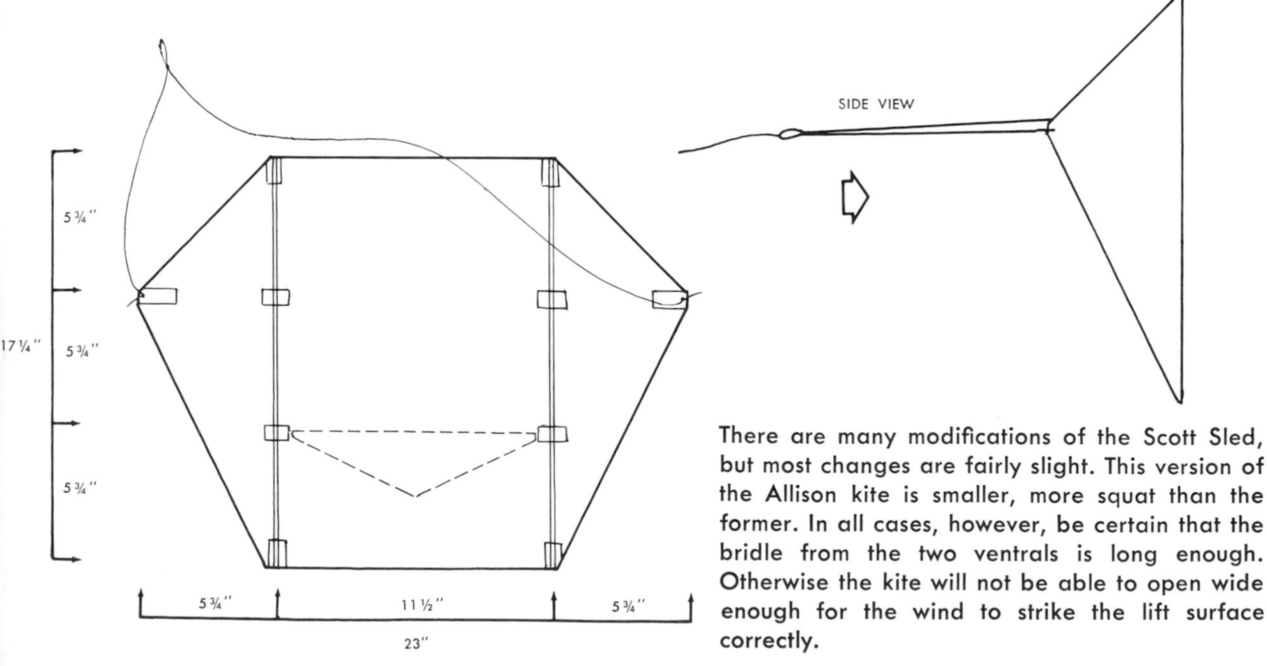

There are many modifications of the Scott Sled, but most changes are fairly slight. This version of the Allison kite is smaller, more squat than the former. In all cases, however, be certain that the bridle from the two ventrals is long enough. Otherwise the kite will not be able to open wide enough for the wind to strike the lift surface correctly.

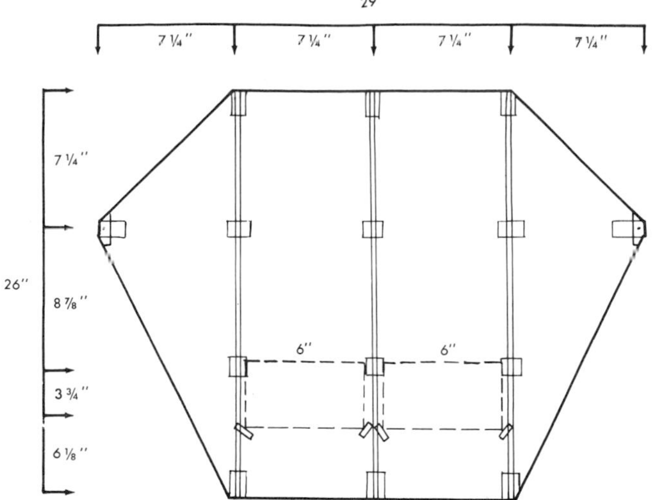

Seeking to modify the Scott Sled to fly in all winds, Kenneth and Keith Shields of Ambridge, Pa., recommend a smaller-than-standard version with rectangular vents. It is made of a 30″ x 37″ polyethylene trash bag, three balsa sticks, Mystik cloth tape, and flies with a 52″ bridle of 20-lb. test line.

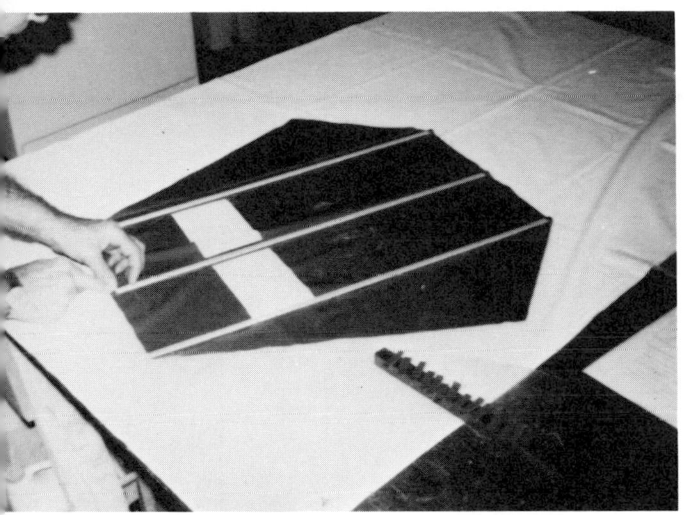

You might also like to experiment with other variations in the Allison kite genre.

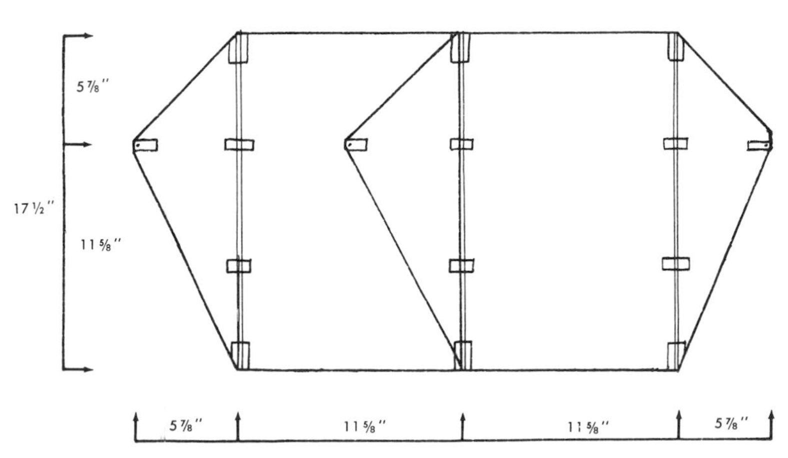

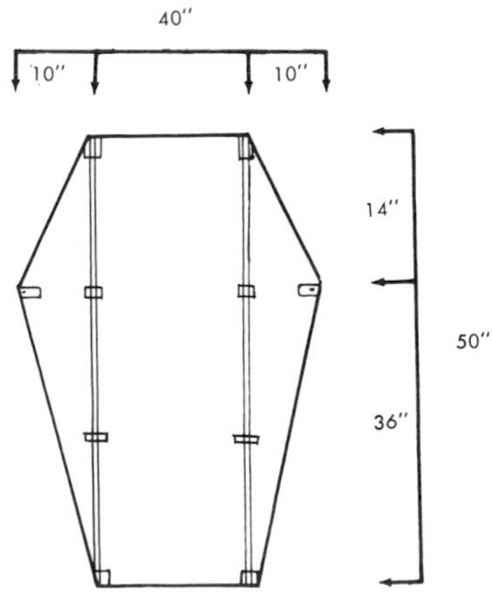

THE JALBERT PARAFOIL

In 1943, the year when Rogallo was just developing his parawing nonrigid kite design which would rely on the wind for lift and shape, Domina Jalbert was also striving to harness the energy of the wind. Throughout a long career dedicated to utilizing the wind, Jalbert had worked with balloons, kites, kite-balloons, and even parachutes. But after fifty years of aeronautical engineering and a lifetime of kiting, Jalbert had become disillusioned with the modified giant Conyne kites which he had demonstrated in the '40s. After just a few hours of flight, the rigid, weighty wooden supports would warp or break, and they limited the flying and carrying potential of the kite.

The question was how to create the perfect tethered airfoil—a kite of minimum weight and maximum lift. The vision came in 1953. With a yardstick, Jalbert measured depth, width, and shape of the wing of his Beechcraft airplane and proceeded to duplicate this airfoil standard using only fabric and thread.

The result was a cross of balloon, airplane wing, parachute, and kite—a new kite design which, even more than Rogallo's design, employed the air to provide shape and lift. The parafoil was born. Looking like an airborne mattress, the parafoil is a series of fabric cambers (cylindrical cells) which take shape when the wind blows head on into them. The multicelled "mattress" inflates, creating the lightest possible lifting surface.

The parafoil is all wing and in most variations is wider than it is long. Necessary lateral stability is provided by a series of ventrals (keels) which are sewn to the underside of the kite. Numerous long shroud lines are attached to the tips of the triangular ventrals. "Notice how tight and wrinkle-free the bottom of the airfoil is and how the air flows between the suspension cloth triangles which give an even distribution of pressure, eliminating the need for any rigid membrane," Jalbert writes. As he claims, the parafoil *is* "the most effective plane surface." Certainly it is one of the most efficient lifting devices yet devised, using air alone as its source of power.

Like the Rogallo nonrigid kite, the dimensions of the parafoil are precise and critical. Also, while not requiring any rigid members, the parafoil has "ribs" (which are really just hems and seams between cells) placed equidistant along the top and bottom of the kite. Like the Rogallo, the parafoil conforms automatically to the airflow. In order to retain the proper pressure inside the airfoil when it is inflated, Jalbert's more sophisticated, larger designs include a sleeve or flutter valve in the underside of the parafoil. This valve (a hinged piece of fabric which permits the escape of some air through nylon mesh) is also nonrigid and is quite effective in retaining the airfoil shape while releasing excess pressure.

The average-sized, toy-marketed parafoil flies best in 8 to 15 mph winds, Jalbert reports. "Any more than this is a destructive force. Few fly well in winds above 15 mph and the experience is frustrating and tiring." But the parafoil has the widest range of any kite—as little as 6 mph and (in more elaborate sizes) as high as 70 or 80 mph. While they can fly in gale winds, "the kite loses heavily in functional performance" according to the Florida-based aeronautical engineer and master kiteman.

"Functional performance" for the Jalbert parafoils has included heavy load transportation, use as a modified parachute, and a 200-square-foot class of parafoil has even been deemed "suitable for sky diving."

Because of the unique suspension (ram-air) system, the parafoil has a great need for extra lateral stability—even more than that offered by the numerous cloth keels. Jalbert recommends a narrow, lengthy tail. Although drogues are typically included with the toy version of the kite, Jalbert insists this is done for the sake of simplicity only. A long narrow tail of various colors is hard to beat for efficiency and beauty. A cloth strip 4 inches wide and 62 feet long was used on a parafoil by Jalbert to stabilize flight in 25 to 30 mph winds after a drogue dragging on 10 feet of line had failed to do the job.

To build your own parafoil requires exact measuring, cutting, hemming, sewing—but it can be done. Since a light, flexible material is best, a Bainbridge cloth like Zephyrlite or Stabilkote is considered the optimal fabric for an average size or small parafoil. Of course the building process isn't the only challenge—flying a parafoil remains one of the true tests of kiting skill. Launch the parafoil in a large open space, because when it comes to landing the kite, unless you are using a power reel, chances are good that you will have to "walk it down." Feed out a few feet of line from the reel and straighten out all shrouds leading to the ventrals. Then, with a firm tug, pull the parafoil upward—it will begin to climb at an outrageous near-90° angle, filling out the cells with the air pressure from your pulls. Quickly the parafoil will assume a nearly flat (near 0°) angle to the wind. When it faces the wind head on like this it will really take off. Since the parafoil most closely resembles the airplane wing and airfoil, it doesn't need to be angled upward to achieve lift. It flies almost flat, and the lift is maximal because the only drag created by such an airfoil is by the tapered leading edge. A single parafoil has been flown as high as 9,000 feet.

Jalbert's one major variation on the parafoil design tries to improve on the ability of the cells to retain necessary air pressure: it is the parasled. The parasled has flaps of cloth tightly covering the leading edge where the air enters the cells. These flaps keep the bottom side flutter valves from being blown forward when there are lulls in wind velocity and all available pressure is needed. As the wind decreases, the cloth strips at the parasled's leading edge snap shut, lodging against a permeable nylon mesh, sealing in the air which gives the sled its mandatory configuration. Like every adjustment Jalbert has made in the original parafoil design (including the flutter valve itself), this is capitalization on a good design.

Domina Jalbert's invention, the parafoil, spotlights him as an innovator in kite design.

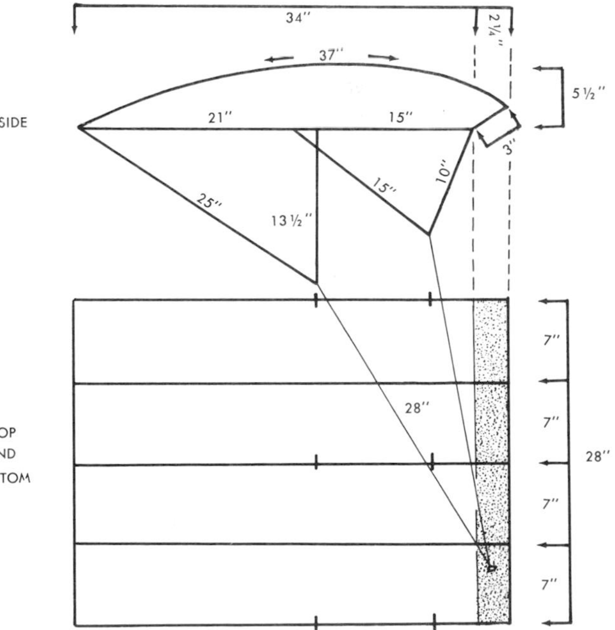

Side and top/bottom views of a simple parafoil design. It must be constructed carefully of a strong lightweight material such as Bainbridge's Zephyrlite or Stabilkote. It has three pairs of ventrals attached to the underside as indicated in the side view.

The parafoil's cousin, the parasled. Constructed just like the parafoil, the parasled has the additional feature of cloth flaps which cover the entrance to the chambers whenever wind velocity drops. This way pressure inside the kite is sustained even in a lull, thereby retaining the essential inflated shape. Courtesy: Mendel Silbert.

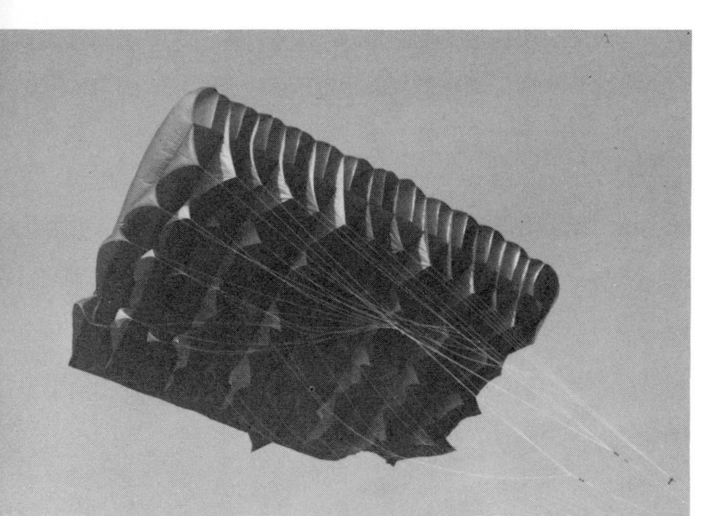

Because of their great efficiency, parafoils develop tremendous lift. They have been used to lift jeeps and other heavy objects, and have been approved for skydiving. A parafoil of this size should only be flown, however, using a power winch. Courtesy: NASA.

Parafoils and parasleds (parasled pictured here) can and have been made in any number of shapes. Each retains the essential airfoil design, however. Bridle shroud lines run from the tip of each ventral.

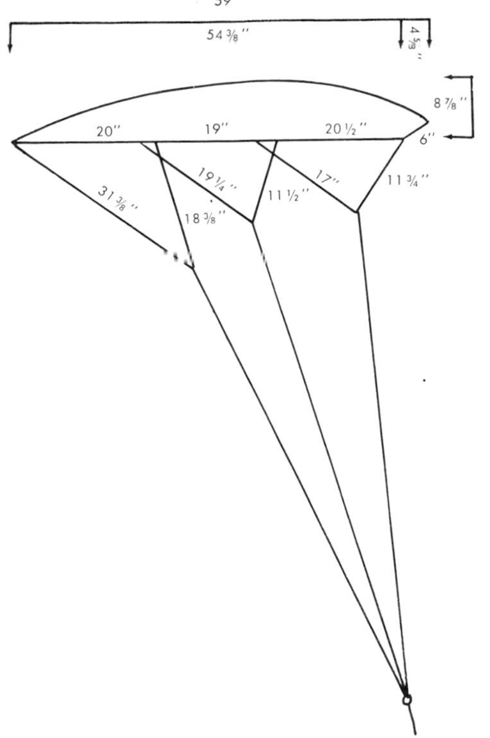

A more complex foil/sled design has the additional feature of flutter valves on the underside of the kite. To make the flutter valves, sew nylon mesh where indicated. Two flaps of kite cloth hinge at the leading edge of the nylon mesh rectangles on the inside of the kite bottom. The flutter valves permit excess air to pass out of the cells, avoiding distortion of shape and uncalled-for stress on seams. To make this parafoil into a parasled add nylon mesh to the leading edge of the kite, covering the entrance to the cells. Nylon, large enough to cover the nylon mesh, should hinge from inside the top edge. Courtesy: NASA.

TOP
AND
BOTTOM

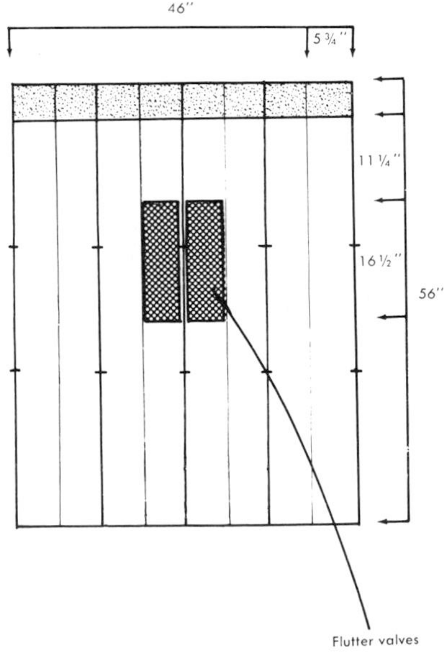

APPENDIX

CLIMBERS

If the kite is stable and flying well, you then have the luxury of a little more fun at the wind's expense—by sending up kite climbers on the flying line.

An elementary but satisfying climber is made with a piece of heavy paper or cardboard. Cut a slit from a center hole to the outer edge so that the paper disc slips onto the line. Now tape the slit closed again. Push this paper disc a few feet up on the line until the wind catches it like a sail, carrying it up the line to the kite bridle.

Variations on this simple messenger design include curling the ends of brightly colored paper (so the climber will spin on its way up), using different shapes of paper cutouts, vents, pinwheels, cones, and the like. Dozens of these may be sent up on a single line.

A cone-shaped messenger can be filled with cut paper or confetti. If there is a rea-

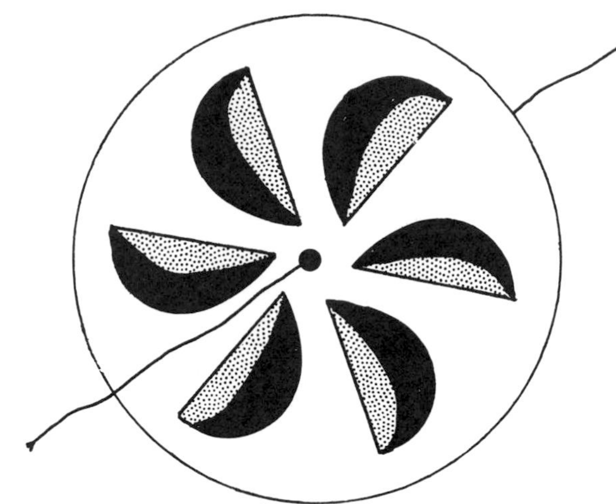

One of the simplest kite climbers is made from a single piece of light cardboard with a hole in the center. You may choose to cut vents within this form or to use brightly colored papers.

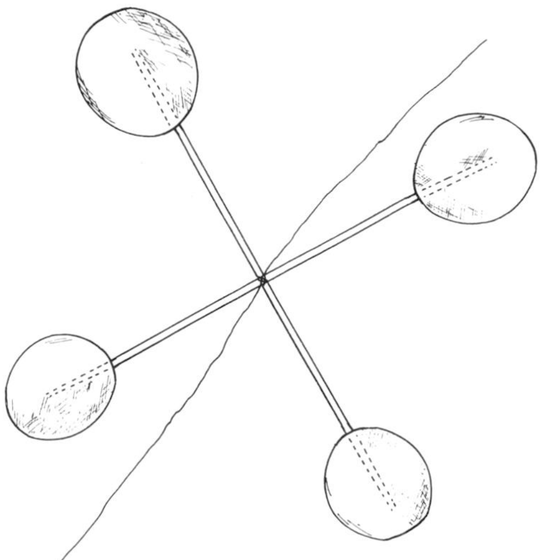

Another kite climber is made of two overlapping strips of bamboo which have paper discs glued to their ends. The discs are not flat; they are turned at slight angles to "slice" the wind and achieve lift the same way a kite does.

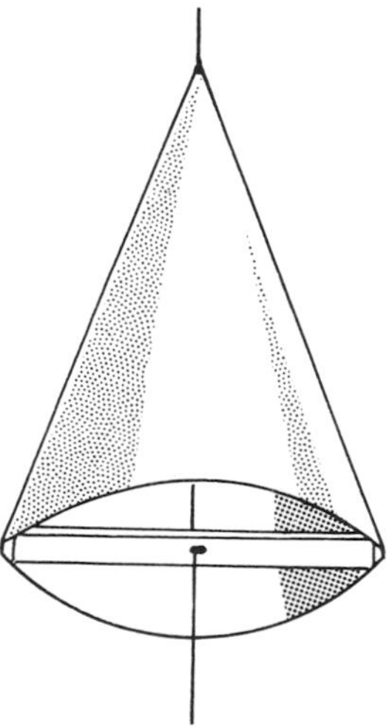

A paper cone attached to a bamboo, wood, or cardboard strip can be stuffed with confetti and sent up the line. The jolt of striking the kite bridle causes the paper (held in place by wind pressure) to be dislodged and flutter earthward.

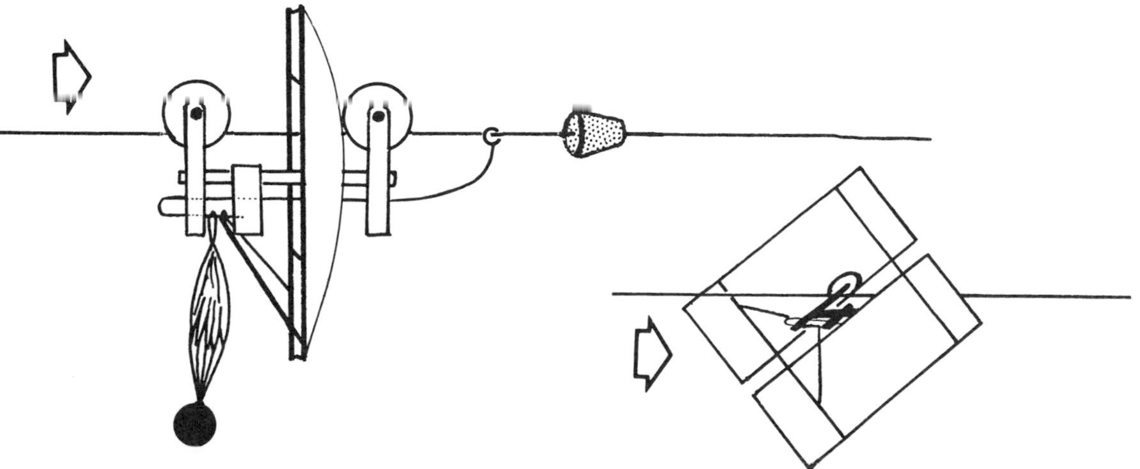

A more sophisticated climber is constructed with two pulley wheels, cloth, bamboo, wood, and wire. The pulley wheels use the flying line as a track. The wheels are flanked by two sails, held stiff to the wind by strings looped around a wire hook. When the climber strikes an obstacle on the line (such as a preset piece of cork) the wire "feeler" which runs in front of the sails will be pushed back. This feeler is part of the same wire which forms a hook on the climber's underside. When the hook is pushed back, the strings that hold the wings in place are collapsed automatically, and at the same time the parachute (also riding on the hook) is released. With the wings parallel to the line and no longer braced to the wind, the climber races back to your hands.

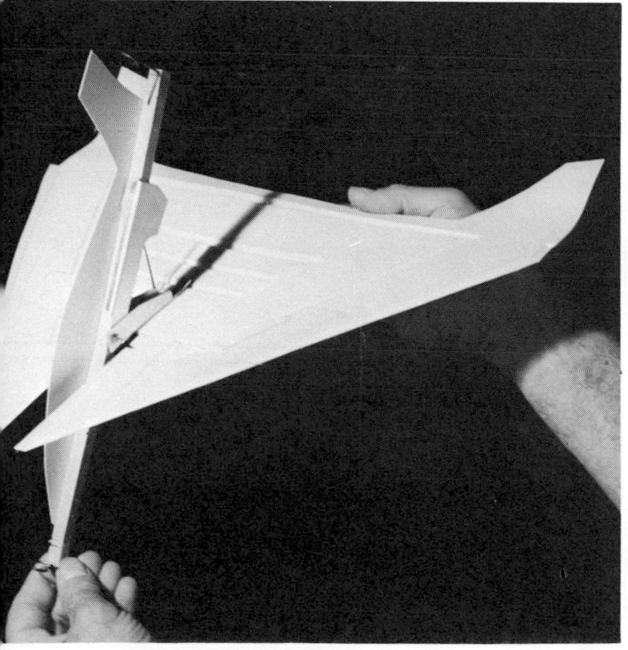

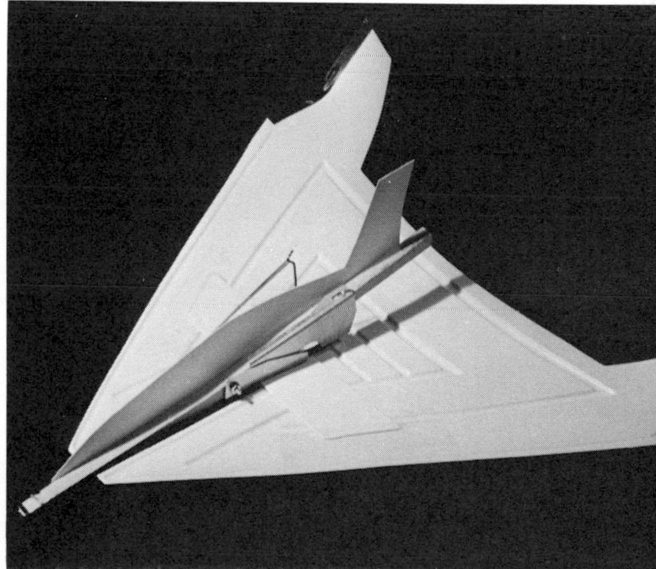

The Astrozoomer® sails up the line like the previous climber. When it hits a stop on the line, its wings fold up and it zips down like a jet until it hits a lower stop which was placed on the line after the Astrozoomer was attached. The wing converts back into sails and it heads back up the line again . . . give this climber enough rope and it will zoom itself.

sonably strong wind, the wind pressure on the inside of the cone should be sufficient to hold confetti inside until the jolt of the cone striking the kite bridle jars the contents loose.

More elaborate kite climbers employ a mechanism combining pulley wheels, strips of bamboo, paper or cloth, and wire. One such device rides up the line with the help of a pair of square sails flanking two pulley wheels. A wire contraption, which is built between the sails as diagrammed, releases a miniparachute "payload" when its leading tip strikes a cork that was fastened to the line earlier. Also released upon impact with the cork bumper are the two cords which kept the wings from folding under the wind pressure. The wings then fold, and the weight of the climber causes it to fall back into your hands.

NOISE ON A STRING

Chinese legend has it that during the Han Dynasty kites were once used to rout an invading army. At night, kites sent aloft over the besiegers, were armed with taut bamboo hummers. The skies literally cried out—or so the invaders thought—and, with a spy-planted rumor that these were gods announcing defeat, the army panicked, bolting into retreat.

Paper-thin rattan or bamboo stretched and bowed taut across the top of a kite (like a bow) has traditionally served throughout the Far East to add another dimension to kite flight. A simpler kite noisemaker is formed by folding and gluing a strip of paper around taut string. The razzing sound is charming. Of course one can also attach already noisy instruments to the kite—such as bells, hollow bamboo wind chimes which clink when they touch, or even firecrackers. With an extended fuse, fireworks attached to a kite tail (at sufficient distance so they don't destroy the kite itself) can suddenly arouse the neighborhood.

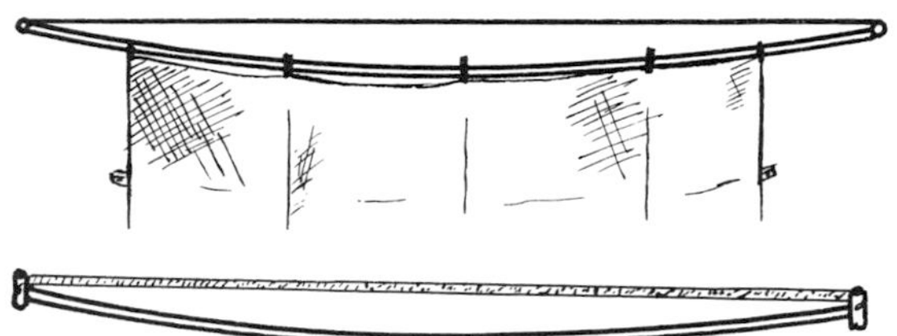

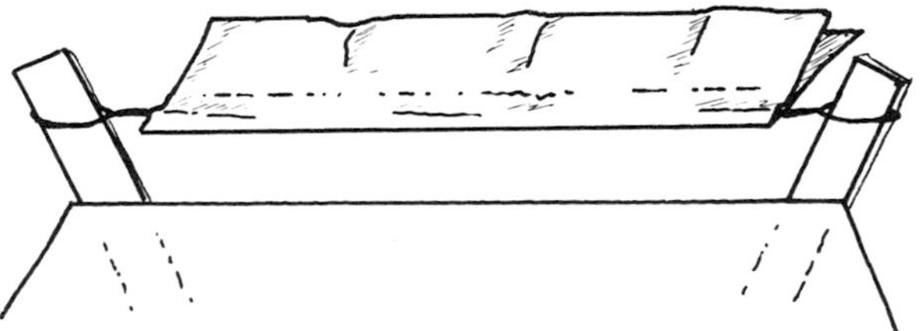

Here are three simple noisemakers that can be attached to a kite. At top (1) is a bamboo stick with a screw eye mounted in each end. A bow of string or paper-thin bamboo is strung across the stick and vibrates, singing in the wind. This bow is a conventional hummer of the Far East. The bow beneath it (2) is also common in Japan. It is made of bamboo with segments of bamboo shaft at the ends, around each of which a thin strip of tough rattan is mounted. The third hummer is simply a narrow piece of paper folded lengthwise and glued around a string stretched between two extended spines of a kite. The flapping ends of the paper strip "razz" quite nicely.

Bamboo hummer.

Bamboo hummer strung with rattan.

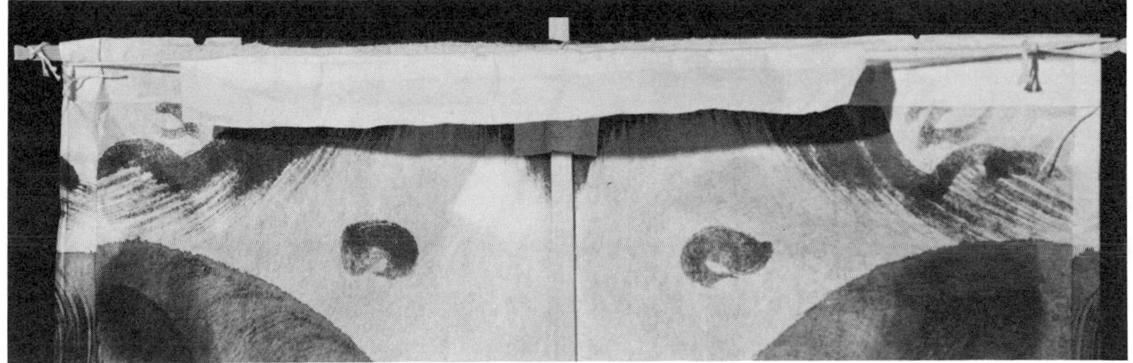

A simple paper hummer.

KITE REELS

All that's needed to fly most kites at moderate altitudes is a stick and some line. But when you start making kites, and especially making kites to fly well, the need develops for more efficient, effective tools for handling great lengths of flying line quickly and neatly.

Hand-winding great lengths of line is, to say the least, tiresome. It also leads to tangled lines. One alternative is to use a winding bobbin—this is a flat piece of wood, about a foot long and several inches wide, with rounded surfaces and a groove at each end for collecting masses of string. The winding bobbin works faster than a mere stick, but still requires patience and much energy for long flights. Winding bobbins of the type shown are simple to construct, however, with a saw and sandpaper. To avoid cutting your line you should be certain that all the edges are sanded smooth.

Another, more sophisticated alternative to the stick and bobbin is a genuine reel. Since a reel, too, is quite simple to make with a few bolts and a little plywood, no serious kitemaker should plan to make lengthy flights without this convenience. To control some kites, reels driven by electric motors are sometimes used. Some kitefliers use a fishing rod and reel. In choosing a design for a reel, make certain that, unless it will be power driven or gear driven, it has a large core. The larger the core of the reel, the more line you can pull in on a single revolution of the crank. The rod with a large-capacity reel is quite popular not only for its reel, but because the extra length offered by even a stubby rod can be helpful in kite control by amplifying your movements.

An assortment of hand reels imported from India by Go Fly a Kite Store.

When reeling in line, hold one end of the stick in the crook of your arm and use the other hand to twirl the reel. Feed in the line so that it covers the spool evenly.

Jackie Monnier uses a flat bobbin and recommends that it also have a finger grip.

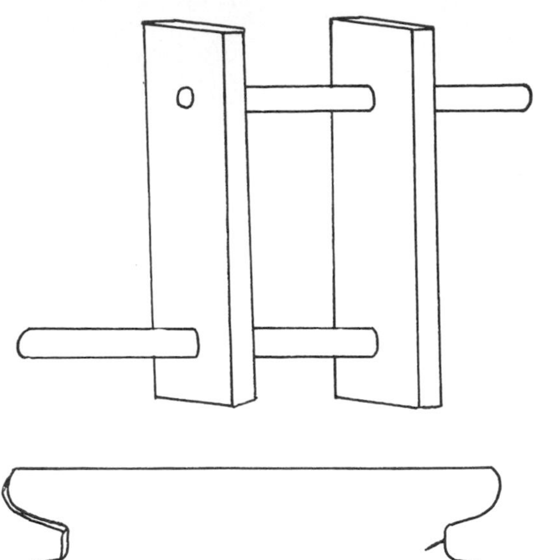

Two varieties of hand bobbins for collecting line. Both are easily constructed from wood scraps. The flat bobbin has a slit in one end for inserting and holding the end of the line.

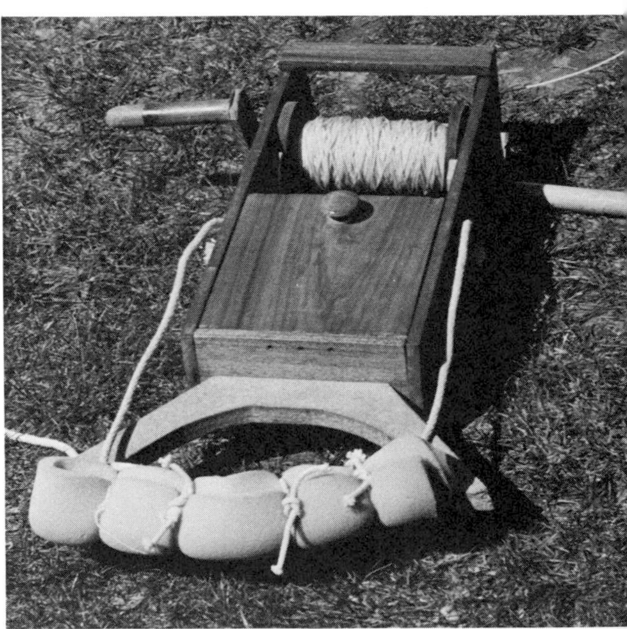

This sophisticated crank bobbin ties around the pilot's waist.

If you plan to construct a genuine reel—an irresistible asset if you fly often—make certain that it has a wide core. The wider the core, the more line you can reel in by a single revolution. This model, built by the late E. A. McCandlish, is only for light lines; it pulls 3′ of line per revolution. Courtesy: Kite Tales.

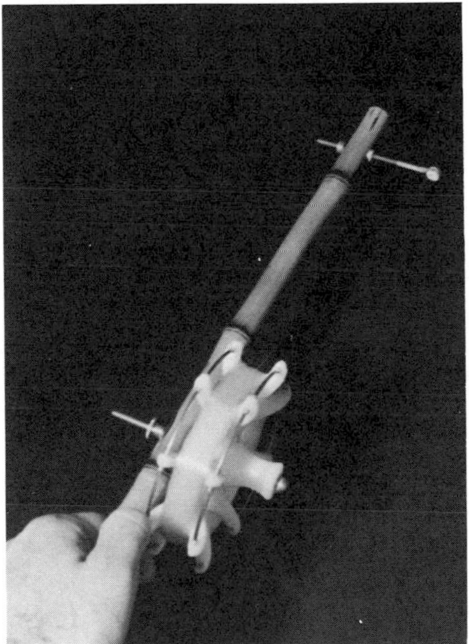

Some kitefliers use a combination rod and reel. This model is made in Taiwan of bamboo and an inexpensive plastic reel with hardware findings.

Planning to do some high flying? Mendel Silbert (and his son, pictured here) use this modified garden hose reel. Courtesy: Mendel Silbert.

For those heavyduty flights there is always the investment called the power reel. Designed by Mendel Silbert, this electric model packs real power for pulling in those monsters which might otherwise need to be walked down for miles. The reel can also be turned manually. Courtesy: Mendel Silbert.

ASSEMBLE A KITE KIT

If you are planning to experiment with kiteflying and kite building, you will soon discover that kites often need a lot of attention directly on the flying field—not just in your workshop. They need adjustments in bridling, changes in flying lines, balancing, minor repairs of tears and snapped sticks. If you come prepared for minor surgery flying will progress more smoothly.

We suggest some items you may want to have on hand whenever you fly. Materials and tools could include:

bamboo and wood dowels
cloth, paper, other swatches of material for kite face repairs
ample flying lines of the proper weight for your kites
lashing cord and/or thin wire
needle and thread
several sharp knives
scissors
portable (folding or tape) ruler
plastic and/or cloth adhesive tape
all-purpose white glue and/or rubber cement
pliers
eyelets and eyeletter
swivel hooks (for attaching the end of line to bridle rings)
extra bridle rings (plastic drapery rings)
a pair of gloves

Include any instruments which you like to use: range or height finders, favorite messengers, wind-velocity meters, line pull devices, and your offerings and talismans for the wind.

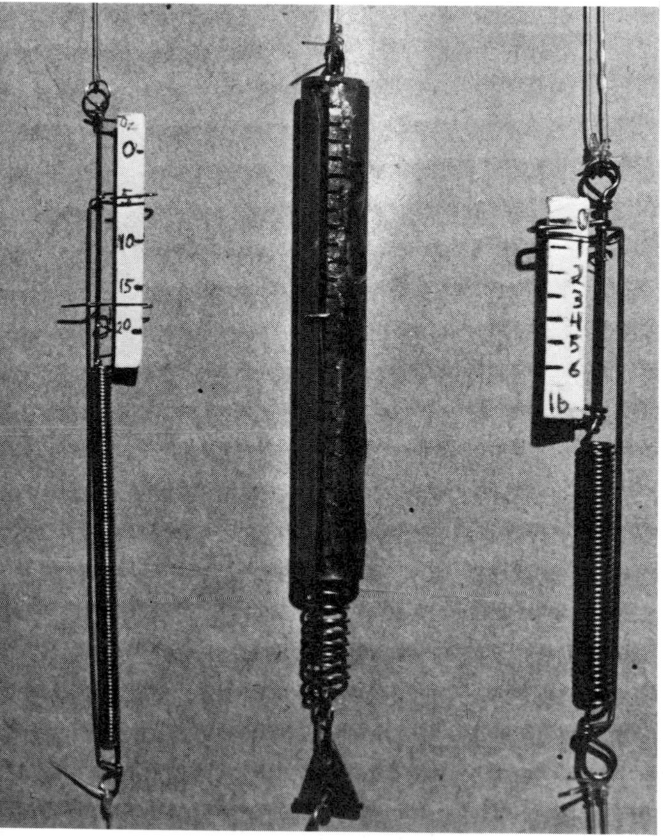

William Bigge builds his own line test gauges from spring wire. Beginning with a single piece of wire, Bigge bends and winds the springs. He then attaches a scale based on standard weights. They are masterpieces of ingenuity and practical tools for determining which weight of line to fly.

Ranging, Inc., offers the Rangematic®, a device for determining distance which is accurate as far as 1000 yards. Popular with hunters and sailors, it has practical applications for kitefliers interested in their kites' progress.

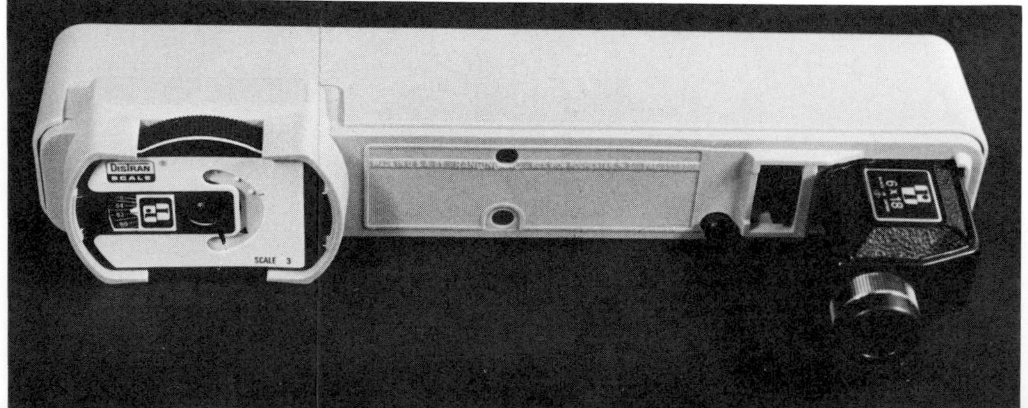

SOURCES OF SUPPLY AND INFORMATION

ORGANIZATIONS AND INFORMATION

American Kitefliers Association
315 North Bayard Street, P.O. Box 1511
Silver City, New Mexico 88061
An organization of kitefliers interested in kite design, building and flying for sport, recreation, and scientific study of aerodynamics. Publishes quarterly magazine *Kite Tales*

Self-Soar Association
P.O. Box 1860
Santa Monica, California 90406
For hang glider enthusiasts. Publishes *Low & Slow* newsletter

Skysurfer Publications
P.O. Box 375
Marlborough, Massachusetts 01752
Publishes *Skysurfer Magazine*, sells a complete line of skysurfing supplies and kite plans

KITE SHOPS

Go Fly a Kite Store
1613 Second Avenue
New York, New York 10028
Sells a complete range of kites from all over the world mail order or direct. Also carries bamboo and reels, kite line, balsa sticks, birch doweling, rice paper, Mylar, madras paper, tissue paper, clear plastic film, fiberglass rods, tyvek, mulberry paper, and other supplies. Hang gliders are also available. Andrea Bahadur, proprietor

Come Fly a Kite
900 North Pt. Ghiradelli Sq.
San Francisco, California 94109
A full range of kites, and reels. Dinesh Bahadur, proprietor

The Kite Shop
810 St. Ann Street
New Orleans, Louisiana 70116
A full range of imported and American kites. Sally Fontana, proprietor

COVERING MATERIALS

Andrews, Nelson, Whitehead
7 Laight Street
New York, New York 10013
Handmade and exotic papers

Cadillac Plastics and Chemical Co.
15841 Second Avenue
P.O. Box 810
Detroit, Michigan 48232
Fiberglass rod, Mylar films
Outlets throughout the country

Crystal Craft Tissue Co.
Middletown, Ohio 45042
Tissue papers

David Davis
530 LaGuardia Place
New York, New York 10012
Handmade and exotic papers

E. I. Du Pont de Nemours & Co., Inc.
Textile Fiber Department
Wilmington, Delaware 19898
Manufacturers of Tyvek and Mylar film

Howe & Bainbridge Inc.
220 Commercial Street
Boston, Massachusetts 02109
Zephyrlite and Stabilkote fabrics and a full range of sailcloths

Industrial Plastics
324 Canal Street
New York, New York 10013
Fiberglass rod, Mylar films

FRAMING MATERIALS

Aircraft Spruce and Specialty Co.
Box 424
Fullerton, California 92632
Spruce and aerolite glue

Sig Manufacturing Co., Inc.
Rt. 1, Box 1
Montezuma, New Mexico 50171
Balsa and spruce woods

KITE LINE

K. T. Netcraft Co.
3101 Sylvania Avenue
Toledo, Ohio 43613
Marine line and braided and monofilament nylon

Shakespeare Company
Box 4470
Columbia, South Carolina 29204
Manufacturers of monofilament and braided monofilaments, lines with break tests from 2 lbs. to 60 lbs.

KITEMAKERS

Airplane Kite Co.
1702 W. Third
Roswell, New Mexico 88201
Blackhawk, Skyscraper, Scott Sled and many other kites

Alan-Whitney Co.
P.O. Box 447
New Haven, Connecticut 06520
Spacebird kite and a full range of other designs

Brookite Ltd.
Francis Terrace
Junction Road
London N. 19
England
Well-made cloth kites, many cellular variations. Outlets in the U.S.

Condor Industries, Ltd.
3914 St. Peters Road
Victoria, B.C.
Canada V8P 2J8
Space platform acrobatic kite

Crunden-Martin Mfg. Co.
P.O. Box 508
St. Louis, Missouri 63166
A line of paper and plastic kites

Fredricks Corp.
300 West Washington Blvd.
Chicago, Illinois 60606
Puffer kites

Gayla Industries
P.O. Box 10800
Houston, Texas 77018
One of the largest producers of colorful paper and plastic-covered kites

Geodestix
P.O. Box 308
Spokane, Washington 99211
Tetrahedral kite kit

Hi-Flier Mfg. Co.
510 Wabash Avenue
Decatur, Illinois 62525
A most complete line of basic kites covered in plastic films and papers, reels and lines

The Kite Factory
P.O. Box 9081
Seattle, Washington 98109
Well-made cloth kites including sleds, parafoils, box kites

Kyte Specialties Co.
433 Avery Street
Elmhurst, Illinois 60126
Kite plans and some accessories

Nantucket Kiteman (Al Hartig)
P.O. Box 1356
Nantucket, Massachusetts 02554
Beautifully handcrafted kites

North Pacific Products, Inc.
P.O. Box 871
Bend, Oregon 97701
Glite, Dual Glite, many other models

Stratton Air Engineering
12821 Martha Ann Drive
Los Alamitos, California 90720
Airplane kite kits

L. G. Striegel Mfg. Co.
1223 Arcade Avenue
Louisville, Kentucky 40215
Superkite (Tyvek, Conyne)

Synestructics, Inc.
9559 Irondale Avenue
Chatsworth, California 91311
A well-made tetrahedral kite kit

ACCESSORIES

W. B. Products Co.
560 South Helberta Avenue
Redondo Beach, California 90277
Astrozoomer kite line flier

Ranging, Inc.
Rochester, New York 14625
Rangematic®, rangefinder

MISCELLANEOUS MATERIALS

Activa Products, Inc.
7 Front Street
San Francisco, California 94111
Celluclay, instant papier-mâché

Aljo Mfg.
116 Prince St.
New York, New York 10012
Dyes for batik and dip-dyeing

Commercial Art Materials Co.
165 Lexington Avenue
New York, New York 10016
Dyes, paints

Hazel Pearson Handicrafts
4128 Temple City Blvd.
Rosemead, California 91770
Craft supplies, full range

Permanent Pigments
2700 Highland Avenue
Norwood
Cincinnati, Ohio 45212
Liquitex acrylic colors and paints

Riverside Paper Corp.
Appleton, Wisconsin 54911
Decomaché, papier-mâché mix

Slomon's Labs, Inc.
32-45 Hunter's Point Avenue
Long Island City, New York 11101
Sobo, Velverette, and Quik glues. Available in stationery, hardware, and arts and crafts stores

BIBLIOGRAPHY

BAHADUR, SURHENDRA. "Indian Fighter Kites." Go Fly a Kite Shop, New York City.

BRUMMITT, WYATT. *Kites*. New York: Golden Press, 1971.

FOWLER, HALLER. *Kites: A Practical Guide to Kite Making and Flying*. New York: The Ronald Press Co., 1953.

HART, CLIVE. *Kites: An Historical Survey*. New York: Frederick A. Praeger, 1967.

———. *Your Book of Kites*. New York: Transatlantic Art, Inc., 1964.

HIROI, TSUTOMU. *Kites: Plastic Art in the Air*. Tokyo: 1972.

HUNT, LESLIE. *Twenty-Five Kites That Fly*. New York: Dover Publications, Inc., 1971.

JUE, DAVID. *Chinese Kites*. Rutland, Vt.: C. E. Tuttle Co., 1967.

NEWMAN, JAY HARTLEY and LEE SCOTT. *Plastics for the Craftsman*. New York: Crown Publishers, Inc., 1972.

NEWMAN, THELMA R., JAY HARTLEY, and LEE SCOTT. *Paper as Art and Craft*. New York: Crown Publishers, Inc., 1973.

ROY, HERMAN. *Kites*. Gregg Reprint Series, 1971.

TADAO, SAITO. *High Fliers*. New York: Japan Publications, Inc., 1969.

WAGENVOORD, JAMES. *Flying Kites*. New York: The Macmillan Company, 1968.

YOLEN, WILL. *The Young Sportsman's Guide to Kite Flying*. New York: Thomas Nelson and Sons, 1963.

INDEX

Page numbers in *italics* refer to illustrations